The Delmonico Cook Book

How To Buy Food, How To Cook It, And How To Serve It

A thousand recipes

By

Alessandro Filippini

RECIPES.

SOUPS.

1. Bouille-à-Baisse. —Chop two medium-sized, peeled, sound onions very fine, with one medium-sized, fine, fresh, green pepper, the same way, and put them in a pan on the hot range, with a gill of sweet oil. When well browned, moisten with three pints of hot white broth (No. 99). Cut three skinned, good-sized, sound, well-washed potatoes into quarters, also three fine, good-sized, sound, red, peeled tomatoes into rather small pieces; put all in the soup. Season with a pinch of salt (the equivalent of a tablespoonful) and half a pinch of pepper, and then boil well for fully one hour and a half, placing into it a strong bouquet (No. 254) at the beginning, also half a teaspoonful of powdered saffron, diluted in a little water; when nearly done, add one pound of boned codfish, cut into small pieces; boil again for three minutes, pour into a hot soup tureen, and serve with six slices of toasted bread.

2. Brunoise. —Pare and cut into small squares three medium-sized carrots, one turnip, half an onion, and two leeks; put these with two ounces of butter in a covered saucepan for a few moments; moisten with three pints of broth (No. 99), season with half a tablespoonful of salt, and a teaspoonful of pepper. Cook for three-quarters of an hour, and then add a handful of chiffonade (No. 132); when ready, serve with six slices of toasted bread.

3. Brunoise with Rice. —The same as for No. 2, adding half a cupful of uncooked rice about seventeen minutes before serving; taste to see if sufficiently seasoned, and serve.

4. Brunoise with Sorr el.—The same, adding two good handfuls of chopped sorrel about two minutes before serving.

5. Beef à l'Anglaise. —Cut up into small squares a quarter of a pound of raw, lean beef; brown them a little in a saucepan on the hot range, then moisten with three pints of broth (No. 99), add half a pint of printanier (No. 51), a handful of barley, and half a pinch each of salt and pepper. Boil thoroughly for half an hour, and a few moments before serving put in one medium-sized sliced tomato, taste to see if sufficiently seasoned, then pour the soup into a hot tureen, and send to the table.

6.Beefàl'Ecossaise,thickened. —Brown in a little fat, in a saucepan, a quarter of a pound of small squares of lean beef and a sliced onion; moisten with three pints of broth (No. 99), adding half a cup of oatmeal, a small glass of Madeira wine, half a tablespoonful of salt and a teaspoonful of pepper. Let cook for thirty minutes, then serve.

7.Busecca. —Brown in a saucepan one pint of raw printanier (No. 51), adding half a pint of chopped celery; let steam gently for about ten minutes, then moisten with three pints of white broth (No. 99) and a quarter of a pound of very finely shred tripe; season with half a tablespoonful of salt and a teaspoonful of pepper. Cook thoroughly for twenty-five minutes, and serve with a little grated cheese, separate.

8.BisqueofClams. —Open twelve large clams, scald them whole in their own juice, and drain. Then pound them in a mortar, and put them back into a saucepan with the same water. Add one quart of white broth (No. 99), one bouquet (No. 254), half a pint of raw rice, a little pepper, but no salt; boil for forty-five minutes, then strain through a fine sieve, adding half a cupful of good cream. Let it heat, but not boil again, and serve with very small squares of fried bread.

9.BisqueofCrabs. —Boil four hard-shelled crabs in salted water for about fifteen minutes; wash and drain them well, and proceed as for No. 8.

10.BisqueofLobster .—The same as for No. 8. Two pounds of lobster boiled in the shell will be sufficient; serve with small squares of boiled lobster claw, cut in dice.

11.Cr oûte-au-Pot.—Take two carrots cut in round slices, one turnip, cut the same, adding a few pieces of celery and half a quarter of chopped-up cabbage; stew them for ten minutes in a covered saucepan, with two ounces of butter; then moisten with three pints of white broth (No. 99), adding half a tablespoonful of salt and a teaspoonful of pepper. Boil well for thirty minutes, and serve with six pieces of dry toasted rolls.

12.FishChowder ,Bostonstyle. —Take a nice live codfish of about six pounds, cut the head off and remove all the bones, then cut the fish into square pieces, place them in a bowl, and add half a pinch of salt and a pint of cold water so as to have the flesh firm. Take the head and bones, place them in a saucepan with two quarts of white broth (No. 99) on the stove, and as soon as it comes to a boil, skim it well. Season with one pinch of salt and half a pinch of pepper. Let boil for twenty minutes. Peel and slice very fine one small, sound onion, place it in a saucepan with one ounce of butter, half an ounce of salt pork, cut in small dice-shaped pieces, let cook for five minutes, then add two tablespoonfuls of flour. Stir well together for three minutes on a brisk fire, being careful not to let it get brown. Strain the broth into a bowl, and when all strained in, add it to the flour, stirring well until all the broth is added. Let boil for ten minutes. Cut two good-sized, sound potatoes in small dice-shaped pieces, add them to the soup. Boil five minutes. Drain the codfish, wash it once more, and add it to the soup. Boil five minutes more; add half a pint of cold milk, being very careful not to allow to boil again; sprinkle a teaspoonful of chopped parsley over, and serve very hot.

13. Clam Chowder .—Wash six fine, medium-sized potatoes, peel and cut them into small dice-shaped pieces, wash again in fresh water, take them up with a skimmer; place them in a stewpan large enough to hold three quarts. Immediately add two quarts of cold water (not placing the pan on the fire until so mentioned). Peel one medium-sized, sound onion, chop it up very fine, and place it on a plate. Take a quarter of a bunch of well-washed parsley greens (suppressing the stalks), place it with the onions; wash well two branches of soup celery, chop it up very fine, place it with the parsley and onions, and add all these in the stewpan. Place the pan on a brisk fire. Season with a light pinch of salt, adding at the same time a light tablespoonful of good butter. Let all cook until the potatoes are nearly done; eighteen minutes will be sufficient. Cut out from a piece of fresh pork, *crosswise*, one slice a third of an inch thick, then cut it in pieces a third of an inch square, fry, and reduce it in a pan on the hot stove for four minutes. Add it to the broth, add also three-quarters of a teaspoonful of branch dry thyme. Lightly scald four fine, medium-sized tomatoes, peel and cut them into small pieces and add them to the preparation. Open and place in a bowl twenty-four medium-sized, fine, fresh clams; pour into another bowl half of their juice. Place the clams on a wooden board, cut each one into four equal pieces, and immediately plunge them into the pan with the rest; gently mix, so as to prevent burning at the bottom while boiling, for two minutes. Range the pan on the corner of the stove to keep warm. Season with a saltspoonful of black pepper, one tablespoonful of Worcestershire sauce, gently stir the whole with a wooden spoon; break in two pilot crackers in small pieces, stir a little again. Leave two minutes longer in the same position, but under no circumstances allow to boil. Pour it into a hot soup-tureen, and serve.

14. Chiffonade. —Wash well, drain, and chop up very fine one quart of sorrel with the green leaves of a lettuce-head. Brown in a saucepan, with two ounces of butter and a sliced onion, seasoning with half a tablespoonful of salt and a teaspoonful of pepper. Moisten with three pints of white broth (No. 99), add a handful of peas, the same of string beans and asparagus tops; boil for three-quarters of an hour with an ounce of butter; serve with six slices of toasted bread.

15. How to Prepare Green Turtle. —Select a medium-sized turtle, cut off the head, and let it bleed for twelve hours. Remove the bones by opening the sides; cut the carcass in pieces, and blanch them for three minutes in boiling water. Lift off the top shell and place it in a saucepan, covering it with white broth (No. 99), a handful of whole pepper, one dozen cloves, half a bunch of thyme, and six bay leaves (all the above spices and herbs carefully tied in a white cloth). Add a handful of salt, and cook for about one hour. Drain, remove the bones, cut the rest in dice-sized squares. Let the broth be reduced to three-fourths its quantity, then put in the white, lean meat, letting it cook for ten minutes, and then add the green part (the shell) of the turtle. Fill some medium-sized pots with this, and when cooled off pour hot lard over the tops. A good glassful of Madeira wine can be added to the broth, according to taste.

16. Green Turtle Soup. —Place a pint of green turtle, cut into pieces (No. 15) in a saucepan with two pints of broth (No. 99); add a bouquet (No. 254), a glassful of Madeira wine, a little bit of red pepper, half a tablespoonful of salt, a little grated nutmeg, a teaspoonful of English sauce, and a cupful of Espagnole sauce (No. 151). Boil for twenty minutes, and serve with six slices of peeled lemon, after suppressing the bouquet.

17. Mock Turtle. —To be prepared as for green turtle (No. 16), substituting a pint of cooked calf's-head for the turtle.

18. Clear Green Turtle. —Proceed the same as for the green turtle (No. 16), omitting the Espagnole sauce, but adding two tablespoonfuls of dissolved corn-starch, also a quarter of a glassful more of Madeira wine before serving.

19. Giblets With Rice. —Take three chicken giblets and brown them in a saucepan, with half an ounce of fat and one sliced onion. Moisten with one quart of white broth (No. 99), adding one thinly sliced carrot, half a sliced turnip, a tablespoonful of well-washed rice, half a tablespoonful of salt, and a very little pepper. Boil for thirty minutes, and then put in one sliced tomato; cook for five minutes more, and serve, adding one teaspoonful of Parisian sauce.

20.Gibletsàl'Ecossaise. —The same as for No. 19, substituting half a cupful of oatmeal for rice ten minutes before serving.

21.GibletswithBarley .—The same as No. 19, substituting barley for rice forty minutes before serving.

22.Gibletsàl'Anglaise. —Brown in a saucepan three minced giblets with a sliced onion; moisten with one quart of white broth (No. 99), adding a cupful of Espagnole sauce (No. 151), a bouquet (No. 254), half a glassful of Madeira wine, a teaspoonful of Parisian sauce, and half a tablespoonful of salt and a teaspoonful of pepper. Cook thoroughly for about thirty minutes, and when done, serve with one chopped hard-boiled egg.

23.GumboW ithFr ogs.—Brown in half an ounce of butter, in a saucepan, one chopped onion with about one ounce of raw ham cut into dice shape, half a green pepper cut in small dice, and half a tablespoonful of salt and a teaspoonful of pepper. Moisten with one quart of white broth (No. 99), or consommé (No. 100), add one tablespoonful of raw rice, six sliced gumbos, and one sliced tomato. Let all cook thoroughly for about twenty minutes; and five minutes before serving add a quarter of a pound of raw frogs cut up into small pieces.

24.GumboofCrabs. —The same as for No. 23; replacing the frogs by three well-washed, minced, soft-shelled crabs five minutes before serving.

25.Fr ogsàl'Espagnole. —The same as No. 23, adding one green pepper and two tomatoes (as green peppers and tomatoes must predominate when frogs are used instead of crabs), and omitting the gumbo.

26.Oysters. —Put thirty medium-sized oysters in their own water, with half a pint of water added, in a saucepan, with a tablespoonful of salt and half a teaspoonful of pepper, and one ounce of good butter. Let it boil once only; then serve, adding half a pint of cold milk.

27.Julienne. —Cut into fine long shreds two carrots, half a turnip, two leaves of celery, one leek, an eighth of a cabbage, and half an onion; brown them in a saucepan with one ounce of butter; moisten with one quart of white broth (No. 99), or consommé (No. 100), and season with half a tablespoonful of salt and a teaspoonful of pepper. Cook for thirty minutes;

add two tablespoonfuls of cooked green peas, and one tablespoonful of cooked string beans. Boil up again, and serve.

28.Jardinièr e.—The same as for No. 27, only the vegetables are cut larger, and omit the cabbage. When ready to serve, add a handful of chiffonade (No. 132) five minutes before serving.

29.ShinofBeefLiée. —Place ten pounds of leg of beef (shin) in a saucepan, with one gallon of cold water, on the fire. When it comes to a boil, thoroughly skim off all the scum. Add one good-sized carrot, one sound onion, six cloves, eighteen whole peppers, a well-garnished bouquet (No. 254), and two pinches of salt. Let all boil on a moderate fire for four hours. Place in a saucepan two ounces of butter, four tablespoonfuls of flour, mix well together, and place it also on a moderate fire, stirring it once in a while until it has obtained a light brown color, which will take six minutes. When the broth has boiled for four hours, strain either through a napkin or a sieve into a vessel and let cool for five minutes; then gradually add it to the flour, stirring until all is added; place it on the fire, and when it boils skim it once more, and let cook for ten minutes. Cut a piece of four ounces of the meat of the cooked shin of beef into small dice-shape pieces half an inch square, add them to the soup, let all boil ten minutes; squeeze in the juice of one medium-sized sound lemon, add a glassful of Madeira wine, and serve in hot tureen.

30.MuttonwithBarley .—Cut in small squares a quarter of a pound of lean mutton, and brown them in saucepan, with a little fat, on the hot range, with half a chopped sound onion. Moisten with three pints of white broth (No. 99), and season with half a pinch of salt, and half a pinch of pepper; add half a pint of printanier (No. 51), a little cut-up celery, and a tablespoonful of well-washed barley. Boil well together for forty minutes; pour into a hot soup-tureen and serve.

31.Muttonàl'Ecossaise. —The same as for No. 30, substituting half a cupful of oatmeal for the barley ten minutes before serving.

32.Mikado. —Cut half of a small breast of chicken, a quarter of a pound of very lean veal, and a quarter of a pound of lean mutton, into small equal-sized dice-shaped pieces, and put them in a saucepan on the hot stove, with two ounces of good butter. Cook for five minutes, stirring with the spatula; then moisten with two quarts of broth (No. 99), adding a finely chopped medium-sized onion, the same of green pepper, two tablespoonfuls of diluted curry, and a bouquet (No. 254). Season with a tablespoonful of salt and a teaspoonful of pepper, and, after cooking for thirty minutes, add three tablespoonfuls of raw rice and cook again for thirty minutes. Remove the bouquet, skim thoroughly, and pour the soup into a hot soup-tureen to serve.

33.W estmorelandSoup. —Put into a saucepan one quart of broth (No. 99), one quart of Espagnole sauce (No. 151), three tablespoonfuls of Parisian sauce, a little cayenne pepper (about the equivalent of a green pea), and a bouquet (No. 254); place the saucepan on the hot stove, and add two cooked and boned calf's feet, cut into small square pieces, and pour in a glassful of good Madeira wine. Cook for thirty minutes, remove the bouquet, and skim the fat from the surface; pour the soup into a hot tureen; add eighteen cooked chicken quenelles (No. 226), then send to the table.

34.Mulligatawney. —Cut a quarter of a medium-sized raw chicken in pieces, with half a green pepper, half an ounce of lean raw ham, and half a finely sliced onion. Brown the whole for five minutes in a saucepan; moisten with one quart of white broth (No. 99), adding a quarter of a pint of very finely cut printanier (No. 51), a teaspoonful of curry, and half a green apple cut into small pieces, one slice of egg-plant cut into small pieces, and a tablespoonful of uncooked rice. Season with half a tablespoonful of salt and a teaspoonful of pepper; boil for twenty-five minutes and serve.

35.MulligatawneyàlaDelmonico. —The same as for No. 34, but instead of the printanier use two tablespoonfuls of rice, adding twelve medium-sized oysters two minutes before serving.

36.Menestra. —Cut up all together into fine pieces two carrots, half a turnip, two leeks, a quarter of a cabbage, half an onion, and one stalk of celery, and steam them in two ounces of butter for about ten minutes in a covered saucepan; moisten with three pints of white broth (No. 99), adding one tablespoonful of washed rice, a bouquet (No. 254), and half a tablespoonful of salt and a teaspoonful of pepper. Boil well for thirty minutes, and serve with two tablespoonfuls of grated cheese separately for each person.

37.Napolitaine. —Cut into small pieces a quarter of a raw chicken; brown them well in one ounce of butter, with an ounce of lean raw ham, half a green pepper, half a sliced onion, also one carrot cut in the same way. Steam for ten minutes in a saucepan, then moisten with three pints of white broth (No. 99); season with half a tablespoonful of salt and a teaspoonful of pepper, and add one tablespoonful of raw rice. Let it simmer until half cooked (about fifteen minutes), then throw in one ounce of pieces of macaroni and half a tomato. Boil again for ten minutes, and serve with two tablespoonfuls of grated cheese separately.

38. Ox-Tail with Barley .—Cut a small ox-tail into little pieces, wash well, drain them, then place in a saucepan with a quarter of an ounce of butter, fry for ten minutes on the hot stove. Moisten with three pints of consommé (No. 100); season with half a pinch of salt and half a pinch of pepper. Cook for one hour. Then add half a pint of printanier (No. 51), one tablespoonful of well-washed barley, and a teaspoonful of Parisian sauce. Cook for forty minutes, then skim the fat off, and a few moments before serving add one medium-sized, red, sliced tomato to the soup.

39. Ox-Tail à l'Ecossaise. —The same as for No. 38, substituting half a cupful of oatmeal for the barley ten minutes before serving.

40. Ox-Tail à l'Anglaise. —Cut a small ox-tail into pieces, and fry them the same as in No. 38. Moisten with a quart of consommé (No. 100), and one pint of Espagnole sauce (No. 151). Cook for one hour, then season with a pinch of pepper, add one tablespoonful of well-washed barley, one teaspoonful of Worcestershire sauce, half a glass of Madeira wine, and a bouquet (No. 254). Boil thoroughly for forty-five minutes, skim off the fat, then serve with six slices of lemon, and one chopped hard-boiled egg, and suppressing the bouquet.

41. Sorrel with Asparagus-tops. —Chop up fine one quart of well picked and washed sorrel; put it in a saucepan with two ounces of butter. Let it steam for ten minutes; then moisten with three pints of white broth (No. 99), adding half a cupful of asparagus-tops, and half a tablespoonful of salt and a teaspoonful of pepper. Cook together for twenty-five minutes, and when about serving thicken it with the yolk of one egg in half a cupful of cream. Serve with six sippets of toast.

42. Sorrel with Rice. —The same as for No. 41, using two tablespoonfuls of rice twenty minutes before serving, instead of the asparagus, and omitting the sippets of toast.

43. Purée Jackson. —Cut one pint of potatoes into pieces and cover them with one quart of white broth (No. 99) in a saucepan. Press the broth through a napkin, adding about two ounces of butter and a bouquet (No. 254.) Season with half a tablespoonful of salt and a teaspoonful of pepper, cook well for thirty minutes, then strain the soup, adding half a cupful of cream, and serve with six sippets of toast. Do not let it boil again after the cream has been added.

44. Purée Parmentier .—The same as for No. 43, adding one bunch of cut-up leeks fifteen minutes before serving.

45. Purée Br etonne.—The same as for No. 43, substituting one pint of dried white beans, previously soaked for four hours in cold water, for the potatoes.

46. Purée Faubonne. —The same as for No. 43, using one pint of lentils instead of potatoes. (Lentils must also be soaked for four hours before using.) Throw in two tablespoonfuls of cooked green peas and a pinch of chopped parsley one minute before serving.

47. Purée Crécy .—Steam four medium-sized finely chopped carrots for fifteen minutes in a saucepan, with two ounces of butter; then moisten with one quart of white broth (No. 99), adding half a cupful of raw rice, one bouquet (No. 254), and half a tablespoonful of salt and a teaspoonful of pepper. Cook thoroughly for thirty minutes, then strain through a fine colander. Finish with half a cupful of cream, and serve with two tablespoonfuls of croûtons (No. 133).

48. Purée Condé. —Place in a saucepan on the fire one pint of red beans, previously soaked for four hours in cold water. Moisten with one quart of white broth (No. 99), and add two ounces of blanched salt pork, one onion, one carrot, a bouquet (No. 254), and a teaspoonful of pepper. Cook thoroughly for one hour; then strain, add half a glassful of claret, and then serve with two tablespoonfuls of square croûtons of fried bread (No. 133).

49. Purée of Gr eenPeas. —The same as for No. 48, using a pint of green peas instead of red beans, and adding half a cupful of cream in the place of claret, and one ounce of butter, one minute before serving.

50. Purée Mongole. —Boil in a saucepan half a cupful of dried peas in two gills of white broth (No. 99), for one hour; if fresh peas, half an hour will be sufficient. Cut up in julienne shape, one medium-sized sound carrot, one small turnip, and one leek; place them in a saucepan with half an ounce of butter on the hot stove, cover the pan, and let simmer for five minutes. Peel two good-sized ripe tomatoes, cut them into quarters, put them in a saucepan with a quarter of an ounce of butter; season with one pinch of salt and half a pinch of pepper, add one gill of white broth (No. 99). Let cook for twenty minutes on a brisk fire. Then strain the tomatoes through a fine sieve into a bowl, add them now to julienne, let all cook five minutes longer; strain the peas through the sieve into the julienne, let the whole come to a boil, and serve in a hot soup-tureen.

51. Printanier Grenat.—Cut into small pieces two carrots, half a turnip, half an onion, two leaves of celery, and two leeks; steam them well for ten minutes in a saucepan with one ounce of butter; then moisten with three pints of consommé (No. 100), adding two tablespoonfuls of rice, half a pinch each of salt and pepper. Cook thoroughly for thirty minutes and five minutes before serving put in one cut-up raw tomato.

52. Printanier Chasseur.—Proceed as for No. 51, only replacing the tomato with half the breast of a cooked grouse, partridge, or any other game, cut into small pieces, and twelve quenelles (No. 221).

53. Paysanne.—Cut in square-shaped pieces two carrots, half a turnip, an eighth of a cabbage, half an onion, one potato, and two leaves of celery. Steam them for ten minutes with two ounces of butter in a saucepan; then moisten with three pints of white broth (No. 99); season with half a tablespoonful of salt, and a teaspoonful of pepper. Cook for thirty minutes, and when serving add six thin slices of bread.

54. Pot-au-Feu.—Family Soup.—Thoroughly wash twice in cold water, either six pounds of brisket or eight pounds of shin of beef. Place it in the stock-pot, and entirely cover with cold water; place it on the fire, and be very careful, as soon as it comes to a boil, to thoroughly skim off all the scum. Add two medium-sized, sound, well-cleaned carrots, one turnip, one good-sized, well-peeled onion with six cloves stuck in it, and two leeks tied together. Season with two pinches of salt, and eighteen whole peppers; let boil for four hours. Strain either through a napkin or a sieve into a bowl; cut the carrots into round pieces, quarter of an inch thick, turnip the same, as also the leeks; add all these to the broth, and serve with six quarters of toasted rolls.

55. Ala Russe.—Cut into pieces one ounce each of lean, raw ham, mutton, beef, and veal; brown them well in one ounce of butter with the half of a finely shred onion for five minutes. Moisten with one quart of white broth (No. 99), then throw in half a pint of prepared printanier as for No. 109, and a tablespoonful of raw rice. Boil thoroughly for thirty minutes, season with two teaspoonfuls of pepper, and five minutes before serving add a handful of chiffonade (No. 132).

56. Spaghetti with Tomatoes.—Pour into a saucepan one pint of white broth (No. 99), one pint of tomato sauce (No. 205), and season with half a pinch each of salt and pepper. Let it boil well for ten minutes; then throw in half a pint of cooked spaghetti—cut about three-quarters of an inch in length; cook again for five minutes, tossing them well meanwhile, and serve very hot.

57. T omatoeswithRice. —The same as for No. 56, using three tablespoonfuls of raw rice twenty minutes before serving instead of the cooked spaghetti.

58. T omatoesàl'Andalouse. —Boil together in a saucepan one pint of tomato sauce (No. 205), and three pints of consommé (No. 100). Add half a tablespoonful of salt and a teaspoonful of pepper; then put in two tablespoonfuls of tapioca, stirring it well all the time. Cook for fifteen minutes, and add twelve chicken quenelles (No. 226); then serve.

59. T omatowithSago. —Boil for ten minutes in a saucepan one pint of tomato sauce (No. 205), and three pints of consommé (No. 100), seasoning with half a pinch each of salt and pepper; add two tablespoonfuls of sago, cook again for fifteen minutes, gently stirring, and serve.

60. T errapin—howtopr epareit. —Take live terrapin, and blanch them in boiling water for two minutes. Remove the skin from the feet, and put them back to cook with some salt in the saucepan until they feel soft to the touch; then put them aside to cool. Remove the carcass, cut it in medium-sized pieces, removing the entrails, being careful not to break the gall-bag. Put the pieces in a smaller saucepan, adding two teaspoonfuls of pepper, a little nutmeg, according to the quantity, a tablespoonful of salt, and a glassful of Madeira wine. Cook for five minutes, and put it away in the ice-box for further use.

61. T errapinSoup. —Put in a saucepan one pint of Espagnole sauce (No. 151) and half a pint of consommé (No. 100). Add a good bouquet (No. 254), one tablespoonful of Parisian sauce, a very little red pepper, the same of nutmeg, and half a glassful of Madeira wine. Boil for twenty minutes, being careful to remove the fat, if any; add half a pint of terrapin prepared as above (No. 60), and boil for ten minutes longer. Then serve with six slices of lemon, always removing the bouquet.

62. ChickenàlaRichmond. —Place a quarter of a medium-sized chicken, previously boned, into a saucepan with one ounce of butter or fat, one finely shred onion, and half a green pepper, also shred. Fry well together for ten minutes; then moisten with three pints of white broth (No. 99), adding a teaspoonful of powdered curry, diluted in two tablespoonfuls of broth, good bouquet (No. 254), a spoonful of Lima beans, two tablespoonfuls of fresh corn, and six cut-up gumbos, suppressing the stalks.

Season with half a tablespoonful of salt, and a teaspoonful of pepper; cook thoroughly for thirty-five minutes; remove the bouquet and serve.

63.ChickenPiémontaise. —The same as No. 37, omitting the carrots and rice.

64.ChickenHollandaise. —Cut one quarter of a medium-sized raw chicken into small pieces with half an onion; brown well together for ten minutes in a saucepan with an ounce of butter, and moisten with three pints of consommé (No. 100). Add three tablespoonfuls of raw rice, half a tablespoonful of salt, a very little red pepper, and a bouquet (No. 254). Boil thoroughly for twenty minutes; remove the bouquet, and serve.

65.ChickenàlaCréole. —The same as for No. 64, adding half a chopped green pepper, one ounce of lean, raw ham, cut in small pieces. Five minutes before serving put one cut tomato in the soup.

66.ChickenàlaPortugaise. —Prepare the chicken as for No. 64; add half a pint of cooked printanier (No. 51) cut very fine five minutes before serving.

67.Chickenàl'Okra. —The same as for No. 65, adding twelve raw okras cut in small pieces ten minutes before serving.

68.ChickenwithLeeks. —Brown for ten minutes, in one ounce of butter in a saucepan, one quarter of a medium-sized chicken with half a cut-up small onion; moisten with three pints of consommé (No. 100), adding three leeks cut in pieces, a bouquet (No. 254), and half a tablespoonful of salt and a teaspoonful of pepper. Boil thoroughly for thirty minutes and serve, suppressing the bouquet.

69.ChickenàlaT urque.—Brown in a saucepan a quarter of a raw chicken in one ounce of butter, with one ounce of raw ham and a sliced onion, moisten with a quart of consommé (No. 100), and half a pint of tomato sauce (No. 205), add two tablespoonfuls of raw rice, a bouquet (No. 254), half a tablespoonful of salt, half a cut-up green pepper, and one teaspoonful of diluted curry. Boil for thirty minutes and serve, removing the bouquet.

70.Cr eamofAsparagus. —Put two ounces of butter in a saucepan, adding three tablespoonfuls of flour; stir well, and moisten with three pints of white broth (No. 99). Put in the equivalent of half a bunch of asparagus; add a bouquet (No. 254), twelve whole peppers, and half a tablespoonful of salt. Boil thoroughly for thirty minutes; then strain through a fine sieve, add half a cupful of cream, and serve either with a handful of cooked asparagus tops or croûtons soufflés (No. 134).

71. Cream of Celery .—Heat half a pint of mirepoix (No. 138) in a saucepan with an ounce of butter, adding three tablespoonfuls of flour; moisten with three pints of white broth (No. 99), put in half a bunch of celery with a little nutmeg, and half a tablespoonful of salt; let boil well for forty-five minutes then strain through a sieve; add half a cupful of cream, and serve with two tablespoonfuls of croûtons (No. 133).

72. Cream of Artichokes. —Heat half a pint of mirepoix (No. 138) in a saucepan with one ounce of butter, adding three tablespoonfuls of flour, and half a tablespoonful of salt; moisten with three pints of white broth (No. 99), and put in two well-pared, fresh, or three canned, artichokes, and cook well for thirty minutes; strain through a sieve, stir in half a cupful of cream, and serve with a handful of croûtons soufflés (No. 134).

73. Cream of Cauliflower .—Proceed the same as for No. 72, omitting the mirepoix, and substituting half a medium-sized cauliflower instead of artichokes.

74. Cream Palestine. —Boil for about twenty-five minutes half a pound of Jerusalem artichokes; peel and mash them well, then put them in a saucepan with one ounce of butter, moistening with three pints of white broth (No. 99), and half a pint of mirepoix (No. 138). Add three tablespoonfuls of raw rice, and half a tablespoonful of salt. Cook thoroughly for thirty minutes; then strain through a sieve, and finish with half a cupful of cream, and a handful of croûtons soufflés (No. 134).

75. Cream of Lima Beans. —Put two ounces of butter in a saucepan with half a pint of mirepoix (No. 138), a tablespoonful of flour, and one pint of Lima beans, seasoning with half a tablespoonful of salt. Moisten with three pints of white broth (No. 99); cook for thirty minutes; then strain through a sieve, and serve with half a cupful of cream and a handful of croûtons soufflés (No. 134).

76. Cream of Dried Green Peas. —Soak one pint of dried peas for four hours; then cover them with three pints of white broth (No. 99), or water. Put them in a saucepan, adding a bouquet (No. 254), a good-sized piece of salt pork (about two ounces), one carrot, one onion, three cloves, and twelve whole peppers. Cook for forty-five minutes; then rub through a sieve, add two ounces of good butter, and half a cupful of cream, and serve with sippets of fried bread. Should water be used instead of broth, taste before serving to see if sufficiently seasoned.

77. Cream of Barley.—Moisten half a pint of well-washed barley with one quart of white broth (No. 99), adding a bouquet (No. 254), and one whole onion; boil in the saucepan on the stove for forty-five minutes, and season with half a tablespoonful of salt and a teaspoonful of pepper. Strain through a coarse colander, and removing the bouquet, serve with a thickening made of a cupful of cream and the yolks of two raw eggs, and a handful of sippets of bread fried in butter.

78. Cream of Rice.—Same as for No. 77, using rice instead of barley, and letting it cook thirty minutes.

79. Cream of Sorrel.—Steam three good handfuls of well-cleaned sorrel with one ounce of butter. After cooking ten minutes, rub through a sieve into a saucepan; add a quart of white broth (No. 99), and one pint of béchamel sauce (No. 154); season with half a tablespoonful of salt and a teaspoonful of pepper and let boil for fifteen minutes. Thicken the soup before serving with half a cupful of cream and the yolks of two raw eggs well beaten together, adding six slices of bread.

80. Cream of Sorrel and Rice.—The same as for No. 79, adding three tablespoonfuls of raw rice, and cooking for twenty minutes longer.

81. Cream of Sorrel, fermière.—Steam three good handfuls of well-cleaned sorrel with one ounce of butter for ten minutes, and then strain it as for the above. Moisten with three pints of broth (No. 99), adding one more ounce of butter, one sliced, raw potato, two leeks cut in small squares, half an onion, also cut, half a tablespoonful of salt, and a teaspoonful of pepper. Cook well for thirty minutes, and serve with six slices of bread, but add no thickening.

82. Cream of Chicken.—Pound half a boiled chicken in a mortar, then put it in a saucepan, and moisten with three pints of white broth (No.99), adding one cupful of raw rice, one bouquet (No. 254), half a tablespoonful of salt, twelve whole peppers, and three cloves. Boil thoroughly for thirty minutes; then strain through a fine sieve; put in half a cupful of cream, and serve with two tablespoonfuls of small pieces of cooked chicken in the tureen, or croûtons soufflés instead of the chicken.

83. Cream of Game.—The same as for No. 82, using game instead of chicken; the same quantity of each being needed.

84. Cream à l'Allemande.

—Heat half a pint of mirepoix (No. 138) in a saucepan with one ounce of butter, adding two tablespoonfuls of flour, and moistening with three pints of white broth (No. 99); season with half a tablespoonful of salt and three cloves. Boil for thirty minutes, then strain, and after adding an ounce of good butter, serve with two ounces of very finely cut noodles (No. 1182) which have been previously boiled in salted water.

85. Cream of Turnips.—Put three medium sized cut-up raw turnips in a saucepan with one ounce of butter; steam them for thirty minutes, then add one pint of good béchamel sauce (No. 154); rub through a sieve and moisten with one quart of white broth (No. 99); season with a tablespoonful of salt and a teaspoonful of pepper. Heat it while stirring continually, and serve with half a cupful of cream beaten with two egg yolks.

86. Cream of Celery à l'Espagnole. —Put two stalks of celery, cut into fine strips, in a covered saucepan, with one ounce of butter; add a pint of good broth (No. 99), with half a tablespoonful of salt and a teaspoonful of pepper. Boil for thirty minutes; then rub through a sieve, moisten with one quart of broth, and before serving thicken with two egg yolks diluted in half a cupful of cold consommé (No. 100). Add three tablespoonfuls of boiled rice, and, two minutes before serving, one ounce of butter. After the egg yolks have been added to the soup it should not be allowed to boil again.

87. Cream of Lettuce. —Wash thoroughly the green leaves of three good-sized heads of lettuce; drain and chop them up; place them in a saucepan with a quarter of a pound of butter, and cook for five minutes, stirring it lightly. Moisten with two quarts of white broth (No. 99); season with a tablespoonful of salt, a teaspoonful of pepper, and half a teaspoonful of grated nutmeg; add a bouquet (No. 254), and four ounces of well-cleaned, raw rice; cover the saucepan, and cook for forty-five minutes. Remove the bouquet and strain the soup through a fine sieve. Clean the saucepan well, replace the cream in it, and let it heat thoroughly, but do not let it boil, meanwhile stirring it gently with the spatula. Pour in a pint of sweet cream, stir a little more, and throw it into a hot soup tureen, serving it with croûtons soufflés (No. 134).

88. Cream of Lentils à la Major-domo.—Soak one pint of lentils for four hours in cold water; then put them on to boil in a saucepan, with two quarts of water, one carrot, one onion, two ounces of salt pork, six whole peppers, a bouquet (No. 254), and the bones of one partridge; also half a tablespoonful of salt. Cook for forty-five minutes, then rub through a sieve;

cut half the breast of a partridge in slices, lay them in the soup-tureen with an ounce of butter, pour the purée over, and serve with a handful of fried sippets of bread, suppressing the bouquet.

89. Purée of Partridge à la Destaing. —Pound in a mortar the bones of a partridge, and half a pint of purée of chestnuts (No. 131). Put the whole into a saucepan, and moisten with three pints of white broth (No. 99), one ounce of butter, and half a tablespoonful of salt and a teaspoonful of pepper. Boil for forty-five minutes; then rub through a wire sieve, adding about an ounce more butter and three tablespoonfuls of cooked rice just before serving.

90. Purée of Partridge à la Gentilhomme. —Pound well the bones of one of any kind of game, place them in a saucepan, add half a pint of purée of lentils with three pints of white broth (No. 99), half a tablespoonful of salt and a teaspoonful of pepper, and one ounce of butter. Boil forty-five minutes, then rub through a fine sieve, stir well while on the fire, not letting it come to a boil, and finish with one ounce of fresh butter. Serve with twelve small game quenelles (No. 228).

91. Purée of Chestnuts à la Jardinièr e.—Place in a saucepan one pint of purée of chestnuts (No. 131), moisten it with one pint of white broth (No. 99) and a glassful of Madeira wine; boil for thirty minutes, then put in a quarter of a carrot, the same of turnip cut with a tin tube, a tablespoonful of asparagus-tops, six Brussels sprouts, and a piece of cut-up cauliflower the size of an egg. Boil all together for fifteen minutes, and serve after seasoning with half a tablespoonful of salt and a teaspoonful of pepper.

92. Purée of Beans Soubise. —After soaking a pint of white beans for four hours, cook them in a saucepan with one ounce of butter and two sliced onions, and moisten with three pints of white broth (No. 99); season with half a tablespoonful of salt and a teaspoonful of pepper. Boil for forty-five minutes; then rub through a fine sieve, and serve with a thickening of two egg yolks and half a cupful of cream. Add twelve quenelles to the soup (No. 231), and serve.

93. Potage à la Diplomate. —Blanch a beef palate for two minutes in boiling water, then scrape it well, drain, cook again for one hour, and then cut it up in dice shape. Place it in a stewpan with one pint of consommé (No. 100), half a glassful of Madeira wine, and half a pinch each of salt and pepper; pour the liquid over and cook for thirty minutes. Now prepare, in another saucepan, one quart of a stock such as clear green turtle (No. 18), add the beef palates, and twelve chicken quenelles or forcemeat balls (No. 226) and serve.

94. Potage à la Windsor.—Boil for one hour, in two quarts of white broth (No. 99) and one quart of water, three calf's feet; when done, bone and cut them into pieces (they are preferable if cold); moisten with three pints of their own broth, adding a bouquet (No. 254), half a glassful of Madeira wine, half a tablespoonful of salt, and a very little cayenne pepper. Boil again for ten minutes, then strain through a fine sieve, darken the soup with a little essence of caramel, and when serving add twelve crawfish quenelles (No. 227).

95. Potage à la McDonald.—Pound a cooked calf's brain in a mortar; add two cooked onions, three raw egg yolks, and a teaspoonful of curry powder; rub well through a fine sieve, and when ready to serve pour it into three pints of white broth (No. 99) in the saucepan, adding a peeled and baked cucumber cut in slices. Then serve.

96. Potage à la D'Orsay.—Place in a saucepan a pint of béchamel (No. 154). One pint of white broth (No. 99), half a tablespoonful of salt and a teaspoonful of pepper, and let simmer on the corner of the fire for fifteen minutes. Add to this half a pint of cream of asparagus (No. 70) and one ounce of butter; when finished boiling, put in the tureen six soft-boiled and well-pared pigeon eggs, and the breast of one pigeon cut in julienne; pour the soup over, and serve.

97. Potage Montmorency.—Add to one quart of boiling consommé (No. 100), in a saucepan, half a cupful of noodles (No. 1182) previously blanched in salted water; thicken with the yolks of two beaten eggs, a tablespoonful of grated Parmesan cheese, half a cupful of cream, and one ounce of butter; pour into the tureen, adding either the minced leg or wing of a cooked chicken, and serve with three heads of baked lettuce cut in two, on a separate dish.

98. Potage of Rice à la Maintenon.—Take one quart of white broth (No. 99), one pint of béchamel (No. 154), half a tablespoonful of salt and a teaspoonful of pepper, and add to it half a raw chicken; cook for twenty minutes in the saucepan on the fire, then take the chicken out and thicken the soup with the yolks of two beaten eggs, and a teaspoonful of powdered curry, mixed with half a cupful of cream; rub all through a fine sieve, and serve, adding two tablespoonfuls of boiled rice, and the breast of the half chicken previously cooked in the soup, and cut into small pieces.

99. Bouillon Blanc—White broth.—Place in a large stock-urn on a moderate fire a good heavy knuckle of a fine white veal with all the débris, or scraps of meat, including bones, remaining in the kitchen (but not of game); cover fully with cold water, adding a handful of salt; and as it comes to a boil, be very careful to skim all the scum off—no particle of scum should be left on—and then put in two large, sound, well-scraped carrots (whole), one whole, cleaned, sound turnip, one whole, peeled, large, sound onion, one well-cleaned parsley root, three thoroughly washed leeks, and a few leaves of cleaned celery. Boil very slowly for six hours on the corner of the range, keenly skim the grease off; then strain well through a wet cloth into a china bowl or a stone jar, and put it away in a cool place for general use.

100. Consommé pure—Consommé plain.—Chop up a shin of beef of twelve pounds, *using a machine if practicable*; put it in a large soup kettle with two sound, well-scraped, good-sized carrots, two peeled, sound onions, three well-washed and pared leeks, a few branches of celery, and one bunch of parsley roots, all well-scraped, washed, and shred, six cloves, eighteen whole peppers, a bay-leaf, and the whites of six raw eggs, including their shells. Mix all well together, and then moisten with two gallons of cold white broth (No. 99), one quart of cold water (all this should be done before the soup-kettle has been placed on the hot range). Stir thoroughly for two or three minutes without ceasing; and then place it on the hot range, add some débris of chicken if any at hand. Boil slowly for about four hours, skim the grease off thoroughly, and then strain through a wet cloth into a china bowl or stone jar, and put away in a cool place for general use. Should the white broth that you employ be hot, replace the cold water by a piece of ice well cracked, and the equivalent of a quart of water, adding it to the consommé very gradually at the beginning, but continually increasing, and stirring till all added. (Always taste if sufficiently seasoned before serving).

101. Consommé Dubourg.—Cut half a pint of royal (No. 107) into pieces; put three tablespoonfuls of cooked rice into a soup-tureen, and pour three pints of boiling consommé over it, and serve.

102. Consommé Massena.—Add half a glassful of Madeira wine and a bouquet (No. 254) to three pints of game-stock (No. 219), and boil well together for two hours. Have ready three tablespoonfuls of purée of chestnuts (No. 131), mixing in three egg yolks, adding a very little salt and the same of pepper. Take six small timbale-molds, butter them well, and fill them with the above preparation. Poach them for two minutes; take them out, and let them get cool before unmolding them. Put them in a soup-tureen and serve, adding the boiling game-stock.

103. Consommé aux Pâtes. —When one quart of consommé is boiling very hard, add three-quarters of a cupful of paste, such as vermicelli or any other Italian paste; let them cook for six minutes, stirring frequently; then serve. (Pastes such as macaroni, rice, spaghetti, noodles &c., must first be parboiled, and, when necessary, broken into pieces before being added to the soup.)

104. Consommé à la Semoule, or Tapioca.

—Into one quart of boiling consommé (No. 100), sprinkle four tablespoonfuls of semolina, or tapioca, stirring constantly; boil thoroughly for ten minutes, and skim the surface just previous to serving.

105. Consommé Tapioca or Semoule à la Creme.—The same as for No. 104, adding to the tureen a thickening of two egg yolks with half a cupful of cream when ready to serve.

106. Consommé à la Sevigne.—With chicken forcemeat (No. 226) fill six very small timbale-molds; let them poach for two minutes in hot water, then set them aside to cool, turn them out, and put them into the tureen with two tablespoonfuls of cooked asparagus-tops, and two tablespoonfuls of cooked green peas; pour over it one quart of boiling consommé (No. 100), and serve.

107. Consommé Royal.—Take six egg yolks and two whole eggs, half a teaspoonful of nutmeg, half a tablespoonful of salt, and a scant teaspoonful of cayenne pepper; beat well together in a bowl, adding half a pint of cream; strain through a fine hair sieve and fill up six small timbale-molds, being careful that they are previously well buttered. Cook them in a stewpan with boiling water to half their height; then place them in the oven until they become firm, which will take about fifteen minutes; immediately after taking them from their moulds, cut them in slices, and add them to one quart of boiling consommé (No. 100) when ready to serve in a tureen.

108. Consommé Deslignac.—Make a royal consommé for three timbales (No. 107), but instead of cream use consommé; unmold, cut them dice-shaped, and put them in the tureen with half a cupful of cooked printanier (No. 109) and one quart of boiling hot consommé (No. 100); then serve.

109. Consommé Printanier.—Cut out, with a vegetable scoop, two carrots and one turnip; simmer them for twenty minutes in water and with a tablespoonful of salt, then drain and throw them into a quart of consommé (No. 100) in a saucepan with two tablespoonfuls of cooked green peas, and two tablespoonfuls of cooked string beans cut into small pieces. Add a handful of chiffonade (No. 132), cook five minutes more, and serve in a hot tureen.

110. Consommé à la D'Orleans.—Add a little crawfish butter (No. 150) to eight fish quenelles; fill six long-shaped quenelle molds with this and poach them in salted water for two minutes; drain, and after unmolding put them in a tureen with two tablespoonfuls of cooked green peas and as much boiled rice; pour one quart of boiling consommé (No. 100) over it, and serve.

111. Consommé à l'Imperiale.—Place four tablespoonfuls of chicken forcemeat (No. 226) in a paper cornet; cut away the end of the cornet. Butter a pan, and with the contents of the cornet, make eighteen round quenelles; put on top of each quenelle a small slice of truffle; poach them for two minutes in white broth (No. 99); then drain through a sieve, and serve in the tureen, after pouring one quart of consommé (No. 100) over them and adding a tablespoonful of cooked green peas and six cock's combs.

112. Consommé Garibaldi.—Proceed the same as for No. 107; have two green timbales, two red ones; use a very little carmine Broton, then use two more plain timbales, and serve.

113. Consommé Princesse.—Wash well three tablespoonfuls of barley, drain, and place it in a saucepan with three pints of consommé (No. 100), and let boil for forty minutes. Add two tablespoonfuls of cooked breast of chicken cut in dice, two tablespoonfuls of cooked green peas, and serve in a hot tureen.

114. Consommé Douglas.—Pare and blanch for ten minutes half a root of celery as for a julienne (No. 27); then place it in a saucepan, adding two tablespoonfuls of boiled rice, half an ounce of smoked, cooked tongue, and six mushrooms, both shred very small; pour one quart of hot consommé (No. 100) over it and serve.

115. Consommé Renaissance.—With two ounces of pâté-à-chou (No. 1240) make a handful of croûtons, the size of the little finger; cook them on a tin dish in the oven for ten minutes, and when done fill them inside with chicken forcemeat (No. 226) pressed through a cornet. Put them in a tureen with two tablespoonfuls of cooked peas, and two spoonfuls of sliced mushrooms; pour one quart of consommé (No. 100) over them, and serve.

116. Consommé à l'Africaine.—Cut one cooked artichoke bottom dice-shaped, also one slice of fried egg-plant cut in pieces; drain them on a cloth to remove all the fat, then add two tablespoonfuls of cooked rice, and a teaspoonful of powdered curry diluted in water; put these in a soup tureen with one quart of consommé (No. 100) poured over them, and serve.

117. Consommé à l'Andalouse.—Boil three tablespoonfuls of tapioca in one quart of consommé (No. 100); add half a pint of thin tomato sauce (No.

205), boil for ten minutes, and serve with twelve small quenelles of godiveau. (No. 221).

118. Consommé Celestine.—Make two light French pancakes (No. 1186) cover one with chicken forcemeat (No. 226), and sprinkle over it a little grated Parmesan cheese; then put the other one on top, and cut them in twelve slices with a tube, and serve in one quart of boiling consommé (No. 100) in a hot tureen.

119. Consommé à l'Anglaise.—Add half a cupful of minced cooked chicken, and three tablespoonfuls of cooked green peas to one quart of boiling consommé (No. 100), and serve in a hot tureen.

120. Consommé Colbert.—Add six poached eggs (No. 404) to one quart of boiling consommé (No. 100) before serving.

121. Consommé Printanier Colbert.—The same as for the above, adding half a pint of cooked printanier (No. 51).

122. Consommé Suèdoise.—Cut three rolls in halves, and take out the crumbs; make a preparation, cutting up together one carrot, half a turnip, one leaf of a white cabbage, two tablespoonfuls of peas, and one tablespoonful of string beans; add one ounce of butter, half a tablespoonful of salt, and very little pepper. Leave it very thick, and cook for twenty minutes in a saucepan, adding two tablespoonfuls of grated Parmesan cheese. Fill the rolls with this mixture, and sprinkle the tops with more cheese and a few drops of drawn butter; place them in the oven for two minutes, and serve with three pints of consommé (No. 100) in a hot soup-tureen.

123. Consommé Rachel.—Decorate the bottom and sides of twelve quenelle molds with sliced truffles, and the same of smoked cooked tongue, being careful to have them well buttered. Fill them with chicken forcemeat (No. 226); poach them in salted water for two minutes, unmold, and serve with one quart of boiling consommé (No. 100) in the hot tureen.

124. Consommé Printanier Royale.—Add to one quart of boiling consommé (No. 100) three royals (No. 107) cut into pieces, also half a pint of cooked printanier (No. 51), and serve.

125. Consommé Duchesse.—Butter and cover a tin plate with two ounces of pâté-à-chou (No. 1240), about the height of a quarter of an inch. Cook it in the oven for six minutes, then remove, and fill it with forcemeat (No. 226) pressed through a cornet; cut it with a paste cutter into twelve equal-sized pieces, put them in the tureen, pour one quart of boiling consommé (No. 100) over them, and serve.

126. Consommé Patti.—Cut half a breast of a cooked chicken into small pieces; put them in a tureen, adding two tablespoonfuls of boiled rice, two tablespoonfuls of cooked green peas, and one truffle cut dice-shaped. Pour one quart of boiling consommé (No. 100) over it, and serve with grated cheese separate.

127. Consommé Napolitaine.—Cut two ounces of cooked spaghetti into pieces, adding half an ounce of cut-up, cooked tongue, half an ounce of lean, cooked ham, and three mushrooms cut into small pieces. Pour all into a tureen with one quart of consommé (No. 100), and serve with grated cheese separate.

128. Consommé Chatelaine.—Take three molds. Add to the four whites of well-beaten eggs half a pint of purée of onions (Soubise No. 250), and a quarter of a pint of cream; beat well together with a very little grated nutmeg, and half a tablespoonful of salt. Fill the molds, previously well buttered; then poach them in water to half their height for six minutes, and unmold. Cut them into twelve pieces, and put them in the soup-tureen, adding two tablespoonfuls of cooked asparagus-tops, and the same quantity of green peas. Pour one quart of consommé (No. 100) over it, and serve very hot.

129. Consommé aux Quenelles.—Have ready eighteen small godiveau quenelles (No. 221). Arrange them in a well-buttered stewpan, being careful they do not touch each other; pour some salted water over them, and let them poach for two minutes. Drain on a perfectly dry sieve, and put them in the tureen with one quart of boiling consommé (No. 100), and serve.

130. Onion Soup.—Brown two onions in a saucepan with one ounce of butter, stir in a little flour, and moisten with three pints of white broth (No. 99); season with half a tablespoonful of salt and a teaspoonful of pepper, and cook for ten minutes. Place six pieces of toasted bread in a bowl; cover them with fine slices of Swiss cheese, pour the broth over them, add a few more slices of cheese on top, and put it in the oven five minutes before serving.

131. Purée of Chestnuts.—Boil one pound of chestnuts for ten minutes; peel and skin them immediately, put them in a saucepan with one quart of white broth (No. 99), a tablespoonful of salt, and two teaspoonfuls of pepper and a quarter of a pound of butter. Let all boil well for thirty minutes; rub through a sieve, and use when needed.

132. Chiffonade for Soups.—Chop well together half a head of lettuce, half a handful of sorrel, a few branches of chervil, and a little parsley. Use it in soups five minutes before serving.

133. Croûtons for Soups.—Cut some dice-shaped pieces of bread, and fry them in a pan with clarified butter; when a rich golden color, drain, and add to the soup when needed.

133½. Croûtons for Garnishing.—Cut six rather thin slices out of an American loaf of bread; neatly pare, then cut them into heart-shaped croûtons. Lay them on a tin plate, drip a little clarified butter over them, place in the hot oven for four minutes, to let get a good golden color. Take from out the oven, and use when required.

134. Croûtons Soufflés.—Make some pâté-à-chou (No. 1240), spread it out to the thickness of macaroni, and cut with a knife the size of a pea. Put them in a sieve, sprinkle with flour, shake well, and fry in hot lard; when done, which will take five minutes, drain through a cloth, and serve with the soup when needed.

A pinch of salt represents 205 grains, or a tablespoonful.

Half a pinch of pepper represents 38 grains, or a teaspoonful.

A third of a pinch of nutmeg represents 13 grains, or half a teaspoonful.

STOCKS, SAUCES, FORCEMEATS, AND GARNISHINGS.

135. White-Roux.—Put in a saucepan two ounces of butter, and place it on the corner of the hot range, add to it two tablespoonfuls of flour; keep stirring constantly for seven minutes. Then let it cool, and when cold, use in various sauces, as directed.

136. Brown-Roux.—Place two ounces of good butter in a saucepan on the hot range; mix in two tablespoonfuls of flour, and cook rapidly for about seven minutes, or until it assumes a rich brown color. Let it thoroughly cool off, and then use in different sauces, as mentioned.

137. White Stock—for one gallon.—Reduce in saucepan on the hot range, one ounce of very good, finely shred, salt pork, previously well washed, and the same of beef suet. Add one carrot, one onion, a bouquet of aromatic herbs (No. 254), twelve whole peppers, and four cloves. Brown these well on a moderate fire for four minutes. Add four ounces of flour; stir well, and moisten with a glassful of white wine and three quarts of white broth (No. 99). Add one tablespoonful of salt, and stir until it comes to a boil; then let it cook thoroughly for one hour; strain through a fine sieve. This stock should be used without any further thickening.

138. Mirepoix.—Stew in a saucepan two ounces of fat, two carrots, one onion, one sprig of thyme, one bay-leaf, six whole peppers, three cloves, and, if handy, a ham bone cut into pieces. Add two sprigs of celery and half a bunch of parsley roots; cook for fifteen minutes, and use when directed in other recipes. Scraps of baked veal may also be added, if at hand.

139. Marinade Stock, cooked—for one gallon.—Stew together a finely sliced sound onion and four parsley roots, adding one pint of vinegar and four quarts of fresh water, also a quarter of a bunch of thyme, six bay-leaves, twenty-four whole peppers, and twelve cloves. Cook well for thirty minutes on a brisk fire, then place in a stone jar, and keep it in a cool place for general use.

140. Marinade Stock, raw—for six persons.—Finely slice one medium-sized, sound, peeled onion, place it in an earthen crock, with three slices of lemon, two bay-leaves, twelve whole peppers, four cloves, three whole mace, and three sprigs of parsley roots. Add to these two tablespoonfuls of sweet oil, a cupful of vinegar, and a pinch of salt. Place the meat or fish in this, and leave it to souse as long as necessary, or about six hours.

141. Meat Glaze—Glace de Viande.—As this meat glaze, when properly made, will keep in perfect condition for any length of time, I would advise that half a pint be made at a time, in the following manner. Place in a large saucepan ten quarts of white broth (No. 99), or nine quarts of consommé (No. 100), and reduce it on a moderate fire for fully four hours, at which time it should be reduced to half a pint. Transfer it in a stone jar or bowl; put a cover on, and keep in a cool place for general use.

142. Court Bouillon.—Cut up one good-sized, peeled and well-washed carrot, with a sound onion, and half a bunch of parsley roots, also cut up; brown them in a glassful of white or red wine, according to the fish; add to it any well-washed pieces of fish-heads and a pint of water. Season with half a pinch each of salt and pepper. Boil well for five minutes; let cool; strain through a napkin or a sieve into a jar, and use when needed. Always avoid straining anything acid into tin or copper vessels—to prevent blackening.

143. Cooked Fine Herbs.—Chop up one sound onion and two well-peeled shallots; brown them in a saucepan with one ounce of butter, for five minutes, then add double the quantity of finely minced mushrooms and a grain of garlic; season with half a tablespoonful of salt and a teaspoonful of pepper, and finish with a tablespoonful of chopped parsley. Cook ten minutes longer, and then let it cool.

144. Raw Fine Herbs.—Chop separately, half an onion, two shallots, two sprigs of parsley, four hairs of chives, and the same of chervil; mix thoroughly before using.

145. Butter, maître d'hôtel.—Put one ounce of good butter in a bowl with a teaspoonful of very finely chopped parsley, adding the juice of half a sound lemon. Mingle well with a very little nutmeg, and keep it in a cool place to use when needed.

146. Anchovy Butter.—To one ounce of good butter, add one teaspoonful of anchovy essence; mix well, and keep it on ice—for general use.

147. Butter à la Ravigote.—Pound together in a mortar one sprig of parsley, the same of tarragon, very little chives, the same of chervil, and one small, peeled shallot. Add half a teaspoonful of anchovy essence, one ounce of good butter, and half a drop of spinach-green. Rub through a fine sieve, and keep it in a cool place for general use.

148. Horseradish Butter.—Pound in a mortar one teaspoonful of grated horseradish with one ounce of good butter, and season with very little red pepper—third of a saltspoonful. Rub through a fine sieve, and keep it in a cool place. When this butter is added to other sauces, it should not boil again.

149. Lobster Butter.—Extract the coral from one cooked lobster (the eggs may be used instead); pound it in a mortar to a paste, mixing it with one ounce of good butter and a teaspoonful of mustard. Rub through a fine sieve, and keep in a cool place. The butter can also be used for coloring purposes.

150. Crawfish Butter.—Pick the meat from the tails of twelve boiled crawfish; dry the shells, and pound them all together in a mortar, adding one ounce of good butter; then place it in a saucepan on a moderate fire, stirring, until it clarifies, for about five minutes; then strain through a napkin, letting it drop into cold water. When it is congealed, take it out, and place it in a warm basin, stirring until it assumes the desired color. The same method can be used for lobsters and shrimps.

151. Sauce Espagnole—for one gallon.—Mix one pint of raw, strong mirepoix (No. 138) with two ounces of good fat (chicken's fat is preferable). Mix with the compound four ounces of flour, and moisten with one gallon of white broth (No. 99). Stir well, and then add, if handy, some baked veal and ham bones. Boil for three hours, and then remove the fat very carefully; rub the sauce through a very fine sieve, and keep it for many purposes in cooking.

152. Sauce Velouté.—Melt one ounce of good butter in a saucepan, adding two tablespoonfuls of flour, and stir well, not letting it get brown. Moisten with a pint and a half of good veal and chicken stock, the stronger the better. Throw in a garnished bouquet (No. 254), half a cupful of mushroom liquor, if at hand, six whole peppers, half a pinch of salt, and a very little nutmeg. Boil for twenty minutes, stirring continuously with a wooden spatula; then remove to the side of the fire, skim thoroughly, and let it continue simmering slowly for one hour. Then rub through a fine sieve. This sauce will make the foundation for any kind of good white stock.

153. Sauce Villeroi.—Strain and place in a saucepan with one ounce of butter, two tablespoonfuls of raw mirepoix (No. 138), adding two tablespoonfuls of flour. Cook, and mix well together for five minutes; moisten with three pints of white broth (No. 99), and season with half a tablespoonful of salt. Boil for one hour; then strain through a fine sieve and use when needed.

154. Béchamel Sauce.—Place in a saucepan two ounces of butter, add two tablespoonfuls of flour, and stir constantly for five minutes. Moisten with a pint and a half of boiling milk, being careful to pour it in gradually; then beat it well with a whisk. Add half a teaspoonful of grated nutmeg, a pinch of salt, a bouquet (No. 254), twelve whole peppers, and a little mushroom liquor, if at hand. Cook well for fifteen minutes, and when done rub through a fine sieve.

155. Melted Butter Sauce.—Put one ounce of good butter in a saucepan on a slow fire, stir, and when melted add the juice of half a lemon. Serve in a sauce bowl.

156. Nut-brown Butter Sauce.—Place one ounce of good butter in a frying-pan, let it heat until it assumes a nut-brown color, then add one drop of vinegar, and use when needed.

157. Black Butter Sauce.—Warm one ounce of good butter in the frying-pan until it becomes brown; add six parsley leaves, heat again for one minute, then throw in five drops of vinegar. Pour it into a sauce-bowl and serve.

158. Lobster Sauce.—Pour one pint of Hollandaise sauce (No. 160) into a saucepan; place it on the hot stove, but do not allow it to boil. Add the claw of a good-sized boiled lobster cut into lozenge-shaped pieces; heat well for five minutes, stirring it lightly, add a quarter of an ounce of lobster butter (No. 149), and serve when needed.

159. Drawn-Butter Sauce.—Put two ounces of butter in a saucepan, adding two tablespoonfuls of flour while stirring; moisten with one quart of water, and season with one tablespoonful of salt and half a teaspoonful of pepper. Let it simmer on the side of the stove for thirty minutes until it thickens; then add, little by little, half an ounce of butter, beating it continuously until it becomes perfectly white. Squeeze in the juice of a lemon; stir once more, strain through a hair sieve and serve.

160. Sauce Hollandaise.—Place one sound, sliced onion, six whole peppers and a bay-leaf in a saucepan with two ounces of good butter on the hot stove; stir in two tablespoonfuls of flour to thicken, then moisten with a pint and a half of either chicken or white broth (No. 99); mix well with a whisk or wooden spatula, being careful to remove any accumulated fat. Add half a teaspoonful of grated nutmeg and half a tablespoonful of salt, and cook for twenty-five minutes. Beat the yolks of three eggs separately with the juice of half a medium-sized sound lemon. Pour them gradually into the sauce, being careful not to boil it again after they have been added. Rub through a hair sieve into a serving bowl, and finish with half an ounce of good butter, mixing it well, and serve.

161. Egg Sauce.—Use one pint of the Hollandaise sauce (No. 160), and when ready to serve sprinkle it with two chopped hard-boiled eggs and a teaspoonful of minced parsley.

162. Bread Sauce.—Crumble one and a half ounces of fresh bread crumbs, and place them in a saucepan with not quite half a cupful of cold water; add half an ounce of butter, half a tablespoonful of salt, and six whole peppers. Cook for five minutes; then pour in half a cupful of cream or milk. Cook again for five minutes, and serve in a sauce-bowl, removing the peppers.

163. Anchovy Sauce.—To three-quarters of a pint of drawn-butter sauce (No. 159), or Hollandaise sauce (No. 160), add one tablespoonful of anchovy essence; beat well together and serve.

164. Horseradish Sauce.—Add two tablespoonfuls of grated horseradish to three-quarters of a pint of béchamel sauce (No. 154); also half a pinch of powdered sugar, a third of a pinch of cayenne pepper, and half a pinch of salt. Boil for five minutes. Should the sauce be too thick add a little cream or milk, and three drops of vinegar in case the horseradish be fresh.

165. Sauce Percillade.—Pour half a cupful of sweet oil into an earthen bowl with the juice of half a lemon, half a tablespoonful of salt, and a scant teaspoonful of pepper. Beat well with a spoon or whisk, adding one teaspoonful of parsley, half the quantity of chervil, the same of tarragon and chives all chopped very fine together, and a teaspoonful of mustard. Mix the whole well before serving.

166. Sauce Béarnaise.—Chop very fine two medium-sized, sound, well-peeled shallots; place them in a small saucepan on the hot range, with two tablespoonfuls of either tarragon or chervil vinegar, and five whole crushed peppers. Reduce until nearly dry, then put away to cool. Mingle with it six fresh raw egg yolks, sharply stirring meanwhile, then gradually add one and a half ounce of good fresh butter; seasoning with half a tablespoonful of salt, half a teaspoonful of grated nutmeg, and twelve finely chopped sound tarragon leaves. Have a much wider pan on the fire with boiling water, place the small one containing the ingredients into the other, and see that the boiling water reaches up to half its height; thoroughly heat up, beating briskly with the whisk; when the sauce is firm add one teaspoonful of melted meat-glaze (No. 141), beat lightly for two seconds longer, then strain through an ordinary, clean kitchen towel, neatly arrange the sauce on a hot dish to be sent to the table; and dress over it any article required to be served.

167. Sauce Trianon.—The same as for Béarnaise sauce (No. 166), but pour the sauce over the article to be served, instead of under; finish with two medium-sized sliced truffles, nicely arranged on top.

168. Apple Sauce.—Core, peel and quarter four sour apples. Place them in a saucepan with half a glassful of water, half a tablespoonful of salt, and two ounces of sugar. Cover and cook for about twenty-five minutes, or until the apples are reduced to a marmalade; then strain through a colander, and add the third of a pinch of cinnamon, if necessary.

169. Mint Sauce.—Take one-quarter of a bunch of finely minced mint-leaves, moistening with half a cupful of water and half a cupful of broth (No. 99), or consommé (No. 100); add four tablespoonfuls of vinegar, a tablespoonful of salt, and half an ounce of sugar; stir well and serve in a sauce-bowl.

170. Green Sauce.—Pound in a mortar one sprig of parsley and three hairs of chervil; add three medium-sized vinegar-pickles, half a small, white onion, one anchovy, and a teaspoonful of capers. Mix these with soaked bread the size of an egg, and pound all well together. When the preparation is reduced to a paste, rub it through a fine sieve, put it in a bowl and stir well, adding half a cupful of sweet oil, two tablespoonfuls of vinegar, half a teaspoonful of pepper, and half a tablespoonful of salt. This sauce must be consistent and of a green color.

171. Suprême Sauce.—Clean thoroughly the carcass of one raw chicken and place it in a saucepan, covering it with water; cook quickly, and at the first boil take it off, drain and wash the carcass well. Put it back into a very clean saucepan, covering it with one quart of white broth (No. 99), adding a bouquet (No. 254) and half a tablespoonful of salt. Cook for forty-five minutes; have two tablespoonfuls of white roux (No. 135) separate; pour the broth over it, continuing to stir; reduce to half, and strain through a fine Chinese strainer. Add half a cupful of good cream and an ounce of fresh butter and finish with the juice of half a lemon.

172. Tarragon Sauce.—Put half a pint sauce velouté (No. 152) to boil in a saucepan on the hot stove. Add half a cupful of white broth (No. 99) and two sprigs of tarragon. Season with a very little salt, and cook for ten minutes. Cut up very fine, and add to the sauce when serving twelve blanched tarragon leaves.

173. Oyster Sauce.—Open eighteen medium-sized, fine Shrewsbury oysters and put them in a saucepan with one ounce of good butter, placing the pan on the stove. Cook for four minutes; remove half the liquid from the pan and add a pint of hot Allemande sauce (No. 210). Then with the spatula mix lightly together without allowing it to boil, and serve.

174. Indian Sauce.—Brown in a saucepan one sliced onion, one ounce of raw lean ham, one sprig of thyme, and twelve whole peppers, with one ounce of butter. Add a teaspoonful of powdered curry diluted in a pint of sauce velouté (No. 152); boil for ten minutes. Then strain through a Chinese strainer into another saucepan, being careful to pour in half a cupful of cream, the juice of half a lemon and two egg yolks. Then serve.

175. Sauce Normande, for Fish.—To a pint of sauce velouté (No. 152) add two tablespoonfuls of mushroom liquor. Reduce the sauce for ten minutes, and place in it two tablespoonfuls of fish-stock (No. 214). Let it just boil again, then add two egg yolks and the juice of half a lemon; strain through a fine sieve and stir in half an ounce of fresh butter. This sauce should be consistent.

175½. Normande, garnishing for Meat.—Neatly peel and wash well twelve celery knobs, drain, and then place six of them in a saucepan with one tablespoonful of butter, one pinch of salt, half a pinch of pepper, and a gill of white broth (No. 99), and cook for twenty minutes on a moderate fire; then mash them as you would potatoes; when thoroughly mashed place them in a warm place for further action. Take the other six celery knobs, cut out very carefully the centres with the aid of a vegetable scoop, leaving about half an inch uncut at the bottom to prevent burning. Season with one pinch of salt only, evenly divided. Stuff them with the above farce; then place them in a saucepan with half a medium-sized, sound, scraped and sliced carrot, half a peeled and sliced onion, and a tablespoonful of butter. Cook three minutes on a moderate fire. Add a wine-glassful of good cider and a gill of white broth (No. 99). Cook again for twenty minutes. Arrange the remaining mashed celery in the centre of the hot serving dish, place the meat over it, nicely surround the dish with the six stuffed celery knobs, strain the gravy over, arranging a small piece of cooked cauliflower on top of each, and serve very hot.

176. Sauce à la Toulouse.—To a pint of Hollandaise sauce (No. 160) add two tablespoonfuls of white wine, one sliced truffle, and six minced mushrooms. Heat well without boiling, and when serving add a little meat-glaze (No. 141).

177. Sauce maître d'hôtel, liée.—Add to half a pint of warm Hollandaise sauce (No. 160), a teaspoonful of chopped parsley, half an ounce of butter, a scant teaspoonful of pepper, and half a teaspoonful of nutmeg; then serve.

178. Shrimp Sauce.—Place half an ounce of shrimp butter (No. 150) in half a pint of Hollandaise sauce (No. 160); stir well on the fire for five minutes, and when ready to serve add twelve picked shrimp tails and the juice of half a lemon. Heat without boiling, and serve.

179. Sauce à la Venitienne.—Reduce for four minutes one tablespoonful of tarragon-vinegar and chervil-vinegar with six whole peppers, one ounce of lean cooked ham cut into small dice, six parsley roots, one sprig of thyme, and one bay-leaf. Then strain through a napkin into a bowl; moisten with half a pint of sauce velouté (No. 152), and finish the sauce with twelve leaves of finely cut tarragon, two drops of spinach green, and a teaspoonful of chopped parsley.

180. Sauce à la Matelote.—Reduce for five minutes one glassful of good red wine with a bouquet (No. 254) and a small glassful of mushroom liquor; then add half a pint of velouté (No. 152) and boil for five minutes. Strain, and then add the third of a tablespoonful of salt and a scant teaspoonful of pepper, and throw in twelve small, cooked, glazed onions (No. 972), four mushrooms cut into quarters, and one ounce of cooked salt pork cut in dice. Cook again for five minutes, and serve.

181. Cream Sauce.—Take half a pint of béchamel sauce (No. 154); add half an ounce of butter, and beat them together carefully, adding half a cupful of sweet cream. Then serve.

182. Sauce à l'Aurore.—To half a pint of hot, highly seasoned béchamel sauce (No. 154) in a saucepan add a small glassful of mushroom liquor, half an ounce of butter, and three tablespoonfuls of very red tomato sauce (No. 205). Stir well on the fire for five minutes, then add square cuts of six whole mushrooms, and serve.

183. Sauce à la Duchesse.—Cut up in small dice-shaped pieces half an ounce of cooked ham and two truffles, place these in a saucepan on the fire, with half a wine-glassful of white wine; let reduce for three minutes on a brisk fire. Add one gill of good tomato sauce (No. 205). Boil for one minute with a tablespoonful of glace de viande (No. 141). Add half a pint of Allemande sauce (No. 210). Toss well while heating, but do not allow to boil again, and serve very hot.

184. Sauce Princesse.—Take eighteen chicken quenelles, two truffles cut in slices, and one blanched chicken liver cut in dice shape; place all in a saucepan on the fire with half a glassful of white wine, and let reduce for three minutes; then add one tablespoonful of glace de viande (No. 141), let come to a boil; add half a pint of good Allemande sauce (No. 210). Toss well together, but do not allow to boil, and serve very hot.

185. Sauce Demi-Glace, or Madeira.—Add one small glassful of mushroom liquor to one pint of good Espagnole sauce (No. 151); also a small glassful of Madeira wine, a bouquet (No. 254), and a scant teaspoonful of pepper. Remove the fat carefully and cook for thirty minutes, leaving the sauce in a rather liquid state; then strain and use when needed. This takes the place of all Madeira sauces.

186. Sauce Bordelaise.—Chop up two shallots very fine; put them with half a glassful of red wine in a saucepan on the fire, reduce to half, and then add three-quarters of a pint of good Espagnole sauce (No. 151) and a scant teaspoonful of red pepper. Cook for twenty minutes, and before serving place eighteen round slices of blanched marron in the sauce.

187. Sauce à la Génoise.—Strain about two tablespoonfuls of cooked mirepoix (No. 138), and moisten it with half a glassful of red wine; reduce to half on the hot stove, then add half a pint of Espagnole (No. 151), two tablespoonfuls of white broth (No. 99), and a scant tablespoonful of pepper. Cook for ten minutes, then strain through a sieve; put in half an ounce of good butter and a teaspoonful of anchovy sauce (No. 163), and serve.

188. Sauce Italienne.—Brown two medium-sized, fine, peeled, and chopped-up shallots in a saucepan with a quarter of an ounce of butter, adding half an ounce of cooked, lean ham cut into small dice shape, four minced mushrooms, one finely minced truffle, and a glassful of Madeira wine. Let all cook together for five minutes; then add half a pint of Espagnole sauce (No. 151); let it then come to a boil, and serve very hot.

189. Sauce Duxelle.—Reduce half a pint of Madeira sauce (No. 185) with half a glassful of white wine; add to it twelve very finely chopped mushrooms, two shallots also chopped up and browned in a very little butter for five minutes, and half an ounce of chopped, cooked beef-tongue. Boil again for five minutes and serve.

190. Sauce Colbert.—Put in a saucepan half a pint of very thick Madeira sauce (No. 185); add to it very gradually one ounce of good, fresh butter, also two tablespoonfuls of meat-glaze (No. 141). Mix well together without boiling; then squeeze in the juice of half a sound lemon, and add one teaspoonful of chopped parsley when serving.

191. Sauce Perigueux.—Chop up very fine two fine truffles; place them in a sautoire with a glassful of Madeira wine. Reduce on the hot stove for five minutes. Add half a pint of Espagnole sauce (No. 151). Just allow to come to a boil, and serve very hot.

192. Sauce Robert.—Slice half an onion and fry it in a saucepan with half an ounce of butter and a teaspoonful of sugar until it is of a golden color, or about five minutes; then moisten with half a glassful of white wine and half a pint of Espagnole sauce (No. 151). Boil for ten minutes; then add a teaspoonful of dry English mustard, diluted in cold broth or gravy; stir carefully, and finally rub through a hair sieve and serve.

193. Sauce Salmi.—Place in a saucepan two tablespoonfuls of fumet of game (No. 213) with a half pint of Madeira sauce (No. 185); add two or three livers of any kind of game at hand, cut into small dice-shape pieces. Cook together on a moderate fire for ten minutes; then strain through a colander; mix in the zest of a sound lemon just before serving.

194. Sauce Poivrade.—Fry in half an ounce of butter half an onion and half a carrot, cut up, a sprig of thyme, one bay-leaf, six whole peppers, three cloves, a quarter of a bunch of parsley-roots, and half an ounce of raw ham cut in pieces. Cook it together for five minutes, then moisten with two tablespoonfuls of vinegar, and a pint of Espagnole sauce (No. 151). Boil thoroughly for twenty minutes, then strain through a colander, being careful to remove every particle of grease.

195. Sauce Napolitaine.—Reduce in a saucepan two tablespoonfuls of raw mirepoix (No. 138) with half an ounce of butter; after five minutes moisten with a small glassful of Madeira wine, half a pint of Espagnole sauce (No. 151), two tablespoonfuls of tomato sauce (No. 205), and two tablespoonfuls of fumet of game (No. 218), if any on hand. Reduce for ten minutes, and rub through a sieve.

196. Sauce Hachée.—Chop up very fine two shallots and fry them lightly in a saucepan with half an ounce of butter; add a tablespoonful of capers and three small chopped vinegar-pickles, also a teaspoonful of vinegar. Reduce the sauce for ten minutes; then moisten with half a pint of Espagnole sauce (No. 151), adding a tablespoonful of cooked fine herbs (No. 143). Cook again for ten minutes, and serve.

197. Sauce Chasseur.—Reduce in a saucepan half a pint of Espagnole sauce (No. 151) with two tablespoonfuls of fumet of game (No. 218); after five minutes thicken it with two tablespoonfuls of hare's blood—the blood of any other kind of game will answer—mixed with six drops of vinegar. Do not let it boil after the blood is added to the sauce.

198. Sauce Diable.—Pour a pint of Espagnole sauce (No. 151) into a saucepan with a teaspoonful of dry mustard, diluted in two teaspoonfuls of Parisian sauce, adding a third of a saltspoonful of red pepper. Mix well together. Cook for five minutes and serve.

199. Crapaudine Sauce.—Place half a pint of light piquante sauce (No. 203) in a saucepan on the fire, add four chopped mushrooms, and a teaspoonful of dry mustard, diluted in two teaspoonfuls of tarragon-vinegar. Boil for five minutes and serve.

200. Celery Sauce.—Clean well, nicely pare, and cut into dice-shaped pieces, and then wash thoroughly in fresh water three roots of fine celery, using only the white parts. Lift them out with the hand, so that the sand and dirt remain at the bottom of the pan, and place them in a saucepan. Cover them with fresh water, adding two pinches of salt and half an ounce of butter. Put on the lid, and cook on the hot stove for twenty-five minutes. Drain, and place the celery in the saucepan again with a pint of hot Allemande sauce (No. 210); toss well for just a little while, and serve.

201. Vinaigrette Sauce.—Chop up together very fine one shallot, two branches of parsley, the same of chervil and chives, and when very fine place them in a sauce-bowl with a tablespoonful of salt, a teaspoonful of pepper, and three tablespoonfuls of vinegar. Stir all well together; then add four tablespoonfuls of good oil, mix well again, and serve.

202. Mustard Sauce.—Dilute in a saucepan one tablespoonful of ground English mustard with a tablespoonful of tarragon-vinegar, and half the same quantity of Parisian sauce; strain into this a pint of Espagnole sauce (No. 151), and place the pan on the hot stove. Beat continually until thoroughly heated, then add a teaspoonful of chopped parsley. This sauce must not be allowed to boil.

203. Sauce Piquante.—Place one onion chopped up very fine in a saucepan with half a cupful of vinegar; reduce until almost dry, and then add one pint of Espagnole sauce (No. 151), one tablespoonful of capers, three small gherkins and three mushrooms, all finely chopped up together. Cook for ten minutes; season with the third of a tablespoonful of salt, and a scant teaspoonful of pepper, and serve.

204. Champagne Sauce.—Place two cloves, six whole peppers, one bay-leaf, half a tablespoonful of powdered sugar in a saucepan with a good glassful of champagne; place it on the fire, and reduce for five minutes. Then moisten with three-quarters of a pint of Espagnole sauce (No. 151), and cook for fifteen minutes longer; strain through a Chinese strainer, and serve.

205. Tomato Sauce.—Place two tablespoonfuls of raw mirepoix (No. 138) in a saucepan with one ounce of butter; cook on a moderate fire for five minutes, then add two tablespoonfuls of flour, brown all well. Select one quart of well-washed, ripe, sound, fresh tomatoes, cut them into quarters, and plunge them into the saucepan with the rest, stirring briskly with a wooden spoon until they boil. Season with a good pinch of salt, half a pinch of pepper, and half a teaspoonful of powdered sugar. Boil the whole for forty-five minutes, then strain through a sieve into a vessel, and use when needed. This sauce can also be made with canned tomatoes, in which case cook them for only thirty minutes.

206. Sauce Mayonnaise.—Place two fresh egg yolks into an earthen bowl, with half a teaspoonful of ground English mustard, half a pinch of salt, half a saltspoonful of red pepper; sharply stir with a wooden spoon for two or three minutes without ceasing. Pour in, drop by drop, one and a half cupfuls of the best olive oil. Should it become too thick, add, drop by drop, the equivalent of a teaspoonful of very good vinegar, stirring vigorously with the wooden spoon meanwhile. Taste, and if found a little too acid, gradually add a tablespoonful of oil, stirring continually until all added. The whole operation to prepare the above sauce will take from ten to twelve minutes. To avoid spoiling the sauce, the sweet oil should always be kept in a place of moderate temperature, say, from 70° to 75° Fahrenheit.

207. Sauce Tartare.—Chop up one shallot exceedingly fine, with half a tablespoonful of chervil, and the same of tarragon, and twelve capers chopped exceedingly fine. Place these in an earthen bowl with half a teaspoonful of ground English mustard, two raw egg yolks, a teaspoonful of vinegar (a small drop at a time), half a pinch of salt, and a third of a pinch of pepper. Pour in very lightly, while continuing to stir, a cupful of good olive oil, and if too thick, add a little more vinegar. Taste it to find whether the seasoning is correct; if too salt, add a little more mustard and oil.

208. Victoria Sauce.—Pound one tablespoonful of lobster coral very fine with half an ounce of fresh butter. Then lay it aside. In three-quarters of a pint of Allemande sauce (No. 210), place half a glassful of white wine and six chopped mushrooms; let it warm thoroughly, without boiling, in a saucepan, and then mix in the lobster coral. Stir well, and serve. A few sliced truffles can be used, according to the quality of the dinner.

209. Remoulade Sauce.—Chop up very fine twelve capers, one shallot, three small vinegar-pickles, and add one-half a tablespoonful of chives, with one tablespoonful of parsley. Place them in a bowl with a whole raw egg, a teaspoonful of ground English mustard, half a pinch of salt, and half a pinch of pepper. Incorporate well together, adding four tablespoonfuls of oil and four of vinegar, but keep the sauce sufficiently liquid. Serve when required.

210. Sauce Allemande.—Melt two ounces of butter in a saucepan on a slow fire, with three tablespoonfuls of flour to thicken. Stir well, not letting it brown; then moisten with one pint of white broth (No. 99), beating constantly, and cook for ten minutes. Dilute three egg yolks separately in a bowl; pour the sauce over the eggs, a very little at a time; strain through a Chinese strainer, and finish with half an ounce of good butter and the juice of half a lemon, taking care that it does not boil a second time.

211. Prussian Sauce.—Add to three-quarters of a pint of hot béchamel sauce (No. 154), a teaspoonful of powdered sugar, a scant teaspoonful of red pepper, three tablespoonfuls of grated horseradish, and two tablespoonfuls of cold cream. Let it boil for four minutes, meanwhile stirring it well, and use when needed.

212. Sauce Chambord.—Place one truffle and three mushrooms, sliced very thin, in half a pint of Espagnole sauce (No. 151), adding three tablespoonfuls of Court bouillon (No. 142), six fish quenelles (No. 227), and twelve medium-sized, whole, blanched oysters. Cook slowly for five minutes, and serve.

213. Sauce Montglas.—Cut very carefully into small julienne-shaped pieces one ounce of cooked smoked beef tongue, one ounce of cooked chicken, two truffles, and four mushrooms. Place all in a saucepan, with half a wineglassful of good Madeira wine; place the pan on a brisk fire, and let reduce for three minutes. Then add half a pint of Espagnole sauce (No. 151), and one gill of good tomato sauce (No. 205). Let all cook for five minutes longer, and serve very hot.

214. Cuisson de Poisson—Fish Broth. For one Gallon—Fill a saucepan with three quarts of water, a good handful of salt, half a glassful of vinegar, one carrot, and one onion (both sliced), half a handful of whole peppers, one bunch of parsley-roots, three sprigs of thyme, and three bay-leaves. Cook on a moderate fire for fifteen minutes. Cool, and use when needed for various methods of cooking fish.

215. Duxelle.—Reduce half a pint of cooked, fine herbs (No. 143) in a saucepan, with a quarter of a pint of Madeira sauce (No. 185), on a moderate stove for about ten minutes, when it will then be of a proper consistency and ready to serve.

216. Clear Gravy—For One Gallon.—Place two carrots and one onion cut in slices in a saucepan, with two ounces of uncooked, sliced, salt pork, one sprig of thyme, two bay-leaves, and half a bunch of parsley-roots. Add any scraps of meat, such as shin-bone of veal or beef, or chicken giblets, and a handful of salt; cover well, as it should not color, and moisten with one and a half gallons of water. Cook thoroughly for an hour and a half, then press through a napkin; place it in a stone jar, and use it after carefully removing all the fat.

217. Chicken Essence.—Press one quart of chicken broth through a napkin, and then reduce it in a saucepan until there remains only one-half a pint, and use when needed.

218. Fumet of Game.—Pare and slice one sound carrot and half a medium-sized onion; place them with half a sprig of thyme, one bay-leaf, a small piece of raw, lean ham, also cut up, and the carcass of any kind of raw game in a covered saucepan. Let them brown well; add a glassful of Madeira wine, let it come to a boil; then moisten with one quart of white broth (No. 99), or consommé (No. 100); add a pinch of salt, twelve whole peppers. Cook well for forty-five minutes, then press through a napkin.

219. Game Stock.—Place in a saucepan two game carcasses and one pint of mirepoix (No. 138); cover them with water, adding a pinch of salt. Cook for twenty minutes, and use when needed.

220. Sausage Forcement.—Cut up one pound of fresh pork into small pieces, season it with one pinch of salt, a saltspoonful of pepper, half a saltspoonful of grated nutmeg, and the same quantity of powdered thyme, and chop all up very fine. A quarter of a pound of lean, raw meat can be added if desired. Use when needed.

221. Godiveaux Forcemeat.—Remove the stringy tissue from half a pound of veal suet, pound it in a mortar; take the same quantity of lean veal, chopped in the machine, a quarter of a pound of very consistent pâte-à-chou (No. 1240), omitting the eggs, and pound all together. Season highly with a tablespoonful of salt, a teaspoonful of pepper, and half a teaspoonful of nutmeg. Add four raw egg yolks and two whole ones, and when well incorporated strain through a sieve, and put it on ice to be used when required in other recipes. Poach it for three minutes before serving.

This recipe can be prepared with poultry or game instead of veal.

222. Lobster Forcemeat.

—Fry an onion, chopped very fine, in one ounce of good butter until it is of a golden brown color, adding one tablespoonful of flour to make a roux (No. 135). Moisten with half a pint of white stock (No. 137), stirring well and constantly until the sauce hardens. Season with half a tablespoonful of salt, a scant teaspoonful of white pepper, the same of cayenne, one tablespoonful of English sauce, half a teaspoonful of mustard, a crushed grain of garlic, and one teaspoonful of chopped parsley. Stir well, adding two pounds of cooked lobster, cut up very fine, with twelve mushrooms, also chopped. Cook for thirty minutes in a saucepan, then put it back off the hot fire; add four egg yolks, stir again for a moment, cool, and serve when required.

223. Crab Forcemeat.—The same as for No. 222, using twelve crabs in the place of lobster.

224. Clam Forcemeat.—Proceed the same as for No. 222, seasoning it more highly, and having twenty-four clams blanched and minced exceedingly fine, so that they will better incorporate in the forcemeat.

225. Chicken Forcemeat à la Crême.—Cut two raw chicken breasts in slices, pound them well in a mortar, adding the whites of three eggs; bruise well together, and season with half a tablespoonful of salt, a scant teaspoonful of pepper, and a teaspoonful of nutmeg. Add three tablespoonfuls of very fresh cream, strain through a sieve, cool on the ice, and use when required.

226. Chicken Forcemeat.—Cut in large pieces two raw chicken breasts, pound them in a mortar, adding the same quantity of bread soaked in milk, a teaspoonful of fresh butter and four egg yolks, seasoning with half a tablespoonful of salt, a scant teaspoonful of pepper, and a teaspoonful of nutmeg. Mix all together; strain, and put it in a bowl with three tablespoonfuls of velouté sauce (No. 152).

227. Forcemeat Quenelles of Fish.—Select one pound of firm fish (bass is preferable), remove the skin and take out the bones. Pound it well in a mortar, adding the whites of three eggs a little at a time. When well pounded add half a pint of cream, half a tablespoonful of salt, and a little white pepper and nutmeg. Mix well, and use when needed.

228. Partridge Forcemeat.—Cut two breasts of partridges into large pieces, pound them well in a mortar, gradually adding the same quantity of bread soaked in milk, four egg yolks, one after another, and a teaspoonful of butter. Season with half a pinch of salt, the third of a pinch of pepper, and the same quantity of grated nutmeg; thoroughly pound all together, then rub through a sieve. If not sufficiently consistent, add one more egg yolk.

When game other than partridge is used add two pounded truffles, and use when required.

229. American Forcemeat.—Place on the fire in a saucepan for five minutes two very finely chopped onions with an ounce of butter. Soak in water for fifteen minutes the crumbs of a loaf of bread; press out all the water either with the hands or through a cloth, put the crumbs in a bowl with three whole raw eggs, a tablespoonful of salt, two teaspoonfuls of pepper, a tablespoonful of sage, a large half teaspoonful of nutmeg, three skinned sausages, and a pinch of chopped parsley. Add the cooked onions, and mix well together; use the forcemeat when needed in other recipes.

230. Mushroom Garnishing.—Mince finely twelve mushrooms and place them in a saucepan with half a pint of Madeira sauce (No. 185). Cook for five minutes, and serve.

231. Garnishing Bayard.—Cut into very thin round slices with a tube one good-sized truffle, one ounce of cooked smoked beef-tongue, three mushrooms, and two artichoke bottoms. Place all in a saucepan on the fire with half a wine-glassful of Madeira wine. Reduce to one-half, which will take about five minutes. Then add half a pint of Espagnole sauce (No. 151), and cook for fifteen minutes. Surround the dish with croûtons of bread (No. 133) covered with thin slices of pâté-de-foie-gras.

232. Garnishing à la Chipolata—for one gallon.—Fry a quarter of a pound of salt pork, cut dice-shaped, for two minutes in a saucepan; then add half a pint of carrots cut tubular shaped, half a pint of onions browned and glazed in the oven (No. 972), one pint of blanched and peeled chestnuts, half a pint of mushrooms, and six small sausages cut in pieces. Add two quarts of Espagnole sauce (No. 151), half a pint of tomato sauce (No. 205), a tablespoonful of salt, and a large teaspoonful of pepper. Cook for thirty minutes, and use when needed.

233. Garnishing Vanderbilt.—Peel one green pepper; chop it very fine, and place it in a stewpan with one tomato cut into small pieces. Add an ounce of butter and eighteen canned, picked, and chopped-up shrimps; season with a third of a tablespoonful of salt and a scant teaspoonful of pepper. Cook for ten minutes, and use for garnishing.

234. Garnishing Valencienne.—Cut in long shreds one truffle, three mushrooms, and a very little cooked tongue, adding three tablespoonfuls of cooked rice; put all together in a stewpan with three tablespoonfuls of tomato sauce (No. 205), a third of a tablespoonful of salt, a scant teaspoonful of pepper, and one tablespoonful of grated cheese. Boil for five minutes, and serve when needed.

235. Garnishing Régence.—Take one pint of hot Allemande sauce (No. 210), add to it six mushrooms cut into large pieces, two truffles, six quenelles, either of godiveau (No. 221) or chicken, according to the usage, pieces of sweetbreads, six cocks combs (if handy) and six kidneys. This garnishing must be poached, before adding it to the sauce, in half a glassful of white wine, seasoned with a little salt and pepper. Let cook for six minutes, and add it to the sauce; warm it for three minutes, and serve. The same for fish, omitting the sweetbreads.

236. Garnishing à la St. Nazaire.—Add three tablespoonfuls of court bouillon (No. 142) to a small glassful of white wine, also one tablespoonful of cooked fine herbs (No. 143); add half a pint of Allemande sauce (No. 210), and a third of a pinch each of salt and pepper; pour the sauce over the fish to be served, and garnish with six very small, hot, stuffed clams (No. 376).

237. Garnishing à la Grecque—for roast or broiled meats.—Cut off both ends from twelve medium-sized whole okras, parboil them in boiling water for five minutes, drain, and put them into any kind of meat-juice or Madeira sauce (No. 185). Cook for ten minutes, and serve arranged in clusters with a quarter of a pint of Béarnaise sauce (No. 166).

238. Godard Garnishing.—Take six godiveau quenelles (No. 221), two truffles cut dice-shaped, six cocks' combs, six cocks' kidneys, and three mushrooms cut into square pieces; add half a glassful of Madeira wine, a pinch of salt, and half a pinch of pepper. Cook in a saucepan for five minutes, then add a pint of Madeira sauce (No. 185); boil again for five minutes, and serve when needed.

239. Tortue Garnishing.—Boil three chicken livers in water for three minutes, let them get cool, then cut them up into three pieces each, put them in a saucepan with six stoned and blanched olives, two truffles, four mushrooms, and a throat sweetbread, all cut dice-shaped; add a glassful of Madeira wine, half a pinch of salt, and the third of a pinch each of pepper and nutmeg. Let cook for five minutes, then put in half a pint of Madeira sauce (No. 185), and cook for five minutes longer. Serve with six bread croûtons (No. 133) and six fried eggs (No. 413) as garnishing.

240. Garnishing Parisienne.—Put in a saucepan half a glassful of Madeira wine, six sliced mushrooms, three sliced truffles, and let cook for four minutes. Add half a pint of Madeira sauce (No. 185), cook again for five minutes, then serve.

241. Garnishing Gourmet.—Take a cooked artichoke bottom, either fresh or conserved, and cut it into six pieces; place them in a saucepan with four mushrooms, two truffles, and a piece of cooked palate, all cut dice-shaped; add half a glassful of Madeira wine, and let cook five minutes; pour in half a pint of Madeira sauce (No. 185), cook again for five minutes, and serve.

242. Garnishing Cêpes.—Cut four cêpes into pieces; cook them in a sautoire for three minutes with a tablespoonful of olive oil, half a tablespoonful of salt, a teaspoonful of pepper, and half a clove of crushed garlic. Moisten with half a pint of Espagnole sauce (No. 151), and serve.

243. Bordelaise Garnishing, for tenderloins and steaks.—Place a peeled shallot chopped very fine in a sautoire with half a glassful of red wine, and cook for five minutes; add half a pint of Espagnole sauce (No. 151), a small pinch of red pepper, and cook for five minutes longer. Serve it poured over the fillets or steaks, placing on each one six slices of beef marrow, previously parboiled for one-half a minute.

244. Marrow Garnishing.—Open two fine marrow bones by setting them upright on the table, the narrow part on top, and with a sharp blow of the hatchet cleaving them in two, striking on one side only. Remove the marrow, put it into fresh salted water, and let it remain in for one hour. Then take it up, drain, and cut it into slices. Heat half a pint of Madeira sauce (No. 185), add the pieces of marrow, and let it boil up once with a few drops of tarragon-vinegar. Serve with the slices of marrow on top.

245. Garnishing à la Patti.—Wash well two ounces of rice; drain, dry, and then put it in a saucepan with a pint of good white broth (No. 99). Pound the wing of a cooked chicken in a mortar and add it to the rice; season with a tablespoonful of salt and a teaspoonful of white pepper. Cook on a moderate fire for thirty minutes; strain through a fine sieve, return it to the saucepan with half an ounce of good butter and three tablespoonfuls of sweet cream, and heat slowly on the stove without boiling. Dress this garnishing in an artistic crown-shape around the hot serving dish; arrange the suprêmes in the centre, and decorate the garnishing with thin slices of truffles; with a light hair-brush drip a little meat-glaze (No. 141) over it and serve.

Suprêmes of partridges, quails, cotelettes of squabs, or sweetbreads à la Patti, are all to be served this way.

246. Garnishing Financière.—Cut a blanched, throat sweetbread into dice-sized pieces, put it in a saucepan with two truffles, six mushrooms, twelve stoned olives, six godiveau quenelles (No. 221), and two blanched chicken livers cut in pieces. Moisten with half a glassful of sherry or Madeira wine, and season with half a pinch each of salt and pepper, and a quarter of a pinch of nutmeg; add a pint of Madeira sauce (No. 185), cook again for ten minutes, skim off the fat, and serve when required.

247. Garnishing Ecarlate.—Cook in a saucepan half a pint of tomato sauce (No. 205) with half a pint of Espagnole sauce (No. 151), and a little cooked, smoked beef-tongue, chopped very fine; let cook for six minutes, then serve.

248. Garnishing à la Stanley.—Pour a pint of very hot Russian sauce (No. 211) upon the hot serving-dish. Lay the mignons filets, or any other meat, including broiled fillets, sirloin steaks, etc., on top, and garnish with six fried bananas cut in halves, and send to the table immediately.

249. Garnishing à la Montebello.—Place a pint of tomato sauce (No. 205) in a saucepan; add a pint of Béarnaise sauce (No. 166) and three good-sized, nicely sliced truffles; heat well by means of the Bain-Marie, without boiling, and serve.

250. Garnishing Soubise.—Cut up three medium-sized, white onions, and place them in a saucepan with an ounce of butter, half a cupful of white broth (No. 99), a tablespoonful of salt, and a small saltspoonful of white pepper. Cover the saucepan and cook for twenty minutes, stirring frequently. Add one pint of béchamel sauce (No. 154), and boil again for five minutes. Strain the sauce through a tammy, return it to the saucepan, season it a little more, if necessary, adding a little grated nutmeg and a little warm milk, in case it should be too thick; warm it well again, and serve.

251. Garnishing Milanaise.—Cut into julienne-shaped pieces two medium-sized truffles, six mushrooms, and the same quantity of smoked, cooked tongue, and place them in a saucepan with a pint of cooked rice, half a pint of tomato sauce (No. 205), half a pint of Madeira sauce (No. 185), a tablespoonful of salt, very little pepper, and three tablespoonfuls of grated cheese, either Parmesan or Swiss. Cook for ten minutes and serve.

252. Garnishing Rouennaise.—Cut three medium-sized turnips into six pieces, clove-of-garlic-shaped, pare them nicely and put them in a sautoire with one ounce of butter, sprinkling over them a little powdered sugar. Put the lid on tightly and cook in the oven for ten minutes, shaking it by the handle frequently. Moisten with a pint of Espagnole sauce (No. 151); add a pinch each of salt and pepper; cook again for twenty minutes, skim off the fat, and serve.

253. Garnishing Robinson.—Cut the gall away carefully from twelve chicken livers, wash clean and wipe them well, and then fry them with an ounce of butter in a frying-pan. Season them with a tablespoonful of salt and two teaspoonfuls of pepper, and after cooking three minutes, put them in a saucepan, with a pint of Madeira sauce (No. 185); boil for five minutes and serve.

254. A Bouquet.—how to prepare.—Take four branches of well-washed parsley-stalks—if the branches be small, take six—one branch of soup-celery, well washed; one blade of bay-leaf, one sprig of thyme, and two cloves, placed in the centre of the parsley, so as to prevent cloves, thyme, and bay-leaf from dropping out of the bouquet while cooking; fold it well, and tightly tie with a string, and use when required in various recipes.

A pinch of salt represents 205 grains, or a tablespoonful.

Half a pinch of pepper represents 38 grains, or a teaspoonful.

A third of a pinch of nutmeg represents 13 grains, or half a teaspoonful.

———

HORS D'OEUVRES.

255. Salpicon Royal.—Cut a blanched throat sweetbread (No. 601) into small pieces, and put them into a saucepan, with half an ounce of good butter, six mushrooms, and one truffle, all nicely cut into dice-shape. Thicken with half a pint of good béchamel sauce (No. 154), or Allemande sauce (No. 210), and let cook on a slow fire for five minutes, gently tossing meanwhile. Finish by adding half an ounce of crawfish-butter (No. 150); stir well, and it will then be ready to use for the desired garnishing.

256. Salpicon à la Financière.—Take either the leg or the breast of a roasted chicken. Cut it into dice-shaped pieces, and put them into a saucepan with half an ounce of good butter, adding four mushrooms, one truffle, half an ounce of cooked, smoked beef-tongue, all cut in dice-shaped pieces, and twelve small godiveau quenelles (No. 221); thicken with half a pint of Madeira sauce (No. 185), and let cook for five minutes. It will then be ready for any garnishing desired.

257. Salpicon au Chasseur.—Cut the breast of a fine cooked partridge into dice-shaped pieces, and put them into a saucepan on the hot range, with half an ounce of butter, half a glassful of good sherry wine, three blanched chicken livers, one truffle, four mushrooms, and half an ounce of cooked, smoked beef-tongue, all cut into dice. Thicken with half a pint of hot salmi sauce (No. 193), and let all cook for five minutes, and use it for any garnishing desired.

258. Salpicon of Lobster, Crawfish, or Shrimps.—Put a pint of good béchamel (No. 154) into a saucepan, with four mushrooms, one truffle, and the meat from the claw of a cooked lobster, cutting them all into dice-shaped pieces. Thicken well and let cook for five minutes, and serve. If a lobster cannot be obtained, the meat of three cooked crawfish, or of six prawns or shrimps, may be used instead.

259. Salpicon à la Montglas.—Mince, as for a julienne, four mushrooms, one truffle, the breast of a small cooked chicken, or of any game, and half an ounce of cooked ham, or the same quantity of cooked, smoked beef-tongue. Put all into a saucepan, adding a gill of well reduced Madeira sauce (No. 185) and a gill of tomato sauce (No. 205); let cook for five minutes; then use when needed.

260. Salpicon, Sauce Madère.—Place half an ounce of good butter in a saucepan, adding half a glassful of sherry wine, a blanched throat sweetbread (No. 601) nicely cut into dice-shaped pieces, four mushrooms, one truffle, and an ounce of cooked, smoked beef-tongue, all cut the same as the sweetbread. Let cook for five minutes, then add half a pint of Madeira sauce (No. 185), and let cook again for five minutes. It will now be ready to use for the desired garnishing.

261. Timbales à l'Ecossaise.—Butter well six small timbale-molds, and line them with cuts of plain, unsweetened pancake (No. 1186). Take a preparation of purée of chicken (No. 226), and the same quantity of raw forcemeat (No. 220), add to it a reduced salpicon (No. 256), and with this fill the molds. Cover with small round pieces of the pancake. Then steam them in a moderate oven for eight minutes. Unmold, dress them on a hot dish, pour a gill of hot Madeira sauce (No. 185) over, and serve.

262. Timbales de Nouilles à la Genoise.—Sprinkle the insides of six well-buttered timbale-molds with grated, fresh bread-crumbs; line them with thin foundation paste (No. 1078), and fill with finely shred, boiled nouilles (No. 1182), adding an ounce of good butter, and seasoning with half a pinch each of salt and pepper, and the third of a pinch of nutmeg; also half an ounce of grated Parmesan cheese. Thicken with a gill of strong Madeira sauce (No. 185). Cover the molds with pieces of the foundation paste, and put them into a brisk oven for six minutes. Unmold, and arrange them on a hot dish containing a gill of hot Madeira sauce (No. 185), and with the timbales on top.

263. Timbales Russe à la Schultze.—Prepare six light timbales as for No. 262, one and a quarter inches high by two and a quarter inches in diameter. Arrange them on a dessert dish with a folded napkin, and lay them in a cool place until needed. Put into a china bowl half of a fine, well-cleaned, sound Camembert cheese, mash it thoroughly with a fork, and drop on to it very gradually one and a half ponies of old brandy. Cut into small pieces two medium-sized, cooked, throat sweetbreads (No. 601), and add them to the cheese, mixing well together. Season with half a teaspoonful of salt, a saltspoonful of pepper, and the same quantity of grated nutmeg, stirring well for a minute longer. Then add four medium-sized, chopped truffles, and mix again. Divide the above preparation equally into the six timbales, cover each with a thin slice of truffle, previously dipped in brandy, and send to the table.

264. Croustade à la Régence.—Spread out a quarter of a pound of pâte-à-foncer (No. 1078) an eighth of an inch thick. Clean well six tartlet moulds; line them with the paste, then fill them with cracker-dust; cover them with a buttered paper, place them in the hot oven on a tin plate, and bake for ten or twelve minutes. Take from out the oven and let cool. Remove all the cracker-dust, and they will be ready for use. Fill them with a pint of hot régence (No. 235), evenly divided; dress on a hot dish with a folded napkin, and send to the table.

265. Croustades de Riz à la Victoria.—Wash thoroughly and boil in a saucepan one quart of rice with two quarts of broth and one ounce of butter. Keep it as dry as possible so that it remains firm, and add to it half an ounce of grated Parmesan cheese, half a pinch of pepper, and a third of a pinch of nutmeg. Mix well with a wooden spoon; then put it in a buttered sautoire, spreading it an inch and three-quarters thick, and cover with a buttered paper. Leave it to cool with a weight pressed down on the top. Then cut it out with a No. 8 paste-cutter into six croustades (being careful to dip the cutter in warm water each time it is used), and with a No. 4 paste-cutter make a mark on the surface of each without cutting. Dip the pieces in beaten egg, roll them in bread-crumbs (No. 301), and repeat this. Then fry them in very hot fat for five minutes; drain, empty them with a vegetable spoon, and fill the insides with a pint of hot salpicon of shrimps (No. 258), mushrooms, and cream sauce (No. 181). Put the covers on top, and serve the same as the croustades à la régence (No. 264).

266. Small Hot Patties à l'Anglaise.—Line with fine pâte-à-foncer (No. 1078) six small, hot patty-molds, fluted, and provided with hinges. Pinch the tops and fill them with common flour. Bake in a moderate oven for fifteen minutes; empty them, and leave them to dry at the oven door for five minutes. Fill them with a pint of hot salpicon royal (No. 255), place a slice of truffle on the top of each instead of a cover, and serve on a hot dish with a folded napkin.

267. Ortolan Patties.—Make six patties the same as for the above, (No. 266), only use them when cold. Place at the bottom of each a tablespoonful of salpicon royal (No. 255), and then place in each patty two well-picked, fine, fat, raw, seasoned reed-birds, covered with a slice of thin lard; lay them on a small roasting-pan, place in a moderate oven and roast for fifteen minutes. Remove from the oven, take off the lard from the birds, moisten each patty with two tablespoonfuls of good, hot, Madeira sauce (No. 185), and serve on a hot dish with a folded napkin over it.

268. Cromesquis aux Truffles.—Bone a cooked chicken, hash the meat very fine, and put it in a sautoire with a pint of very strong velouté sauce (No. 152), adding two well-hashed truffles, and seasoning with a good pinch of salt, half a pinch of pepper, and the third of a pinch of nutmeg. Let cook for ten minutes, stirring occasionally, then transfer it to a flat tin plate and let it cool. Spread it out an inch thick; then divide it into six parts, and wrap each one in a veal udder, or a piece of crepinette well rolled around. Immerse them in flour batter (No. 1185), and plunge them into boiling fat for five minutes, or until they are slightly browned. Drain on a cloth, and serve on a hot dish with a folded napkin, decorating with fried parsley.

All cromesquis are made the same way, only serving with different garnishing or sauces.

269. Canapé Madison.

—Prepare six medium-sized slices of bread, all the same shape. Toast them to a good golden color and lay them on a dish. Cover each toast with a very thin slice of lean, cooked ham; spread a little mustard over; then cover with a layer of garnishing à la provençale (No. 642), dredge grated Parmesan cheese on top, and strew a little fresh bread-crumbs over all. Place them in the hot oven and bake for ten minutes; remove, dress them on a hot dish with a folded napkin, and send to the table.

270. Small Bouchées à la Reine.—Roll three-quarters of a pound of feuilletage paste (No. 1076) to a quarter of an inch thick; let it rest for ten minutes in a cold place, then cut six rounds out of the paste with a No. 4 channeled paste-cutter. Lay them on a borderless, buttered tin baking-dish, slightly apart from each other; cover with beaten egg, and make a mark on the surface of each with a paste-cutter, No. 2, being careful to dip the cutter each time in hot water, so that the marked outline may remain perfect. Put them in a brisk oven for twelve minutes; then lift the covers with a knife, and fill each one with a white salpicon royal (No. 256) made of truffles, mushrooms, and finely shred chicken. Set the covers on, and serve on a hot dish with a folded napkin.

All bouchées are made the same way, adding different garnishings according to taste.

271. Coquilles of Chicken à l'Anglaise.—Fill six table-shells with a thick chicken and truffle salpicon (No. 256); besprinkle the tops with grated, fresh bread-crumbs, spread a little clarified butter over each, and lay them on a very even baking-dish. Place them in a very hot oven for about six minutes, or until they are of a golden brown color, then serve the same as for the above.

272. Coquilles of Oysters au Gratin.—Blanch twenty-four medium-sized oysters in their own liquor for five minutes; add half a pinch of pepper and half an ounce of butter; then drain them, keeping the liquor for further use. Add to the oysters half a pint of velouté sauce (No. 152), mixed with three tablespoonfuls of the oyster liquor; keep it thick, and be very careful not to break the oysters. Fill six table-shells with this preparation, sprinkle with grated, fresh bread-crumbs and a very little clarified butter, and brown well in the oven for six minutes. Dress on a hot dish with a folded napkin, and serve.

273. Oysters in Shells à l'Anglaise.—Select eighteen large oysters. Put three into each of six table-shells and season with a pinch of pepper, besprinkle with slightly fried bread-crumbs, and lay them on a flat roasting-pan. Place them in a very brisk oven for about four minutes, or until the oysters raise; then serve on a dish with a folded napkin.

274. Lamb Sweetbreads en Petites Caisses.—Blanch, pare, and clean six small lamb sweetbreads as for No. 601. Lay them aside to cool, then lard them with either fresh fat pork or truffles. Place them in a well-buttered sautoire, adding a gill of chicken broth or a gill of Madeira wine. Cover with a buttered paper, and let cook to a golden color in the oven for ten minutes. Then lay them on a dish. Put half a gill of cooked fine herbs (No. 143) and a gill of well-reduced Espagnole sauce (No. 151) into the sautoire, letting it cook for five minutes. Take six small boxes of buttered paper and pour a little of the gravy at the bottom of each; cover with sweetbreads, and place them on a baking-dish; keep them for five minutes in an open oven, then serve on a folded napkin.

275. Oysters en Petites Caisses.—Open and blanch for five minutes twenty-four medium-sized oysters in a sautoire with half a glassful of white wine and half an ounce of butter. Season with half a pinch of pepper and a third of a pinch of nutmeg. Let cook for five minutes; then add one pint of well-reduced velouté sauce (No. 152), and let cook for another five minutes, adding half an ounce of crawfish butter (No. 150), and stirring it occasionally. Fill six buttered paper boxes with four oysters each, and the garnishing equally divided. Sprinkle over a little fresh bread-crumbs, and arrange them on a tin roasting-pan. Spread a very little butter over each patty, and put them in a moderate oven for five minutes. Have a hot dish ready, with a folded napkin nicely arranged on it; dress the patties over, and serve.

276. Chicken Croquettes with Truffles.—Bone and cut up a medium-sized, cooked chicken into small, square pieces; put them in a sautoire with two truffles cut the same way, adding half a pint of strong velouté (No. 152), and let cook for ten minutes. Then incorporate therein half a glassful of Madeira wine, four egg yolks, a pinch of salt, half a pinch of pepper, and the third of a pinch of nutmeg. Stir briskly, then put it away to cool in a flat dish. Now divide the mixture into six even parts; lay them on a cold table, besprinkle with fresh bread-crumbs, and roll them into oblong shapes. Dip each one into a beaten egg, and roll again in fresh bread-crumbs. Fry to a nice color in hot fat for four minutes. Drain thoroughly, and serve on a hot dish with a folded napkin, decorating with a little green parsley.

All chicken croquettes are prepared the same way, only served with different garnishings and sauces, or by omitting the truffles and substituting six hashed mushrooms. Sweetbread croquettes are prepared the same, only substituting four blanched sweetbreads (No. 601) for the chicken.

277. Croquettes of Game.—To be made exactly like the chicken croquettes (No. 276), adding six hashed mushrooms and half a gill of cold fumet de gibier (No. 218).

278. Croquettes of Foie-gras.—Mix half an ounce of cooked, smoked beef-tongue with half a pint of dry salpicon of foie-gras. Put it into a saucepan with a gill of béchamel (No. 154), half a glassful of Madeira or sherry wine, and a tablespoonful of meat-glaze (No. 141). Reduce for ten minutes, stirring well, then transfer to a cold, flat dish, cover with buttered paper, and put aside to cool. Divide the preparation into six parts—each one shaped like a pear—roll them in fresh bread-crumbs, dip in beaten egg, and put a slice of truffle on the top of each. Again roll in bread-crumbs, and fry in boiling fat for four minutes. Remove them, drain well, and serve on a hot dish with a folded napkin. Any desired garnishing may be added.

279. Croquettes of Macaroni.—Boil a quarter of a pound of Italian macaroni in salted water for twenty-five minutes. Drain, and put it in a saucepan with a good ounce of butter, half an ounce of Parmesan cheese, and a quarter of an ounce of cooked, smoked tongue cut into small pieces, and one truffle cut the same. Toss all together, then change it to a well-buttered sautoire, spreading the preparation one inch thick on the bottom. Cover with a buttered paper, press it well down, and put away to cool. Cut the preparation with a plain paste-cutter into six parts; roll each one in grated Parmesan cheese, dip in beaten egg, and roll in grated, fresh, white bread-crumbs. Fry in very hot fat for four minutes, drain well, and serve on a hot dish with a folded napkin.

280. Anchovies on Toast.—Prepare with American bread six dry toasts, spread over them a little anchovy butter (No. 146), and cover each with four half anchovies. Place the toasts on a tin baking-sheet in the oven for one minute. Arrange them on a dish with a folded napkin, and serve.

281. Caviare on Toast.—Prepare six toasts of American bread. Put half the contents of a small box of Russian caviare into a sautoire; add two tablespoonfuls of cream, and heat one and a half minutes on the stove, stirring it carefully meanwhile; pour this over the toasts, and serve on a dish with a folded napkin.

282. Thon Mariné.—Fold a napkin on a radish-dish, and dress on it the desired quantity of Thon Mariné—*pickled tunny*. Decorate with a little fresh parsley, and serve as a *hors-d'œuvre*.

283. Sardines à l'Huile.—Lift the sardines carefully out of the box to avoid breaking them, and lay them on a plate; neatly pare off the loose skin, then dress on a radish-dish, and decorate with parsley.

284. Anchovies à l'Huile.—Take a pint bottle of boned anchovies, drain them on a cloth, then dress them artistically on a radish-dish. Decorate with a hashed, hard-boiled egg and some chopped parsley.

285. Norwegian Anchovies.—These are considered far superior to the bottled anchovies. On taking them out of the keg they should be placed in cold, fresh water for two hours, then drained, and with the hand split in two along the backbone. Lay them in a small bowl and cover with sweet oil, and use as desired.

286. Saucisson de Lyon.—Procure a medium-sized, fine saucisson de Lyon, cut twelve very thin slices from it, dress nicely upon a radish-dish, and place a few parsley-leaves in the centre.

287. Mortadella.—To be served the same as the above (No. 286).

288. Tomatoes, side dish.—Take six fine, firm, red tomatoes, wipe well, then plunge them into boiling water for one minute, drain and peel them. Put them in a cool place, and when thoroughly cold, cut them into slices, arrange them on a radish-dish, sprinkle a little salt, pepper, and vinegar over.

289. Cucumbers, side dish.—Take two medium-sized, fine cucumbers, peel neatly, and cut them in thin slices. Place in a bowl with a good pinch of salt, and put them in a cold place for two hours. Then drain the liquid off, and season with half a pinch of pepper, a tablespoonful of vinegar, and the same quantity of oil. Dress nicely in a radish-dish.

290. Celery, in glass.—Procure a bunch of fine, white Kalamazoo celery, pare off the green stalks, and trim the roots neatly. Be careful to save the clear, white hearts. Cut each plant lengthwise into four equal branches. Wash them well in cold water, and put them into clean water with a piece of ice until ready to serve; then arrange them nicely in a celery glass, or dress on a china radish-dish, with a few pieces of ice in the centre.

291. Celery, frizzled.—Another and economical way to prepare celery for a side dish to decorate the table. Take only one large head of fine celery. Pare off the green stalks, and cut off the root (reserving it for a delicious and wholesome salad). Cut the stalk lengthwise into four equal branches. Wash them well in cold water, then cut each one into pieces about as long as one's finger; by so doing, all the branches will be separated. With the aid of a small, keen knife pare the thin sides a little, making five or six slits in each piece, starting from the top, downwards, leaving half to three-quarters of an inch uncut; place them in cold water with plenty of ice, leaving them in for two hours. Lift it from the ice-water, artistically dress on a round glass dish, and send to the table. Celery arranged and served in this way makes a beautiful effect on the table, but requires a little patience in its preparation.

292. Radishes, how to prepare.—If the radishes be quite large, take three bunches—if small, four bunches—being careful to select them round, firm, and the reddest procurable. Pare off all the leaves and stems except the two prettiest on each radish. Cut away the roots, and also a little of the peel around the roots. With a small, sharp knife divide the remaining peel into five or six equal-sized leaves, beginning at the root end, and cutting toward the green stems, but being careful to avoid detaching the leaves. They can be formed into any desired design by cutting them with care. Place them in cold water until required. When serving, arrange the radishes artistically on a flat saucer, the radishes meeting toward the centre, the green leaves lying outward. Serve with chopped ice over them.

293. Remarks Regarding Radishes.—The following incident happened in my presence over twenty-five years ago. One evening, dinner was served to a party of prominent gentlemen in Lyons, France, among whom were Alexander Dumas, père, the great novelist, and Berger, the famous billiard player. While the waiter was in the act of handing the radishes to M. Dumas, he saw a change come over him; anger was depicted in his face, and he thoroughly expected to see the radishes, radish-dish, etc., flung full at him. He stood amazed, not daring to question the distinguished guest. When his anger subsided, he amiably explained that the cause of his sudden ill-temper was offering to him radishes peeled, and deprived of their green stalks; he asserted that the healthiest and best parts had been removed. After inquiries of more experienced co-laborers, the waiter thoroughly agreed with M. Dumas, and experience has taught him the correctness of his judgment.

Radishes are a luxurious and healthful adjunct to the dinner-table, and can be procured almost the whole year; but in the spring the markets are more plentifully supplied, and that is the most wholesome season to partake of them.

294. Welsh Rarebit.—Take one pound of American cheese; cut up in small pieces. Place them in a sautoire, adding half a glassful of good ale. Season with half a saltspoonful of red pepper. Stir it continually with a wooden spoon until the mass is well melted, which will take about ten minutes. Have six nice, fresh, large pieces of toast; arrange them on a very hot dish, and distribute the preparation equally over, serving the rarebit very hot.

295. Golden Buck.—Proceed as for the above (No. 294), and when ready to serve, dress a poached egg (No. 404) on each piece of toast, and serve very hot.

296. Gherkin Buck.—Prepared the same as Golden Buck (No. 295), only adding to each toast a slice of broiled bacon (No. 754), and sending to the table very hot.

297. Welsh Rarebit au Gratin.—Prepare six toasts of American bread; broil them lightly, remove, and cover each with a slice of Swiss cheese a little less than half an inch thick; lay them in a roasting-pan, sprinkling a very little pepper over. Put in the oven for ten minutes. Arrange the toasts on a very hot dish, and send to the table.

A pinch of salt represents 205 grains, or a tablespoonful.

Half a pinch of pepper represents 38 grains, or a teaspoonful.

A third of a pinch of nutmeg represents 13 grains, or half a teaspoonful.

FISH.

298. How to Serve Oysters for Private Families.—Oysters should be kept in a very cold place before they are opened, and well washed before using, otherwise their appearance will be destroyed. They should, according to the French custom, be opened on the deep shell, so as to better preserve the liquor, then laid on finely chopped ice for a short time—too long destroys their flavor. While they should be kept as cold as possible, they should never be allowed to freeze, therefore they must only be opened shortly before they are needed; for once frozen, they quickly turn sour. The proper way to open them is to place the deep shell in the palm of the left hand, and break them on one side. The Boston stabbing-knife is preferable for this, but if there be none handy use a small block that the oyster can fit into, and stab it on the edge; or even a chopping-block and chopping-knife may be employed in case of necessity. Serve six oysters for each person, nicely arranged on oyster-plates with quarters of lemon.

299. Oysters à l'Alexandre Dumas.—Place in a sauce-bowl a heaped teaspoonful of salt, three-quarters of a teaspoonful of very finely crushed white pepper, one medium-sized, fine, sound, well-peeled, and very finely chopped shallot, one heaped teaspoonful of very finely chopped chives, and half a teaspoonful of parsley, also very finely chopped up. Mix lightly together, then pour in a light teaspoonful of olive oil, six drops of Tabasco sauce, one saltspoonful of Worcestershire sauce, and lastly one light gill, or five and a half tablespoonfuls, of good vinegar. Mix it thoroughly with a spoon; send to the table, and with a teaspoon pour a little of the sauce over each oyster just before eating them.

300. How to serve Clams.—Clams should be served on deep plates, covered previously with finely chopped ice. To have them sweet and fresh, they should be kept as cold as possible. Serve six on each plate with quarters of lemon.

301. To prepare Breaded Fish.—1. After the fish is pared, cleaned, and dried, dip it first in milk, then in flour, and fry in very hot fat.

2. Take very clean fish, dip it in beaten egg, then in freshly grated bread-crumbs, and fry in very hot fat.

3. For certain fish, like whitebait, immerse them in milk, then in flour mixed with pulverized crackers, shake well in a colander, and throw into very hot fat. Oysters are breaded the same way, but should be flattened before frying.

4. For croustades of rice or potatoes, dip in beaten egg and roll in fresh bread-crumbs; repeat three times before frying.

302. Salmon, en Papillotes.—Procure two pounds of very fresh salmon and cut it into six even slices. Season these with a good pinch of salt and a pinch of pepper. Roll them well. Cut out six heart-shaped pieces of paper, oil them nicely, and have twelve thin slices of cooked ham (No. 753), then proceed to prepare them exactly as for mackerel en papillote (No. 330).

303. Salmon, oyster sauce.—Place two pounds of very fresh salmon in a fish-kettle, completely cover with cold water, season with a handful of salt, add one medium-sized, sliced onion, half a wine-glassful of white vinegar, eight whole peppers, two cloves, and two parsley-roots. Range the kettle on a brisk fire. Five minutes after coming to a boil the salmon will be sufficiently cooked. Remove from the kettle, drain it well; dress on a hot dish with a folded napkin, nicely decorate with parsley-greens all around the salmon, and serve with a pint of hot oyster sauce (No. 173) separately.

The necessary time to cook the above to perfection, from beginning to end, will be thirty-five minutes.

304. Salmon Colbert.—Proceed as for the above, and serve with three-quarters of a pint of Colbert sauce (No. 190), also four plain boiled potatoes served separately, and cut in quarters (No. 982).

305. Salmon à la Régence.—Take a fine but very small salmon, fill it with fish forcemeat (No. 227), and put it on a grate in the fish-kettle with half a bunch of parsley-roots, three sprigs of celery, three sliced onions, six cloves, and half a handful of whole pepper. Moisten with half a bottle of white wine, season with a pinch of salt, and cover with a thin *barde* of raw salt pork. Add a little mushroom liquor, if any on hand, and place it in a moderate oven for one and a half to two hours; then lift it from the kettle, removing the pork and herbs. Slide the fish on to a hot dish, strain the broth into a sautoire, reduce it to one-half, and add to the garnish with a régence garnishing (No. 235); glaze the top of the fish with just a little crawfish butter (No. 150) mixed with very little white glaze (No. 141), and serve with the sauce in a sauce-bowl.

306. Salmon à la Genoise.—To be prepared the same as salmon Colbert (No. 304), garnishing with four clusters of mushrooms—four mushrooms on each cluster—and six cooked crawfish instead of the boiled potatoes. Serve with half a pint of Genoise sauce (No. 187) separate.

307. Salmon, rolled à l'Irlandaise.—Bone three pounds of salmon. Parboil it. Besprinkle the sides and insides with a pinch of salt, half a pinch of pepper, and the same of nutmeg; also twelve chopped oysters, one tablespoonful of parsley, and half a cupful of bread-crumbs. Roll it together, then put it in a deep pan with one ounce of butter. Bake in a hot oven for twenty-five minutes and serve on a dish, pouring its own gravy over.

308. Broiled Salmon-tail.—Take three pounds of the tail part of a salmon. Steep it for five or six hours in a marinade composed of three tablespoonfuls of olive oil in a dish with a quarter of a bunch of parsley-roots, two bay-leaves, and a sprig of thyme. Take out the salmon and broil for ten minutes on one side and five minutes on the other (skin side). Dress on a hot dish, and serve with two ounces of melted butter (No. 155), flavored with a light teaspoonful of finely chopped chervil, half a teaspoonful of chives, and the juice of half a medium-sized, sound lemon.

309. Boiled Halibut.—Put a piece of halibut weighing two pounds in a saucepan, and cover it with fresh water; add one sliced onion, half a sliced carrot, and a bouquet (No. 254). Season with a handful of salt and two tablespoonfuls of vinegar. Put on the lid and let cook gently, but no more than five minutes after boiling-point; then lift up the fish alone, drain well; dress it on a hot dish, and serve with any desired sauce.

310. Halibut Steaks, maître d'hôtel.—Wipe well a two-pound piece of fresh halibut, lay it on a dish, and season it with a pinch of salt, a pinch of pepper, and two tablespoonfuls of sweet oil. Roll it well and lay it on a double broiler; then place it on a brisk fire, and broil for eight minutes on each side. Dress the fish on a hot dish, pour a gill of maître d'hôtel sauce (No. 145) over, decorate with parsley-greens, and serve.

311. Trout, shrimp sauce.—Clean, wash, and dry six fine trout, weighing about a quarter of a pound each. Place them on a grate in the fish-kettle, with a pinch of salt, adding one sliced carrot, one sprig of thyme, and two bay-leaves. Moisten with half a glassful of white wine and half a pint of water. Put it on the stove, and let it simmer gently for five minutes after boiling-point; then drain, and serve on a dish garnished with parsley. Send it to the table with half a pint of shrimp sauce (No. 178) in a separate bowl, also four plain, boiled potatoes, cut in quarters, à l'Anglaise (No. 988). Keep the fish-stock for further use.

312. Trout à la Cambacères.—Cook six trout as for the above (No. 311); when cooked, then place on a hot dish. Put in a saucepan two minced truffles, six mushrooms, also minced, and half a pint of Espagnole sauce (No. 151), also twelve olives and three tablespoonfuls of tomato sauce (No. 205). Let cook for ten minutes, then skim off the fat very carefully, and pour the sauce over the trout before serving.

313. Trout à la Chambord.—Clean, wash, and dry three fine trout of half a pound each. Stuff them with fish forcemeat (No. 227), and place them in a deep baking-dish, buttering it well with about half an ounce of butter. Add half a glassful of white wine, a bouquet (No. 254), half a pinch of salt, and half a pinch of pepper. Cook for fifteen minutes in the oven, being very careful to baste it frequently. Take the juice from under the fish, and put it in a saucepan with half a pint of good Espagnole sauce (No. 151). Reduce, and skim off the fat. Add one truffle and four mushrooms, all well-sliced, also twelve blanched oysters. Dress the trout on a hot dish, pour the sauce over, and decorate the fish with six fish quenelles (No. 227).

314. Broiled Trout, maître d'hôtel.—Procure six fine trout, of a quarter of a pound each; clean and wash well, drain them in a napkin, and make three incisions on each side. Place them on a dish with one teaspoonful of oil, a pinch of salt, and half a pinch of pepper; roll gently and put them on the broiler. Cook for four minutes on each side, then lay them on a dish, pour a gill of maître d'hôtel sauce (No. 177) over, and serve with six slices of lemon, or with any other sauce desired.

315. Trout, with fine herbs.—Clean, wash, and dry six fine trout, of a quarter of a pound each. Put them on a buttered dish, adding half a glassful of white wine and one finely chopped shallot. Let cook for ten minutes, then put the gravy in a saucepan, with two tablespoonfuls of cooked herbs (No. 143), moistening with half a pint of Allemande sauce (No. 210). Reduce the gravy to one-half, and pour it over the trout with the juice of half a sound lemon, and serve.

316. Trout en Papillotes.—Take six trout, of a quarter of a pound each, and stuff them with fish forcemeat (No. 227). Oil as many pieces of paper as there are fish; put a *barde* of salt pork on either end of each piece of paper, lay a trout on top, add a little salt and pepper, then fold the paper and tie it securely with string. Cook in a baking-dish in a rather slow oven for about twenty minutes, and serve them in their envelopes, after removing the strings, with any sauces desired.

317. Sole à l'Hollandaise.—Skin and bone well three medium-sized soles; put the fillets in a stewpan, and cover them with salted water, adding a few drops of vinegar. Cook for about six minutes. Then take them off, drain well, and arrange them on a dish. Pour one ounce of melted butter over, with the juice of half a lemon; garnish with green parsley, and serve with twelve pieces of potatoes à l'Anglaise (No. 988) separate.

318. Soles Normande.—Take the fillets from three fine soles, as for the above; fold them in two, and lay them in a buttered, flat saucepan, with half a glassful of white wine, three tablespoonfuls of mushroom liquor, and half a pinch each of salt and pepper. Cover and cook for six minutes; then lift them up, drain, and arrange them on a dish. Reduce the gravy to one-half, add twelve blanched oysters, and six sliced mushrooms, moistening with half a pint of Allemande sauce (No. 210). Thicken the sauce well with a tablespoonful of good butter, tossing well till dissolved, and add the juice of half a lemon. Garnish the sides of the dish with the oysters and mushrooms, and pour the sauce over the fish. Decorate with three small, cooked crawfish, three fried smelts, and three small, round croquettes of potatoes (No. 997).

319. Soles au Gratin.—Proceed as for No. 318. Put three tablespoonfuls of cooked, fine herbs (No. 143) in the bottom of a deep baking-dish, fold the fillets in two, and place them in, crown-shaped. Season with half a pinch each of salt and pepper, then moisten with half a glassful of white wine, and bake for five minutes. Take out the dish, decorate it with twelve mushroom buttons, adding half a pint of good Espagnole sauce (No. 151). Sprinkle over with fresh bread-crumbs, pour on a few drops of melted butter, and bake once more for three minutes, then press the juice of half a lemon over the fillets, add half a pinch of chopped parsley, and serve. (All fish au gratin are prepared the same way.)

320. Fried Soles, sauce Colbert.—Select six small soles, cut off their heads, and make an incision down the backbone. Season with one pinch of salt, half a pinch of pepper, and the juice of half a lemon; roll in fresh bread-crumbs and beaten eggs, then flatten them well, and leave them to drip for a few minutes; fry them for three minutes in very hot fat; drain, add another half a pinch of salt, and arrange them on a dish on a folded napkin. Garnish with a quarter of a bunch of fried parsley, and serve with half a pint of Colbert sauce (No. 190) separate.

321. Fried Soles à la Horly.—Fry twelve fillets of sole as for No. 320, and serve with half a pint of tomato sauce (No. 205) separate.

322. Fillets of Sole, Joinville.

—Take the fillets of three soles, fold them, and lay them crown-shaped in a buttered, flat stewpan, moistening with half a glassful of white wine, and three tablespoonfuls of mushroom liquor. Season with half a pinch each of salt and pepper, and cook on a moderate fire for six minutes. Arrange the fillets on a dish, and put it on the side of the stove; reduce the gravy to half, adding one cooked lobster claw, one truffle, and three mushrooms, all cut julienne-shaped. Add half a pint of Allemande sauce (No. 210); stir it well, and pour it over the soles before serving, inserting a piece of truffle and a mushroom button on each fillet, also in every one stick a picked shrimp, with its head erect, if at hand, and then serve.

323. Sole, with fine herbs.—Proceed as for sole Joinville (No. 322), but replace the truffles and lobster claw by two tablespoonfuls of cooked, fine herbs (No. 143), half a pinch of chopped parsley, and the same of chervil and chives. Garnish with six heart-shaped croûtons (No. 133), and serve.

324. Sole Dieppoise.—Lift the fillets from three medium-sized soles, put them in a buttered stewpan, with one very finely chopped shallot, moistening with half a glassful of white wine, and three tablespoonfuls of mushroom liquor. Cook for six minutes, then lay them on a dish, reduce the gravy to half, adding twelve cooked mussels, six mushroom buttons, and half a pint of good Allemande sauce (No. 210). Thicken it well with a tablespoonful of butter, tossing till well dissolved, and throw it over the fillets with the juice of half a lemon. Serve with six croûtons of fried bread (No. 133) around the dish.

325. Skate or Raie au Naturel.—Pare and cut off the fins from half a skate weighing four pounds the half; divide it into six square pieces, wash them well, being very careful to scrape it with a sharp knife, so as to remove the mucus adhering to it. Put the pieces into a saucepan in which are already placed one sliced carrot, one onion, half a bunch of parsley-roots, one sprig of thyme, two bay-leaves, half a handful of whole peppers, plenty of salt—at least a handful—and half a cupful of vinegar. Cover it well with water, boil on a moderate fire for forty-five minutes, then take it off and lift up the pieces of skate with a skimmer; lay them on a table, and remove the skin from both sides; place them on a deep dish, and strain the stock slowly over, and use, whenever needed, with any kind of sauce desired.

326. Shad, broiled maître d'hôtel.—Pare and cut a small shad in two, scale it and remove the backbone; lay it on a dish, sprinkling it over with a pinch of salt, and baste with one tablespoonful of oil. Leave it for a few moments, then broil it on a slow fire in a double broiler for about fifteen minutes on the flesh side, and for one minute on the skin side, leaving the roe in the inside. Put it on a hot dish, spread a gill of good maître d'hôtel sauce (No. 177) over, and serve with six slices of lemon.

327. Shad, with Sorrel.—Select a small, fine shad, pare and scale it, then let it steep as long as possible in a marinade composed of one tablespoonful of oil, half a sliced lemon, a quarter of a bunch of parsley-roots, and half a sliced onion. When ready, place it in a buttered stewpan, with half a glassful of white wine, three tablespoonfuls of mushroom liquor, also a good bouquet (No. 254). Take two handfuls of picked and washed sorrel, mince it very fine, then put it in the stewpan with the fish, adding a good pinch of salt and half a pinch of pepper; cover it, and let it cook as long as possible on a slow fire—at least two hours; then arrange the shad on a dish. Add one tablespoonful of white roux (No. 135) to the juice, thicken well, and pour the sauce over the fish when serving, with some more of its own gravy in a sauce-bowl.

328. Shad vert-pré.—Pare and scale a small, fine shad, put it on a deep baking-dish, well buttered, and season with one pinch of salt and half a pinch of pepper, adding two finely chopped shallots and half a glassful of white wine. Cover with a piece of buttered paper, and cook in a moderate oven for twenty-five minutes. When done, put the juice in a saucepan, with half a pint of Allemande sauce (No. 210), a pinch of finely chopped chervil, and a little spinach green (Breton essence, a saltspoonful). Let cook again for three minutes, then pour a little of it, through a Chinese strainer, on the fish, and serve the rest in a separate sauce-bowl.

329. Broiled Fresh Mackerel, maître d'hôtel.—Pare and split two good-sized, fresh mackerel through the back, remove the spine, score them slightly, and rub them with one tablespoonful of sweet oil; season with a pinch of salt and half a pinch of pepper, then broil them on a brisk fire for ten minutes on the split side, and one minute on the skin side. Lay them on a dish, pour a gill of maître d'hôtel butter (No. 145) over, and serve with a few parsley-greens and six slices of lemon.

Broiled Spanish-mackerel are prepared in the same way.

330. Mackerel en Papillotes.—Oil three sheets of white paper a little larger than the length of the fish. Cut six thin slices of cooked, lean ham; lay one slice on each piece of paper, and on top a tablespoonful of cooked fine herbs (No. 143). Select three mackerel; make four or five incisions on each side; season with a good pinch of salt and a pinch of pepper, divided evenly on both sides of the fish, then roll them lightly, and lay the mackerel on top of the fine herbs; spread a tablespoonful more herbs over each mackerel, and cover with a slice of ham. Then lift up the other side of the paper and twist the edges together with the fingers, or a simpler way is to fold them the same as trout (No. 316). When ready, put them in a baking-sheet, place them in a moderate oven, and let bake for fifteen minutes. Have a hot dish ready, and after taking them from the oven, use a cake-turner to lift the fish up gently, and dress them on the dish, leaving the paper undisturbed, then serve.

331. Fresh Mackerel aux Fines Herbes.—Choose two fine, fresh mackerel, make six small incisions on both sides, and place them in a buttered baking-dish, with half a glassful of white wine, three tablespoonfuls of mushroom liquor, a finely chopped shallot, and half a pinch of salt, with the third of a pinch of pepper. Cover with a piece of buttered paper, and bake in a moderate oven for fifteen minutes, then place the fish on a dish. Pour the gravy into a stewpan, adding two tablespoonfuls of cooked fine herbs (No. 143), a pint of Allemande sauce (No. 210), and a pinch of chopped parsley. Thicken well with a tablespoonful of butter; stir well until dissolved, and pour it over the mackerel when serving. (All mackerel can be prepared the same way, only adding different sauces to the gravy.)

332. Matelote of Eels.—Pare and then cut one and a half pounds of eels into pieces two inches in length. When well washed, put them in a stewpan with one tablespoonful of butter; fry them for two minutes; add a glassful of red wine, a third of a pinch of nutmeg, half a pinch of salt, and a third of a pinch of pepper, also a bouquet (No. 254), a glassful of fish-stock (No. 214), or white broth (No. 99), and three tablespoonfuls of mushroom liquor. Add six small, glazed onions (No. 972), and six mushroom buttons. Cook for thirty minutes, then put in a tablespoonful of white roux (No. 135); stir well while cooking five minutes longer, and serve with six heart-shaped croûtons (No. 133).

333. Matelote of Eels à la Parisienne.—Proceed the same as for the above (No. 332), only lift out the fish when cooked; reduce the sauce to half, adding three tablespoonfuls of Espagnole (No. 151), six mushroom buttons, six glazed onions (No. 972), and six fish quenelles (No. 227). Stir well while cooking two minutes longer, and serve with six fried pieces of bread garnished with Soubise (No. 250).

334. Matelote of Eels à la Normande.—Cut one and a half pounds of eels into pieces, put them in a saucepan with a tablespoonful of butter; fry two minutes; add a glassful of white wine, and three tablespoonfuls of mushroom liquor. Season well with half a pinch each of salt and pepper, and a third of a pinch of nutmeg. Cook for ten minutes, then add half a pint of good velouté (No. 152), six mushrooms, twelve blanched oysters, six fish quenelles (No. 227), and six small, cooked crawfish tails. Cook again for five minutes, and when ready to serve, beat in three egg yolks, but do not boil again, and garnish with six fried croûtons (No. 133).

335. Blanched Eels.—Select a pound and a half of well-skinned eels, cut them into pieces and tie them in rings; put them with cold water in a saucepan, with a good pinch of salt and a little vinegar, a sprig of thyme, two bay-leaves, twelve whole peppers, a quarter of a bunch of parsley-roots, one onion, and one carrot. Place them on a slow fire, and take them off before they boil; lay them in an earthen jar with the water they were boiled in. (These can be used for frying or boiling, according to need).

336. Bluefish à l'Icarienne.—Scale and score two pounds of bluefish, place it on a well-buttered baking-dish, moistening with three tablespoonfuls of mushroom liquor and half a glassful of white wine. Season with half a pinch of salt and a third of a pinch of pepper, then cover with a buttered paper, and put to cook in a moderately heated oven for fifteen minutes; lift it out, lay it on a dish, and put the gravy into a stewpan, adding three tablespoonfuls of tomato sauce (No. 205) and half an ounce of finely minced, cooked, smoked beef-tongue. Boil for two minutes again, and throw the whole over the fish when serving. Garnish with six small, cooked crawfish, if any on hand.

337. Bluefish à l'Italienne.—Score and scale two pounds of bluefish; place it in a buttered pan, with half a glassful of white wine, three tablespoonfuls of mushroom liquor, half of a very finely chopped onion, and six chopped-up mushrooms. Season with a pinch of salt and half a pinch of pepper. Cover the fish with a buttered paper, and cook in a moderate oven for fifteen minutes; take the fish out, lay it on a serving dish, and put the juice in a stewpan, adding a gill of Espagnole sauce (No. 151), with a small glassful of white wine; reduce for two minutes, then pour it over the fish, with one pinch of finely chopped parsley, and serve with six heart-shaped pieces of croûton (No. 133).

338. Bluefish à la Venitienne.—Prepare the fish as for the above (No. 337), adding to it one tomato cut in pieces, half a pint of Espagnole sauce (No. 151) and six whole mushrooms. Besprinkle lightly with fresh bread-crumbs, and throw over all a few drops of clarified butter; put it in the oven for eight minutes, and serve with half a pinch of chopped parsley.

339. Sheep's-head à la Créole.—Put one chopped onion and one very finely chopped green pepper—the seed extracted—in a stewpan; brown them in a half gill of oil for five minutes, then add one tomato, cut in pieces, four sliced mushrooms, a good bouquet (No. 254), and a clove of garlic. Season well with a pinch of salt and half a pinch of pepper, then moisten with half a pint of Espagnole sauce (No. 151). Cut a fish weighing three pounds in six slices, lay them flat in the stewpan, with three tablespoonfuls of mushroom liquor (if any handy), and let cook for one hour on a very slow fire. When ready to serve, sprinkle over with a pinch of chopped parsley, and decorate with six pieces of heart-shaped croûton (No. 133). (All fish à la Créole are prepared the same way, the time allowed for cooking depending on the firmness of the fish. The fish can be left whole instead of dividing in slices, if desired.)

340. Bouille-à-Baisse, à la Marseillaise.—Brown two sliced onions in a gill of oil for five minutes in a saucepan, then moisten with one quart of fish-stock (No. 214), adding a bouquet (No. 254), three cloves of garlic, bruised and minced exceedingly fine. Dilute a third of a pinch of powdered Spanish saffron in water, and add it to the gravy. Take one small eel, one very small bass, the same of sole, one raw lobster—in fact, all the firm fish ready at hand—cut them in slices, season with a pinch of salt and the third of a saltspoonful of cayenne pepper, and put them all together on a slow fire. Let cook for twenty minutes, and when ready, serve in a deep dish, on which you previously arrange six pieces of toast from a French loaf of bread.

N. B.—The above should be served exceedingly hot.

341. Bass à la Bordelaise.—Cut a deep incision down the back of a three-pound sea-bass, put it in a baking-dish with half a glassful of red wine, half a pinch of salt, and a third of a pinch of pepper. Besprinkle with a finely chopped shallot, cover with a buttered paper, and cook in a moderate oven for fifteen minutes. Lay the bass on a dish, put the juice in a saucepan with a gill of good Espagnole (No. 151), four finely shred mushrooms, and a thin slice of finely chopped garlic; finish cooking for five minutes more, then pour it over the fish. Decorate with six cooked crawfish or shrimps, and serve very hot.

342. Bass, with White Wine.—Lay a three-pound, well-cleaned bass on a well-buttered baking-dish; season with half a pinch of salt and a third of a pinch of pepper; moisten with half a glassful of white wine and three tablespoonfuls of mushroom liquor. Cover with a heavy piece of buttered paper, and cook in a moderate oven for fifteen minutes, then lay the fish on a dish; put the juice in a saucepan, with half a pint of good Allemande (No. 210), thicken well with a tablespoonful of butter till well dissolved, and throw it over the bass, serving with six heart-shaped croûtons (No. 133).

343. Bass à la Chambord.—Lift the middle skin from the back of a three-pound bass, leaving the head and tail covered; lard the fish nicely with a very small larding needle, and then lay it on a buttered, deep baking-pan, adding to it half a glassful of white wine, and half a carrot, and half an onion, both sliced, also a bouquet (No. 254). Season with a pinch of salt and half a pinch of pepper, then cover with a buttered paper; cook it in the oven for thirty minutes, being very careful to baste it frequently, then lift out the fish and lay it on a dish. Strain the gravy into a saucepan, with half a pint of Chambord garnishing (No. 212), moistened with half a pint of Espagnole (No. 151); reduce for five minutes. Decorate the dish with clusters of the garnishing, and three decorated fish quenelles (No. 227) to separate them, also three small, cooked crawfish, and serve.

344. Salt Cod à la Biscaënne.—Take two pounds of boneless cod, and soak it in plenty of cold water for twenty-four hours, changing the water as often as possible. Place it in a saucepan with plenty of fresh water, then let simmer on a slow fire till boiling; take it off, and drain it well; return it to the pan with fresh water, and let come to a boil again, then scale it by separating the bones. Fry together in a saucepan two chopped onions and one green pepper in a gill of oil. Let cook for five minutes, then add one good-sized tomato, cut in pieces, one clove of bruised garlic, and one Chili pepper. Moisten the fish with three pints of broth, add a bouquet (No. 254), three tablespoonfuls of tomato sauce (No. 205), and a pint of Parisian potatoes (No. 986). Let cook for forty-five minutes, then add the codfish; boil again for five minutes more. Dress it on a hot dish, and serve with a teaspoonful of chopped parsley sprinkled over.

345. Codfish, bonne femme.—Have two pounds of cooked, soaked, boneless cod; prepare it the same as for the above (No. 344), then put it in a saucepan, moistening with half a pint of béchamel (No. 154), and half a pint of Allemande (No. 210). Add three sliced potatoes, and three hard-boiled eggs, cut in thin slices, and half a pinch of pepper. (If too thick, put in a little milk.) Cook for about five minutes longer, then serve with a teaspoonful of chopped parsley.

346. Picked-up Codfish.—The same as for the above, only all the materials should be shred smaller, and add three tablespoonfuls of cream.

347. Fish Balls.—Place in a large pan, with plenty of fresh water, three pounds of boneless codfish, and let soak for twelve hours. Drain, and place it in a saucepan on the hot range, with plenty of cold water, and as soon as it begins to boil, drain all the water through a colander. Carefully pick out all the bones from the cod, and return it to the saucepan, adding five medium-sized, well-washed, and peeled sliced potatoes, one gill of cold water or broth, and cook on a moderate fire for twenty minutes, then add half an ounce of butter. Take from off the fire. Season with one pinch of white pepper, then, with the aid of a potato-masher or a pounder, mash all well together right in the pan. Transfer it to a dish, and let cool. Make up small fish balls two inches in diameter by one inch thick, lightly sprinkle them with a very little flour. Heat in a frying-pan one gill of clarified butter; when very hot, put in the fish balls and fry for three minutes on each side, so as to have them of a good brown color. Gently lift them from the pan with a skimmer, dress on a hot dish with a folded napkin, crown-shaped, one overlapping another. Decorate the centre of the dish with parsley-greens, and serve.

Fish Balls à la Mrs. Benjamin Harrison.—To be prepared exactly the same as above (No. 347), dressing them on six dry toasts, placing one poached egg (No. 404) on top of each fish ball, and decorating the dish with six slices of broiled bacon, and serve hot.

348. How to Blanch Codfish-tongues.—Procure eighteen fine, fresh codfish-tongues, wash them thoroughly in cold water, then drain, and place them in a saucepan on the hot stove; cover with fresh water, and season with a handful of salt, six cloves, twelve whole peppers, one sliced onion, a bouquet (No. 254), and half a sliced lemon. Let them come to a boil, then transfer them with the water and garnishings to a stone jar, and use when needed.

349. Codfish-tongues au beurre noir.—Take eighteen blanched codfish-tongues, as for No. 348, heat them in a saucepan with half a gill of their own juice, but do not let them boil; drain well, then dress them on a hot dish, pour a pint of black butter (No. 159) over, and decorate each side of the dish with a few sprigs of parsley, then send to the table.

350. Fried Codfish-tongues.—Take eighteen fine, fresh codfish-tongues, wash them well, drain them in a napkin, dip them in cold milk, and roll them, one by one, in flour. Put one gill of clarified butter in the frying-pan, heat it well, then gently lay in the tongues separately, and let cook for three minutes. Turn them on the other side, using a fork, and cook for three minutes more. Lift them up carefully with a skimmer, and put them on a cloth to drain. Season with one pinch of salt and half a pinch of pepper; dress them on a hot dish with a folded napkin, and decorate with sprigs of parsley. Serve a gill of hot tomato sauce (No. 205) in a separate bowl.

351. Codfish-tongues à la poulette.—Take eighteen blanched tongues, as for No. 348, put them in a saucepan on the stove, adding a pint of sauce Hollandaise (No. 160), half a gill of their own stock, and a teaspoonful of chopped parsley. Heat well for five minutes without boiling, then pour the whole into a deep, hot dish, sprinkle a little chopped parsley over them, and serve.

352. Boiled Codfish, Oyster Sauce.—Cover a three-pound fresh codfish with well-salted fish-stock (No. 214), and let cook thirty minutes without boiling; then take it out and drain it well. Lay it on a dish, and garnish with a few branches of parsley-greens, and twelve pieces of potato à l'Anglaise (No. 988). Serve with three-quarters of a pint of oyster sauce (No. 173) separately. (All codfish with different sauces are prepared the same way.)

353. Broiled Boned Smelts à la Béarnaise.—Split twelve good-sized or eighteen medium-sized smelts up the back, remove the backbone, rub them with one tablespoonful of oil, and season with half a pinch of salt and a third of a pinch of pepper. Broil them in a double broiler for two minutes on each side; pour a little more than a gill of good Béarnaise sauce (No. 166) on a dish, arrange the smelts carefully on top, and serve, finishing with a very little demi-glace sauce (No. 185) around the dish.

354. Smelts à la Toulouse.—Take twelve large or eighteen medium-sized smelts, bone them as for the above, and then close them up again. Put them in a stewpan, with half a glassful of white wine and three tablespoonfuls of mushroom liquor; season with half a pinch of salt and the third of a pinch of pepper, and cook on a moderate fire for six minutes. Arrange the smelts on a dish, add to the sauce twelve mushroom buttons, two sliced truffles, six fish quenelles (No. 227), and moisten with half a pint of Allemande sauce (No. 210). Thicken with a tablespoonful of butter sufficiently, and throw the sauce over the smelts. Neatly dress the garnishing around the dish, and serve with six heart-shaped croûtons (No. 133). (Smelts are all prepared the same way, only adding different garnishings.)

355. Stuffed Smelts.—Cut off the fins, wash, and dry well with a towel, eighteen fine, fresh, medium-sized, Long Island smelts; remove the eggs without splitting the stomachs open, then fill them with a fish forcemeat (No. 227), using a paper cornet for the purpose. Lay the smelts on a well-buttered silver baking-dish (if possible), and cover them with a pint of sauce Italienne (No. 188). Put them in a hot oven and let bake for eight minutes; remove them, squeeze the juice of a good lemon over, and lay the silver dish on top of another to avoid soiling the table-cloth; then serve.

356. Smelts au Gratin.—Clean eighteen smelts, wipe them very dry, and put them on a baking-dish with two tablespoonfuls of cooked fine herbs (No. 143), half a glassful of white wine, half a pinch of salt, and a third of a pinch of pepper. Cover with six whole mushrooms and half a pint of Espagnole sauce (No. 151). Besprinkle lightly with fresh bread-crumbs and six drops of melted butter; place it in a hot oven for ten minutes, and serve with the juice of half a lemon, also a teaspoonful of chopped parsley sprinkled over. (The smelts can be boned if so desired).

357. Lobster à l'Américaine.—Split two fine, good-sized, freshly boiled lobsters; remove all the meat carefully, then cut it up into pieces one inch in length. Have a pan on the hot range with half a gill of good olive oil, and when the oil is very hot add the pieces of lobster. Chop very fine one medium-sized, peeled onion, one fine, sound, green pepper, and half a clove of peeled, very sound garlic; add all to the lobster, and let cook for five minutes, gently mixing meanwhile. Season with a pinch of salt and half a saltspoonful of red pepper, adding also half a wine-glassful of good white wine. Reduce for two minutes, then add one gill of tomato sauce (No. 205) and one medium-sized, sound, red, peeled tomato, cut into small dice-shaped pieces. Cook for ten minutes longer, gently shuffling meanwhile. Pour the whole into a very hot, deep dish, or in a hot tureen, and serve.

358. Lobster with Curry.

—Pick out all the meat from two good-sized, fine, freshly boiled, and split lobsters. Cut the meat up in one-inch-length equal pieces. Have a saucepan on the hot range with an ounce of very good butter; add the lobster to it, and let cook for five minutes. Season with one pinch of salt and half a pinch of pepper. Place in a bowl one tablespoonful of Indian curry, with half a wine-glassful of good white wine, mix well together, then pour it into the lobster. Cook for two minutes. Add two gills of hot Allemande sauce (No. 210), shuffle briskly for one minute longer. Make a border of fresh-boiled rice all around the hot dish; dress the lobster right in the centre of the dish, and serve hot.

359. Lobster à la Newburg.—Split two good-sized, fine, freshly boiled lobsters. Pick all the meat out from the shells, then cut it into one-inch-length equal pieces. Place it in a saucepan on the hot range with one ounce of very good, fresh butter. Season with one pinch of salt and half a saltspoonful of red pepper, adding two medium-sized, sound truffles cut into small dice-shaped pieces. Cook for five minutes; then add a wine-glassful of good Madeira wine. Reduce to one-half, which will take three minutes. Have three egg yolks in a bowl with half a pint of sweet cream, beat well together, and add it to the lobster. Gently shuffle for two minutes longer, or until it thickens well. Pour it into a hot tureen, and serve hot.

360. Lobster à la Bordelaise.—Add to one glassful of red wine in a stewpan one chopped shallot, and half of a small carrot cut into exceedingly small pieces. Boil for five minutes, and then put in pieces of boiled lobster, the same quantity as for the above—about a pound and a half—a pinch of salt, a third of a pinch of pepper and a very little nutmeg, also half a pint of velouté (No. 152). Stew well together for five minutes, then serve.

361. Lobster en Brochette au Petit Salé.—Take one and a half pounds of fresh, shelled, boiled lobster, cut it into two-inch-square, even pieces, lay them in a bowl, then season with a good pinch of salt, a pinch of pepper, the third of a pinch of nutmeg, and a tablespoonful of Parisian sauce, and mix all well together. Have six silver skewers, arrange in the centre of one a piece of lobster, then a mushroom, another piece of lobster and another mushroom; continue the same for the other skewers, then place them on the broiler and broil for eight minutes, turning them over carefully once in a while. Remove them from the broiler, dress them on a hot dish, pour a gill of maître d'hôtel butter (No. 145) over, decorate with six slices of broiled bacon (No. 754), and serve very hot.

362. Lobster en Chevreuse.—To two finely chopped shallots in a stewpan add one glassful of Madeira wine, one ounce of butter, and a pound and a half of pieces of boiled lobster; moisten with one pint of velouté (No. 152), and season with a pinch of salt, half a pinch of pepper, and a very little nutmeg. Let boil for ten minutes, and with this preparation fill six table-shells, or, better still, six small St. Jacques-shells; on top of each lay three slices of truffle and one tablespoonful of good béchamel (No. 154). Put one drop of clarified butter over each, and place them in the oven for five minutes. Serve very hot on a folded napkin.

363. Broiled Lobster à la Ravigote.—Cut three small, raw lobsters into two equal parts, taking out the gravel from the head, season with one pinch of salt and half a pinch of pepper, and rub with a very little oil, then broil the pieces for ten minutes. Take them from the fire, and remove the meat from the head of the lobsters and put it in a salad-bowl with half a pint of ravigote butter (No. 147), and mix well together; take the meat from the balance of the lobster, dip it in the sauce, and return it to its shell; warm again for two minutes in the oven, then serve on a folded napkin, garnishing the shells with parsley-greens, and serving the sauce in a sauce-bowl.

364. Broiled Lobster.—Select three medium-sized, good, live lobsters, split them in halves, and take out the stony pouch and intestines; glaze them slightly with sweet oil, and season them with half a pinch of salt and half a pinch of pepper, and then broil them for seven minutes on each side. Place them on a dish, moisten with a gill of good maître d'hôtel (No. 145), then serve.

365. Lobster Croquettes.—Make some lobster forcemeat (No. 222); form it into the shape of six pears with the hand, roll them in bread-crumbs (No. 301), and fry in very hot fat for three minutes; drain well, then serve on a folded napkin, garnishing with parsley-greens, and add any sauce required in a sauce-bowl.

Salmon croquettes to be prepared the same way, substituting minced, boiled salmon for the lobster forcemeat.

366. Lobster Cutlets, Victoria.—The same as for the above, only giving them the shape of a chop, and when serving stick a lobster leg in the point of each one.

367. Stuffed Lobster.—Fill six empty lobster-tails with forcemeat (No. 222), roll them in bread-crumbs, put them on a baking-dish, smoothing the surface with the blade of a knife; place them in a baking-pan. Pour a little clarified butter over, and brown gently in the oven for six minutes, and serve on a folded napkin with a garnishing of parsley-greens.

368. Fried Soft-shelled Crabs.—Procure six good-sized, live, soft-shelled crabs, cleanse and wash them thoroughly, and dip each one in flour, then in beaten egg, and finally in rasped bread-crumbs or pulverized crackers, using them very lightly. Fry in very hot fat for five minutes, drain, season with one pinch of salt, evenly divided, and serve on a hot dish with a folded napkin with fried parsley around.

369. Broiled Soft-shelled Crabs.—Have six good-sized, fresh, soft-shelled crabs, cleanse and wash them well, then drain them, oil them slightly, and season with a pinch of salt and half a pinch of pepper. Put them on the broiler, and broil for five minutes on each side. Have six pieces of toast ready, lay a crab on top of each, slightly glaze them with a little maître d'hôtel butter (No. 145), and serve. This makes a delicious dish, but must be served very hot.

370. Hard-shelled Crabs à la Diable.—Fill six thoroughly cleaned crab-shells with some crab forcemeat (No. 223), flatten them with the hand, besprinkle with fresh bread-crumbs, smooth the surface with the blade of a knife, moistening the top with a very little clarified butter. Place them on a baking-pan, and bake a little brown for six minutes. Serve on a hot dish with a folded napkin decorated with parsley-greens.

371. Crabs à la St. Jean.—Add double the quantity of onions to some crab forcemeat (No. 223), also garlic, parsley, and chervil (let the crabs be in as large pieces as possible). Then, as for No. 362, fill six St. Jacques-shells, besprinkle with fresh bread-crumbs, smooth the surface with the blade of a knife, moisten slightly with clarified butter, and bake in a brisk oven for six minutes. Serve on a hot dish with a folded napkin decorated with parsley-greens.

372. Crabs à la St. Laurent.—Reduce half a pint of good velouté (No. 152) with half a glassful of white wine, season with one pinch of salt, half a pinch of pepper, and a very little cayenne pepper, adding three tablespoonfuls of grated Parmesan cheese. Take three-quarters of a pound of shelled crabs, put them in the saucepan, and boil them for ten minutes; then lift from the fire and let cool. Prepare six squares of toasted bread, and with a knife spread some of the mixture smoothly over each slice, sprinkle well with grated cheese, and moisten slightly with clarified butter; place them on a baking-dish; bake in a very hot oven for three minutes, and serve on a hot dish with a folded napkin, garnished with parsley-greens.

373. Crabs à l'Anglaise.—Pick twelve boiled, hard-shelled crabs in as large pieces as possible; mix them in a salad-bowl with half a cupful of the white of celery or finely shred lettuce leaves, one pinch of salt, half a pinch of pepper, one tablespoonful of olive oil, and one and a half tablespoonfuls of vinegar. Refill six well-cleaned shells with the salad, and on each one lay a good teaspoonful of mayonnaise sauce (No. 206), sprinkled over with one hard-boiled, finely chopped egg, the yolk and white separated, some crab or lobster coral, and a teaspoonful of chopped parsley, every article to be used separately, so they have each a different color. Serve on a dish with a folded napkin.

374. Oyster-crabs à la Poulette.—Take one and a half pints of oyster-crabs, and proceed the same as for oysters à la poulette (No. 383).

375. Fried Oyster-crabs.—Wash well, and dry one and a half pints of oyster-crabs, dip them in flour, then in cold milk, and finally in cracker-dust; shake them well in a colander, and fry in hot fat for three minutes; serve in shells made of foundation paste, or short paste for tarts (No. 1078), garnishing with parsley-leaves, and sprinkling a very little salt on top.

376. Stuffed Clams.—Refill six good-sized, very clean clam-shells with clam forcemeat (No. 223), and prepare them the same as stuffed crabs (No. 370).

377. Clams à la Marinière.—Open and remove thirty-six small clams from their shells; put them in a stewpan with two ounces of fresh butter, one pinch of chives, and one pinch of finely chopped chervil; add half a cupful of water, so they will not be too salty, with half a pinch of pepper, and two tablespoonfuls of fresh bread-crumbs. Boil for two minutes, and serve with the juice of half a lemon.

378. Mussels à la Marinière.—Steam in a stewpan thirty-six mussels for ten minutes, and proceed as for No. 377, leaving a mussel in each half shell.

379. Mussels à la Poulette.—Steam in a stewpan thirty-six mussels for ten minutes, and proceed the same as oysters à la poulette (No. 383), leaving a mussel in each half shell.

380. Fried Oysters.—Procure twenty-four large freshly opened oysters, or thirty-six of medium size, dip each one separately in flour, then in beaten egg, and lastly in powdered cracker-dust. Fry in very hot fat for four minutes, drain well, and serve on a hot dish with a folded napkin, sprinkling over a very little salt, and garnishing with fried parsley-leaves.

381. Oysters à la Villeroi.—Blanch twenty-four large oysters in their own juice for two minutes, then drain them; take some chicken forcemeat (No. 226), spread it over both sides of the oysters, dip in egg and fresh bread-crumbs, then fry in hot lard for three minutes, and serve with fried parsley.

382. Broiled Oysters.—Dip twenty-four large and freshly opened oysters in half bread-crumbs and half cracker-dust; flatten them with the hand, and broil them on a well-greased broiler for two minutes on each side, then salt them slightly, and serve on six pieces of toast; lightly glaze them with maître d'hôtel sauce on top (No. 177).

383. Oysters à la Poulette.—Put thirty-six freshly opened oysters in a saucepan with a little of their own juice, one ounce of butter, half a pinch of salt, and the same of pepper; parboil for three minutes, adding half a pint of Hollandaise sauce (No. 160), stew well together for two minutes again, but do not let boil, and add one teaspoonful of chopped parsley and the juice of half a lemon. Stir slightly, and serve.

384. Oysters à la Pompadour.—Proceed the same as for No. 383, suppressing the parsley, and adding two chopped truffles.

385. Oysters en Brochette au Petit Salé.—Place twenty-four freshly opened oysters in a stewpan with their own juice; season with a very little salt, half a pinch of pepper; parboil for two minutes. Take six skewers and pass them through the oysters, separating each one by a small square of cooked bacon—that is, alternating each oyster with a piece of the bacon— besprinkle with grated, fresh bread-crumbs, and broil for one and a half minutes on each side. Serve with half a gill of maître d'hôtel sauce (No. 177) poured over, and a bunch of parsley-leaves spread on both sides of the dish.

386. Oysters à la Mali.—Chop an onion very fine; place it in a stewpan with one ounce of butter, and let it get a good golden color, then add a tablespoonful of cooked, finely minced spinach, also a small glassful of white wine. Have eighteen medium-sized oysters chopped exceedingly small, and seasoned with a pinch of salt, and the same of pepper; place these in the stewpan, and let cook for fifteen minutes. Put in one whole egg, also a bruised clove of garlic; stir; then take six large, clean oyster-shells; fill the bottoms with a bed of three parboiled oysters, cover them with the spinach mixture, and besprinkle with fresh bread-crumbs. Flatten the tops with the blade of a knife, pour a very little clarified butter over, and put them for three minutes in the oven. Serve on a folded napkin, garnishing with parsley-leaves.

387. Oyster Patties.—Take twenty-four medium-sized oysters (the least salted oysters are better for this purpose), put them in a stewpan with their own liquor, and add half a pinch of pepper. Cover, and let cook for two minutes; then take half the liquor out, and add to the oysters three-quarters of a pint of béchamel sauce (No. 154), and a very little grated nutmeg; simmer for two minutes, but do not let boil. Take six hot patties (No. 266), fill them up with four oysters each, pour the sauce over, and place the covers on top. Serve on a dish with a folded napkin.

388. Stewed Oysters à la Baltimore.—Open neatly thirty-six medium-sized, fresh Rockaway oysters; place them in a saucepan without their juice, adding one ounce of good butter; cover the pan, put it on the stove, and let cook for two minutes, then add a small glassful of good Madeira wine (about a cocktail glass) and a very little cayenne pepper. Cook together for two minutes longer, then add one gill of Espagnole sauce (No. 151) and one gill of demi-glace (No. 185). Stir thoroughly until boiling, and just before serving squeeze in the juice of a good lemon, add half an ounce of good butter, also a teaspoonful of finely chopped parsley, and serve immediately in a hot tureen.

389. Soft Clams à la George Merrill.—Have thirty-six fresh and rather small soft clams, throw away all the hard part, keeping nothing but the body. Place them in a stewpan with two ounces of butter, half a pinch of pepper, a finely chopped shallot, and half a glassful of Madeira wine. Let cook on the hot stove for seven minutes, then add a gill of Espagnole sauce (No. 151), a pinch of chopped parsley, the juice of a medium-sized, good lemon, and half an ounce of good butter, shuffling the whole well for three minutes longer, without letting it boil, then pour the clams into a hot tureen, and serve.

390. Soft Clams à la Newburg.—Procure forty-two very fresh, soft clams, so that no sand should adhere to them after they are opened; lay them carefully in the palm of the left hand, and with the fingers of the right remove the body gently, but nothing else, being very careful not to break it, and throw away all that remains. When they are all prepared, place them in a stewpan with an ounce of good butter, half a pinch of white pepper, a wine-glassful of good Madeira wine, and two finely hashed, medium-sized truffles. Put on the cover, and let cook gently for eight minutes. Break three egg yolks into a bowl, add a pint of sweet cream; beat well for three minutes, then pour it over the clams; turn well the handle of the saucepan for two or three minutes, very gently shuffling the clams, but it must not boil again or the clams will break, and be very careful not to use either a spoon or fork. Pour them into a hot tureen, and send to the table at once.

391. Canapé Lorenzo.—Cut out from an American bread six slices, the width of the bread, one-quarter of an inch in thickness; neatly pare off the crust, fry them in a sautoire with half an ounce of butter, so as to have them of a light brown color. Boil eighteen hard-shelled crabs in salted water for twelve minutes, remove them, and let cool until they can be handled with bare hands; then remove the upper shell, and with the aid of a pointed knife pick out all the meat; crack both claws, pick the meat out also; place the meat on a plate, season with a tablespoonful of salt and a saltspoonful of red pepper. Place one ounce of butter in a saucepan with half a medium-sized, sound, peeled, and very finely chopped-up onion. Cook on a moderate fire for two minutes, being very careful not to let get brown. Add two tablespoonfuls of flour, stirring constantly for two minutes; then add one gill of broth, stir well again for five minutes while slowly cooking. Add now the crab-meat, and cook for fifteen minutes more, lightly stirring with a wooden spoon once in a while. Transfer it into a vessel, and let cool for fifteen minutes. Place a tablespoonful of good butter in a sautoire on a hot stove, mix in well together one tablespoonful of flour, and cook very slowly for three minutes. Add two ounces of grated Parmesan cheese, and the same quantity of grated Swiss cheese; stir all well together. Then place in a vessel and let cool. Place a layer of crab forcemeat on each toast a quarter of an inch thick. Divide the prepared cheese, etc., into six equal parts, giving them a ball-shaped form two inches in diameter. Arrange them over the layer of the crab forcemeat right in the centre. Place them on a silver dish, and bake in a brisk oven for five minutes. Then take out from the oven, and send to the table in the same dish.

392. Scallops Brestoise.—Blanch in one ounce of butter for ten minutes, and then drain, one pint of scallops; chop up two onions, and put them in a saucepan with an ounce of butter; when brown add one tablespoonful of flour, stirring carefully, and moisten with half a pint of the scallop liquor; if none, white broth (No. 99) will answer. Let reduce while stirring, then season with a good pinch of salt, and half a pinch of white pepper, also a very little cayenne pepper; add the chopped scallops, four egg yolks, and a bruised clove of garlic, also half a cupful of fresh bread-crumbs, and a tablespoonful of chopped parsley. Stir well for two minutes, then put it in a dish and lay aside to cool. Fill six scallop-shells, or St. Jacques-shells with this, besprinkle the tops with fresh bread-crumbs, moisten slightly with clarified butter, and lay them on a baking-sheet; brown them nicely in the oven for five minutes, and serve on a hot dish with a folded napkin garnished with parsley-leaves.

393. Edible Snails à la Bourguignonne.—Have some fine Bourgogne snails; disgorge them well with a little salt for two or three days, then wash them several times in cold water, strain, and place them in a stewpan, covering them with water. Add a bouquet (No. 254), some cloves and whole pepper tied in a cloth, and sufficient salt; cook until the snails fall from their shells, and then empty them, clipping off their tails; clean the shells well. Mix together some good butter, shallots, parsley, and chervil, the whole chopped very fine; put it in a bowl with as much fresh bread-crumbs, and a small glassful of white wine; season to taste with salt and pepper, and knead well. Fill each shell with a little of this mixture, replace the snails, and finish filling with more of the kneaded butter; spread bread-crumbs over, and lay them on a baking-dish, the opened part on the top. Brown in the oven for four minutes, and serve on a dish with a folded napkin.

394. Edible Snails à l'Italienne.—Prepare the snails as for the above, leaving them in their shells; drain, and put them in a saucepan with white wine and a little strong Espagnole sauce (No. 151), a few chopped, fried onions and finely minced mushrooms. Season well with a pinch of salt, cook for a few minutes, and serve.

395. Edible Snails à la Provençale.—Prepare the snails as for No. 393; fry a little chopped onion with oil, add the snails taken from the shells, a little white wine, two cloves of chopped garlic, a little fresh bread-crumbs, and chopped parsley. Cook, add the juice of a lemon; then serve.

396. Terrapin à la Baltimore.—Prepare two medium-sized terrapins as for No. 60, make half a pint of mirepoix (No. 138), add to it a tablespoonful of flour, let cook for fifteen minutes, then moisten with half a glassful of Madeira wine, and a cupful of strong broth. Stir well, and constantly, then season with half a pinch of salt, and a very little cayenne pepper; reduce to half. Cut the terrapin into small pieces, throwing the ends of the claws away; put them in a stewpan, straining the sauce over, and finish with an ounce of fresh butter, also the juice of a lemon.

397. Terrapin à la Maryland.—Carefully cut up two terrapins as described in No. 60; place them in a saucepan with half a wine-glass of good Madeira wine, half a pinch of salt, and a very little cayenne pepper, also an ounce of good butter. Mix well a cupful of good, sweet cream with the yolks of three boiled eggs, and add it to the terrapin, briskly shuffling constantly, while thoroughly heating, but without letting it come to a boil. Pour into a hot tureen, and serve very hot.

Terrapin à la Newburg is prepared exactly the same as above (No. 397), only substituting two raw egg yolks for the three boiled egg yolks, and adding two sound, sliced truffles while heating.

398. Broiled Frogs.—Select eighteen good-sized, fine, fresh frogs, pare off the feet neatly, then lay the frogs on a dish, and pour two tablespoonfuls of sweet oil over, season with a pinch of salt and a pinch of pepper, and squeeze in the juice of a fresh lemon. Roll them around several times in their seasoning, then place them nicely on the broiler, and broil them for four minutes on each side. Take them off, and dress them on a hot dish, pouring a gill of maître d'hôtel butter (No. 145) over, and send to the table immediately.

399. Frogs à la Poulette.—Procure eighteen pieces of medium-sized, fine, fresh frogs; pare off the claws, then place the frogs in a sautoire with two ounces of butter, seasoning with a pinch of salt and a pinch of pepper. Add half a glassful of white wine, cover, and let cook on a brisk stove for five minutes, then add a pint of Hollandaise sauce (No. 160), and two teaspoonfuls of finely chopped parsley, and a little lemon juice; mix well for two minutes, but do not let it boil again; then serve the frogs on a very hot dish.

400. Fried Frogs.—Select eighteen fine, fresh, medium-sized frogs; trim off the claws neatly, and put the frogs in a bowl. Marinade them with a tablespoonful of vinegar, the same of sweet oil, a pinch of salt and a pinch of pepper; mix well together in the bowl, then immerse them in frying batter (No. 1185). Plunge the frogs into very hot fat, one by one, and let fry for five minutes; then drain, and dress them on a hot dish with a folded napkin, decorating with a little parsley-greens. Serve with any desired sauce.

401. Frogs à l'Espagnole.

—Trim nicely eighteen fine, fresh, medium-sized frogs' feet; lay the frogs in a sautoire on the hot stove with two ounces of good butter, season with a pinch of salt and half a pinch of pepper, and add half a glassful of white wine. Let cook for five minutes, then put in it half an empty green pepper and two freshly peeled tomatoes, all cut up into small pieces; cook for ten minutes longer, then dress the frogs on a hot dish, and send to the table.

402. Broiled Shad's Roe, with Bacon.—Procure six pieces of fresh shad's roe, wipe them thoroughly with a towel, then lay them on a dish, and season with a good pinch of salt and two tablespoonfuls of sweet oil. Roll them gently to avoid breaking, then arrange them on a broiler, and broil them for six minutes on each side. Take them off the fire, lay them on a hot dish, and pour a gill of maître d'hôtel butter (No. 145) over; decorate with six slices of broiled bacon (No. 754), and six quarters of lemon; then send to the table.

403. Broiled Sardines on Toast.—Select twelve good-sized, fine, and firm sardines; arrange them in a double broiler, and broil for two minutes on each side on a very brisk fire. Place six fresh, dry toasts on a hot dish, lay the sardines over, being careful not to break them, pour half a gill of maître d'hôtel butter (No. 145) over, decorate with six quarters of lemon, and serve.

A pinch of salt represents 205 grains, or a tablespoonful.

Half a pinch of pepper represents 38 grains, or a teaspoonful.

A third of a pinch of nutmeg represents 13 grains, or half a teaspoonful.

EGGS.

404. Poached.—Boil in a deep saucepan three quarts of water with a heavy pinch of salt and three drops of vinegar. Have easily at hand twelve fresh eggs. When, and only when, the water boils, rapidly but carefully crack six of them, one by one. As success to have them in proper shape and cooked to perfection depends upon how they are handled, special care should be taken to crack them as rapidly as possible, carefully avoiding to break the yolks, and dropping each one right on the spot where the water bubbles, and as near the boiling-point as possible. Poach for one minute and a quarter from the time that the water boils after the eggs were put in. Lift them up with a skimmer, lay them on the freshly prepared toasts, or use for any other desired purpose; and repeat the same with the other six. If handled strictly as above described you will have them to perfection, and no necessity of trimming any superfluous adherings; serve when required.

405. Scrambled Eggs.—Melt three ounces of butter in a saucepan, break into it twelve fresh eggs; season with a pinch of salt, half a pinch of pepper, and a third of a pinch of grated nutmeg. Mix thoroughly without stopping for three minutes, using a spatula, and having the pan on a very hot stove. Turn into a warm tureen, add a little verjuice or lemon juice, and send to the table very hot.

406. Scrambled Eggs with Asparagus-tops.—To be prepared exactly the same as for No. 405. After the eggs have been well mixed with butter in the pan, there is added a quarter of a bunch of freshly boiled asparagus-tops.

407. Scrambled Eggs with Truffles.—Place in a saucepan four good-sized, sliced truffles with a glassful of Madeira wine. Reduce to about half, which will take two minutes; add a tablespoonful of butter; season with one pinch of salt and half a pinch of pepper. Crack into the saucepan twelve eggs, mix all well together with the spatula for three minutes on a very hot stove without stopping. Turn into a hot tureen and serve.

408. Scrambled Eggs with Smoked Beef.—Fry in a sautoire for one minute two ounces of finely minced smoked beef. Scramble twelve eggs as for No. 405, mixing with the above prepared beef. Any kind of garnishing may be added to the scrambled eggs.

409. Scrambled Eggs with Chicory.—Blanch for fifteen minutes a good-sized head of chicory; drain it and cut it into one-inch lengths. Put these in a saucepan on the hot stove with an ounce of butter and one minced onion, fry, and then moisten with half a pint of broth (No. 99), adding a pinch of salt and half a pinch of pepper. Let cook until all the liquid is evaporated (which will take from twenty to twenty-two minutes). Break twelve eggs into a saucepan, add the chicory and another ounce of butter, then scramble with a spatula all together for four minutes, and serve with heart-shaped bread croûtons (No. 133) around the dish.

410. Eggs à la Livingstone.—Cover six pieces of cut toast with pâté-de-foie-gras, lay them on a dish, and pour twelve scrambled eggs over (No. 405), add two tablespoonfuls of demi-glace around the dish and serve (No. 185).

411. Eggs à la Bourguignonne.

—Place in a saucepan one tablespoonful of meat-glaze with one pint of broth (No. 99), or consommé (No. 100). Boil, then crack into it two fresh eggs, and poach for one and a quarter minutes. Carefully lift up with a skimmer, and gently lay them on a hot silver dish. Repeat the same operation with ten more, two at a time; when all on the dish, sprinkle over them an ounce of grated Parmesan cheese. Place in the hot oven to brown for one minute. Reduce the gravy in which they were poached to one-half, then carefully pour the sauce around the eggs, but not over them, and serve hot.

412. Fried Eggs.—Place in a frying-pan on the hot range three tablespoonfuls of very good sweet oil, heat it well, then carefully break into it one fresh egg, being careful not to break the yolk, and with the aid of a table knife fold the white right over the yolk, cook for a quarter of a minute, turn it over with a cake-turner; cook for a quarter of a minute on the other side, lift it up with the cake-turner, dress on a hot dish with a folded napkin. Proceed precisely the same way with eleven more, and then they will be ready to serve for any purpose desired.

N. B.—Mix one pinch of salt, and half a pinch of white pepper, and as soon as the eggs are dressed on the dish season each one evenly with it; taking special care to cook them separately, and no more than a quarter of a minute on each side.

413. Fried Eggs for Garnishing.—Pour half a gill of sweet oil into the frying-pan; when the oil is hot break in one egg, carefully closing up the white part with a skimmer, so as to have it firm, and in a single form. Only one at the time should be cooked, and two minutes will be sufficient.

414. Eggs au Beurre Noir.—Put one ounce of butter in a frying-pan on the hot stove, let heat well, but not brown; break gently into a dish twelve very fresh eggs, slide them carefully into the pan, then season with a pinch of salt and half a pinch of white pepper; let cook slowly for three minutes. Have ready a hot, flat dish, slide the eggs gently onto it, without turning them over, and be careful to avoid breaking them; lay the dish containing the eggs in a warm place. Put two ounces of butter in the same pan, place it on the hot stove, and let the butter get a good brown color for three minutes, then drop in two teaspoonfuls of vinegar. Pour this over the eggs, and send them to the table.

415. Eggs au Soleil.—Put two tablespoonfuls of lard in a frying-pan on the hot stove, break in twelve fresh eggs, dropping them in carefully, one by one; let them cook for two minutes, then with a skimmer take each one up separately and lay it carefully on a dry cloth. Have some fritter-batter (No. 1190) ready, cut a piece of half-cooked bacon into small, square pieces of about an inch, and add them to the batter, then dip in the eggs, one after the other, taking up with each one a piece of the bacon, and with the fingers drop them into very hot grease, and cook to a good golden color for two minutes. Lift them up with the skimmer, lay them on a dry cloth to drain; sprinkle over half a pinch of salt, dress on a hot dish with a folded napkin, and serve.

416. Eggs à la Béchamel.—Pour one pint of béchamel (No. 154) into a saucepan, and put it on the hot stove. Cut twelve hard-boiled eggs in halves, add them to the hot béchamel; season with half a pinch of white pepper, and let heat thoroughly for three minutes, but be careful not to let it boil. Add one ounce of butter and a saltspoonful of grated nutmeg, then pour it on a hot serving-dish, and serve with six heart-shaped croûtons (No. 133).

417. Eggs à la Pauvre Femme.—Heat half an ounce of butter in a dish on the hot stove, then break into it twelve fresh eggs, and sprinkle over two ounces of fresh bread-crumbs. Set the dish in the hot oven, and let bake for two minutes; then pour over the eggs half a pint of well-reduced Espagnole sauce (No. 151), add three ounces of cooked, tender ham, or cooked kidneys cut up finely, and then send to the table.

418. Eggs au Gratin.—Knead well together in a bowl, one tablespoonful of bread-crumbs, two ounces of butter, three chopped anchovies, a pinch of parsley, a pinch of chervil, one chopped shallot, three raw egg yolks, a good pinch of salt, half a pinch of white pepper, and a pinch of grated nutmeg. When ready, put these ingredients into a silver baking-dish (by preference) with one ounce of butter at the bottom. Place it on a slow fire for two minutes, then break over it six eggs, which will be plenty; cook for five minutes in the hot oven, remove, lay the dish on top of another, and serve immediately.

419. Eggs à la Tripe.—Fry two medium-sized, sound, sliced onions in a frying-pan with two ounces of butter, but do not brown them; mix in half a spoonful of flour, and a large cupful of sweet cream; season with a pinch of salt, half a pinch of white pepper, and the third of a pinch of grated nutmeg. Cook for eight minutes, stirring constantly with the spatula; then add twelve sliced, hard-boiled eggs, and heat together thoroughly for two minutes without letting it boil again; pour on a hot dish and serve.

420. Eggs à la Vanderbilt.—Place one ounce of good butter on a silver dish, set it on the hot stove, and break in twelve fresh eggs, being careful not to disturb the yolks; season with a light pinch of salt and the third of a pinch of pepper; then let cook slowly for four minutes. Pour over the eggs a pint of hot Vanderbilt garnishing as for the omelet (No. 471), and serve immediately.

421. Eggs à la Valencienne.—Put into a saucepan half a pint of hot, boiled rice, half a pint of hot tomato sauce (No. 205), two good-sized mushrooms, cut julienne-shaped, one truffle cut the same, and two tablespoonfuls of grated Parmesan cheese; season with half a pinch of salt, half a pinch of pepper, and the third of a pinch of grated nutmeg, and let cook on the hot stove for five minutes, stirring it lightly with the spatula. Leave the pan on the corner of the stove to keep warm, while putting half an ounce of good butter on a silver dish, and when placed on the hot stove, crack in twelve fresh eggs, being careful not to break the yolks; season with half a pinch of salt and the third of a pinch of pepper, then let cook for two minutes. Dress the prepared garnishing in four dome-shaped heaps—one at each end of the dish, and one at each side—and send to the table at once.

422. Eggs à la Provençale.—Pour two tablespoonfuls of oil into a small frying-pan, and set it on the fire. When well heated, break one egg into a bowl, season with a pinch of salt and half a pinch of pepper (divided up for the twelve eggs), then drop it into the oil; baste the egg with a spoon, turn it over, and when a good color on both sides, drain it on a wire sieve. Cook the twelve eggs separately (each one will take two minutes), then pare them nicely, and serve crown-shaped on a dish, putting a piece of fried bread between every other one. Pour over half a pint of reduced Espagnole (No. 151), to which has been added the zest of a lemon, and six sliced mushrooms, and serve very hot.

423. Eggs en Filets.—Mix in a dish that can be put in the oven (a silver one by preference) twelve raw egg yolks, with a spoonful of brandy and a pinch of salt. Cook them for five minutes in a hot oven, then let them cool; cut the preparation into twelve thin fillets or slices, and steep each one in a light pancake batter (No. 1186). Fry them in very hot fat for about two minutes, then lift up with a skimmer, lay them on a napkin to drain, and serve on a folded napkin laid on a hot dish and garnished with fried parsley.

424. Eggs à la Finoise.—Pour a pint of good tomato sauce (No. 205) into a saucepan on the hot stove, add two cut-up, peeled, sweet peppers, fry for two minutes in a tablespoonful of butter, a teaspoonful of chopped chives, and reduce it gradually to about half the quantity, which will take ten minutes. Poach six very fresh eggs, as for No. 404, pare their edges neatly. Place six freshly prepared hot toasts on a warm serving-dish, arrange the eggs carefully on top, and pour the above sauce over all, then send them to the table at once.

425. Eggs au Miroir.—Lightly butter a silver dish large enough to hold twelve eggs, one beside another; carefully break into it twelve eggs, taking care to keep the yolks intact. Evenly sprinkle over them half a pinch of salt. Cook for one minute on the hot stove; then place them in the oven for one and a half minutes. Take out, and place the dish on another, and serve.

426. Eggs with Fresh Mushrooms.—Peel, wash, and drain a quarter of a pound of fine, fresh mushrooms. Place them in a saucepan, with a tablespoonful of very good butter. Season with half a pinch of salt and a third of a pinch of white pepper, squeezing in first two drops of lemon juice. Cover the saucepan, and cook for ten minutes on a moderate fire. Add a quarter of a glassful of good Madeira wine; reduce to one-half, which will take two minutes; add now a gill of béchamel sauce (No. 154), and let come to a boil again. Prepare twelve fresh-poached eggs, as in No. 404; pour the sauce on a hot serving-dish, keeping the mushrooms in the saucepan. Neatly lay the eggs over the sauce around the dish, and dress the mushrooms right in the centre, and serve very hot.

427. Eggs with Celery.—Boil for fifteen minutes, in a quart of white broth (No. 99), two heads of well-washed and neatly pared, sound celery. Remove it from the broth; then cut it up in one-inch-length pieces, and return it to the pan with the broth in which it was first boiled, leaving it on the hot stove. Season with one pinch of salt and the third of a pinch of white pepper. Reduce to three-quarters (which will require ten minutes). Add a gill of hot béchamel sauce (No. 154), let come to a boil. Poach twelve fresh eggs exactly as in No. 404, neatly arrange them on a hot dish, crown-like. Pour the celery sauce right in the centre, and serve very hot.

428. Eggs with Truffles.—Peel three medium-sized, sound truffles. Cut them into thin slices, place in a saucepan with a glassful of Madeira wine; reduce to one-half on a moderate fire. Season with one pinch of salt and the third of a pinch of white pepper; add one gill of béchamel sauce (No. 154); let come to a boil. Prepare twelve heart-shaped croûtons (No. 133); dip the thin parts first into the sauce half an inch in depth, then into fresh, finely chopped-up parsley up to the same depth. Gently dress (arrange) them on the hot serving-dish in star-shape, so that the decorated ends of the croûtons will just reach up to the edge of the dish equally all around. Prepare twelve poached eggs exactly the same as in No. 404; dress an egg on each croûton. Gently pour the above prepared sauce right in the centre of the dish, being careful not to pour any over the eggs. Evenly slice one good-sized, sound truffle into twelve equal slices; dip them in a little hot broth for two seconds; lay one slice on top of each egg, and immediately send to the table.

429. Eggs with Tarragon.—Blanch for one minute in a sautoire a quarter of a bunch of tarragon-leaves, drain, and chop them up very fine. Break twelve eggs into a bowl, add the tarragon, season with a pinch of salt and half a pinch of pepper, and beat well for four minutes; meanwhile adding half a cupful of sweet cream. Then make an omelet, as for No. 450, and roll it on a hot serving dish. Prepare a little roux with flour and butter (No. 135), moisten with half a pint of strong broth and a glassful of white wine; skim off any fat that may accumulate on top, and let it cook slowly for ten minutes. Strain through a fine sieve and pour it around the omelet; then serve.

430. Eggs with Livers.—Remove the gall carefully from about a pint of chicken livers, wash them well, drain, and slice them into small pieces. Place them in a sautoire with one ounce of butter, range the pan on the hot stove, then season with one pinch of salt and half a pinch of pepper; toss the contents gently for two minutes; then add a pinch of chopped parsley, one pinch of chervil, and three well-minced mushrooms, and moisten with half a pint of Madeira sauce (No. 185), and let cook for five minutes; make an omelet of twelve eggs, as for No. 450, and when ready to finish, pour the livers in the centre, reserving two tablespoonfuls of it for further action; close the sides up carefully, cook two seconds longer, then gently turn it on a hot dish, and, with a spoon, pour all the sauce around the omelet. Dress the livers that were reserved, at both ends of the omelet, equally divided, and serve.

431. Eggs au Parmesan.—Beat twelve eggs in a saucepan, with two tablespoonfuls of grated Parmesan cheese, a pinch of pepper, but no salt; stir them well with a whip, and make of this six small omelets, as for No. 450. As soon as they are sufficiently firm, lay them on a dish. Besprinkle the tops with a little grated Parmesan cheese, roll, and trim them nicely, sprinkle more cheese over the tops, wipe off the sides of the dish, and put them in a hot oven for five minutes. Remove from the oven, pour around the omelets one gill of hot Madeira sauce (No. 185); and serve very hot.

432. Eggs à la Bonne Femme.—Slice two large, sound onions, and fry them in two ounces of butter, in a saucepan, stirring frequently, so that they do not burn; when done, dredge in a good pinch of flour, moistening with half a pint of cream or milk, and season with a pinch of salt, half a pinch of pepper, and a saltspoonful of nutmeg. Break six eggs, froth the whites, mix the yolks with the onions, and afterward the beaten whites, stirring well. Lay two pieces of white paper on the bottom of a baking-tin, butter them thoroughly, lay the eggs on top, and set it in the oven for about fifteen minutes. When done, turn them on to a hot dish, remove the papers, add two tablespoonfuls of Espagnole sauce (No. 151) to the eggs, and serve.

433. Eggs à la Paysanne.—Put half a pint of cream into a dish, on the fire, and when it boils, break in twelve fresh eggs, season with a pinch of salt and twelve whole peppers; let cook for two minutes, and then set it in the oven for three minutes, so that the eggs get a good golden color, taking care that they do not harden. Remove from the oven, place the dish on another, and serve.

434. Eggs à la Régence.—Shred an ounce and a half of salt pork into fine pieces (ham will answer the same purpose), also one onion cut into small squares, and six medium-sized mushrooms, all of equal size; moisten with a spoonful of good gravy, and cook for five minutes. When done, reduce with a tablespoonful of mushroom essence (liquor). Break twelve fresh eggs in a dish, with an ounce of melted butter on the bottom, and set it in a moderate oven for five minutes; pour the garnishing over, drip off the fat, wipe the sides of the dish, and add six drops of strong tarragon-vinegar. Remove from the oven, place the dish on another, and serve.

435. Eggs with Melted Cheese.—Grate two ounces of Parmesan cheese on a dish; set it on a slow fire, adding half a glassful of white wine, a pinch of chopped parsley, a pinch of chopped chives, half a pinch of pepper, and a saltspoonful of grated nutmeg, also two ounces of good butter. Stir thoroughly while cooking, and as the cheese melts, break in twelve eggs; cook for five minutes longer, then surround the dish with heart-shaped croûtons (No. 133), set it on another dish, and serve very hot.

436. Eggs en Panade.—Cut out twelve round pieces of bread-crumbs, each one measuring two inches in diameter, and place them in a pie-plate, spreading a little butter over each; brown them in the hot oven for one minute. Break twelve eggs in a bowl, add one pinch of chopped parsley, half a pinch of chives, two tablespoonfuls of thick, sweet cream, one ounce of butter, a pinch of salt, and a very little white pepper. Beat sharply all together for four minutes. Add the twelve pieces of browned bread to the beaten eggs, mix them well together. Place in a frying-pan on the hot range one ounce of clarified butter, heat thoroughly, then fry one egged bread at a time for one and a half minutes on each side. Dress, with the aid of a cake-turner, on a hot dish with a folded napkin; keep in a warm place. Repeat the same process with the others, and serve.

437. Eggs à la Meyerbeer.—Butter a silver dish and break into it twelve fresh eggs; or, if desired, use six small silver dishes, breaking two eggs into each one; then cook them on the stove for two minutes. Cut six mutton kidneys in halves, broil or stew them according to taste, then add them to the eggs, and serve with half a pint of hot Périgueux sauce (No. 191) thrown over.

438. Eggs à la Reine.—Prepare twelve eggs as for the above (No. 437), cook them for two minutes. Make a garnishing of one ounce of cooked chicken-breast, one finely shred, medium-sized truffle, and six minced mushrooms. Moisten with half a pint of good Allemande sauce (No. 210), heat it up well, but do not let it boil; then pour over the eggs and serve immediately.

439. Eggs à la Turque.—Cook twelve eggs the same as for No. 437, and pour over them six chicken livers, tossed gently but rapidly in a saucepan on a brisk fire with one ounce of butter for three minutes, and then with a spoon remove all the butter from the saucepan. Season with a pinch of salt, and half a pinch of white pepper, adding half a glassful of good Madeira wine. Reduce it to one half, then add one gill of hot Madeira sauce (No. 185), heat up a little, and then pour the sauce over the eggs and serve.

440. Eggs à l'Impératrice.—Cook twelve eggs exactly as in No. 437, arranging six small slices of pâté-de-foie-gras, one on top of each egg, and serving very hot.

441. Eggs à la Suisse.—Fry twelve eggs as for No. 437; after cooking for two minutes, cover with half a pint of hot tomato sauce (No. 205), and add three cooked sausages, cut in two, also a little grated cheese, then send to the table.

442. Eggs à la Chipolata.—Prepare twelve eggs as for No. 437, and cover them with a pint of hot Chipolata garnishing (No. 232), and serve very hot.

443. Eggs à l'Alsacienne.—Fry twelve eggs as for No. 437, only putting them on a long dish. Add one chopped onion to four ounces of finely minced calf's liver, quickly toss them on a brisk fire for about eight minutes, then pour in about six to eight drops of vinegar, a pinch of salt, and a little pepper to season. Garnish both ends of the dish with this, then serve.

444. Eggs à l'Aurore.—Boil twelve eggs until hard, then let them cool; shell them, and separate the yolks from the whites, putting the former into a mortar, adding one ounce of fresh butter, a pinch of salt, half a pinch of nutmeg, the same of ground spice, and three raw egg yolks; pound all well together. Mince the whites, and put them in a sautoire with a pint of well reduced béchamel (No. 154), cook without boiling, although letting them attain a good consistency; place them on the dish used for serving, lay the pounded yolks on top, and garnish with twelve square sippets of bread dipped in beaten egg, and put in the oven to brown for about four minutes; then serve.

445. Eggs à la Polonaise.—Cut twelve hard-boiled eggs in halves, separate the whites from the yolks, and pound the latter in a mortar, adding about one ounce of butter, a pinch of salt, half a pinch of ground spice, a saltspoonful of grated nutmeg, and five raw yolks; when well blended, without any lumps, strew half a tablespoonful of very finely chopped parsley over, and add the whites of the five eggs well beaten. Garnish the bottom of a baking-dish with this preparation, laying it in about a finger thick; also fill the whites with a part of it, making them have the appearance of whole eggs. Arrange them tastefully on top, and set the dish in the oven; brown slightly for about five minutes, remove it from the oven, lay the dish on top of another, wipe the sides carefully, and serve immediately.

446. Eggs à la Sauce Robert.—Peel two medium-sized onions, and remove the hearts, cut them in slices (the hearts), and put them with a tablespoonful of butter in a saucepan on a brisk fire, and brown them well. Moisten with a cupful of lean broth, season with a pinch of salt and half a pinch of pepper, cook, and let the sauce reduce for about ten minutes. When ready to serve, cut eight hard-boiled eggs into slices, mix them in the preparation, and let heat together without boiling for two minutes; finish with a teaspoonful of diluted mustard, and then serve.

447. Eggs à la Bennett.—Cut twelve hard-boiled eggs lengthwise, remove the yolks, and place them in a bowl with two ounces of good butter, a teaspoonful of anchovy essence, and a pinch of chopped chives. Beat well together, and fill the whites with it, besprinkle with bread-crumbs, and pour over a few drops of clarified butter; put them in the oven for three minutes on a buttered dish, and serve with half a pint of hot Madeira sauce (No. 185) thrown over.

448. Eggs à la Hyde.—Boil six fresh eggs for seven minutes, then lay them in cold water for five minutes to cool them off; shell them, and put them on a plate. Hash fine half a small canful of mushrooms with two branches of parsley and one medium-sized, sound shallot. Put in a saucepan on the hot stove one ounce of good butter, and when melted add the prepared mushrooms, and let cook rather slowly for fifteen minutes, stirring it occasionally. Add half a pint of Madeira sauce (No. 185), season with a pinch of salt and a light pinch of pepper, then cook again slowly for ten minutes. Strain the whole through a fine sieve into another saucepan, and set it aside to keep warm; cut the six hard-boiled eggs into halves, remove the entire yolks, and mash them thoroughly in a bowl, adding half an ounce of good, fresh butter and half a pint of sweet cream. Season with a light pinch of salt, half a pinch of pepper, and half a teaspoonful of grated nutmeg; mix well together, and with this fill the twelve pieces of egg-white. Lay them on a lightly buttered dish, pour the sauce over, and put them in the oven for eight minutes before sending to the table.

449. Eggs à la Duchesse.—Place a quarter of a pound of powdered sugar in a saucepan, adding half a pint of water, a small piece of lemon peel, and a short stick of cinnamon. Boil until the sugar is reduced to a syrup, then remove the lemon peel and cinnamon, and add half a teaspoonful of orange-flower water. Beat together, then strain twelve egg yolks with a pint of milk or cream, add this to the syrup with a very little salt, then transfer the whole to a silver baking-dish, place it on the hot stove, and let cook for ten minutes, stirring briskly, and when it forms a cream, squeeze in the juice of a fine, sound lemon; remove from the fire, lay the dish on another, and send to the table.

450. Plain Omelet.—Crack into a bowl twelve fresh eggs, season them with a pinch of salt and half a pinch of white pepper, beat them well until the whites and yolks are thoroughly mixed, or for fully four minutes. Place in a No. 8 frying-pan two tablespoonfuls of clarified butter; heat it well on the hot range, and when it crackles pour in the eggs, and with a fork stir all well for two minutes, then let rest for half a minute. Fold up with the fork—the side nearest the handle first—to the centre of the omelet, then the opposite side, so that both sides will meet right in the centre; let rest for half a minute longer; have a hot dish in the left hand, take hold of the handle of the pan with the right, bring both dish and pan to a triangular shape, and with a rapid movement turn the pan right over the centre of the dish, and send to the table. (The omelet should be made on a very brisk range, without taking the lid off the stove.)

Should the pan be smaller than the above-mentioned No. 8 it will require three minutes' stirring, one minute to rest, and half a minute to rest after having been folded.

When making an omelet for one person, for instance, use three fresh eggs, seasoned with half a teaspoonful of salt, and half a saltspoonful of white pepper. Thoroughly heat in a small frying-pan half a teaspoonful of clarified butter; after sharply beating the eggs in the bowl, pour into the pan, and gently mix for one minute on a very brisk range, let rest for a quarter of a minute, fold one side up, rest a quarter of a minute more, then turn on a small hot dish, and serve.

451. Omelet With Fine Herbs.—Break twelve fresh eggs into a bowl, add a pinch of finely chopped parsley, half a pinch of chopped tarragon, and half a pinch of chives; also, if desired, half a cupful of sweet cream. Beat the whole thoroughly without stopping for four minutes; melt one ounce of good butter in a frying-pan on the hot stove; when it is melted, and begins to crackle, pour in the eggs, and mix them gently with a fork, while they cook for three minutes; let them rest for one minute, then bring the sides towards the centre, turn it on a hot dish, and serve.

452. Oyster Omelet.—Blanch eighteen oysters to boiling-point in their own water; drain, and return them to the saucepan, moistening with half a pint of good Allemande (No. 210); season with half a pinch of salt. Make a plain omelet with twelve eggs as for No. 450, bring the sides toward the centre, and fill it with the oyster preparation. Turn it on a hot dish, pour the rest of the sauce around, and serve very hot.

453. Crawfish Omelet.—Stew twelve crawfish tails in a sautoire on the hot stove with half an ounce of butter, letting them cook for five minutes. Break twelve eggs into a bowl, add half a cupful of sweet cream, and a pinch of finely chopped parsley; season with a pinch of salt and half a pinch of pepper, then sharply beat for four minutes. Make an omelet as in No. 450, fold up the side opposite the handle of the pan, place the crawfish right in the centre, fold up the other side, turn it on a hot dish, and serve.

454. Lobster Omelet.—Take six ounces of boiled lobster meat, and cut it into small pieces; put them into a sautoire with half a glassful of white wine and a quarter of an ounce of butter. Moisten with a quarter of a pint of strong, hot béchamel (No. 154), and let cook for five minutes. Make an omelet with twelve eggs as for No. 450, and with a skimmer place the stewed lobster in the middle, fold the opposite side, pour in the garnishing, fold the other side up, turn it on a hot dish, pour the sauce around it, and serve.

455. Crab Omelet.—Proceed exactly the same as for the above (No. 454), substituting six ounces of crab meat cut into small pieces for the lobster.

456. Tomato Omelet.—Break twelve fresh eggs in a bowl, season them with a pinch of salt and half a pinch of pepper, and beat thoroughly for four minutes. Place two ounces of butter in a frying-pan on the hot stove, let it heat well without browning, then pour into it half a pint of freshly cooked stewed tomatoes, suppressing all the liquid. Cook for two minutes, then throw the beaten eggs over, and with a fork mix the whole gently for three minutes; let rest for one minute longer. Bring up the two opposite sides, turn it carefully on a hot dish, and serve.

457. Tomato Omelet à la Provençale.—Peel a medium-sized, sound onion, then chop it fine; place it in a sautoire on the hot stove with one ounce of butter, and let get a good golden color, adding half a pint of stewed tomatoes (No. 1027), or two good-sized, peeled, raw tomatoes cut into small slices, a crushed clove of garlic, and season (should the tomatoes be fresh) with a pinch of salt and half a pinch of pepper, adding a teaspoonful of chopped parsley; let the whole cook together for ten minutes; then proceed as for the tomato omelet (No. 456).

458. Asparagus-top Omelet.—Put a quarter of a bunch of boiled asparagus-tops into a bowl, pour twelve beaten eggs over, season with a pinch of salt and half a pinch of pepper, mix lightly again, and make an omelet exactly as for No. 450.

459. Omelet, with Green Peas.—Break twelve eggs into a bowl, adding half a pint of boiled green peas, a pinch each of salt and pepper, beat well for four minutes, and make into an omelet as for No. 450.

460. Omelet au Cèpes.—Fry six cèpes, cut into small pieces, in half an ounce of butter for two minutes. Beat twelve eggs in a bowl, season with a pinch of salt and half a pinch of pepper, pour them over the cèpes, and make an omelet as for No. 450.

461. Smoked Beef Omelet.—Fry two ounces of finely mixed, smoked beef in a frying-pan, with half an ounce of butter, add twelve well-beaten eggs, and make an omelet as for No. 450.

462. Ham Omelet.—Cut about two ounces of lean ham into small, square pieces, fry them for two minutes with an ounce of butter in a frying-pan, and throw over twelve well beaten eggs; with this make an omelet as for No. 450.

463. Kidney Omelet.—Stew on the hot stove three minced kidneys, with a quarter of a pint of Madeira wine sauce (No. 185), let cook for three minutes. Make a plain omelet with twelve eggs as for No. 450, fold the opposite side up, put the kidneys in the centre, fold the other side up, and turn on a dish, and pour the sauce around; then serve.

464. Chicken Liver Omelet.—The same as for the above (No. 463), substituting six minced chicken livers for the kidneys.

465. Sausage Omelet.—Skin three raw sausages, then put them in a saucepan with a quarter of an ounce of butter; set it on the hot fire for five minutes, and stir well until they cook. Make a plain omelet with twelve eggs, as for No. 450, fold the opposite side, lay the sausages in the centre, fold the other side up, and serve with a quarter of a pint of hot Madeira sauce (No. 185), poured around the omelet.

466. Omelet Bonne Femme.—Cut one ounce of salt pork into small square pieces, also two tablespoonfuls of crust from off a fresh loaf of bread cut the same way; fry them together in a frying-pan with an ounce of butter for about two minutes, adding a boiled potato cut into small squares, a pinch of chopped parsley, half a pinch of chopped chives, half a pinch of salt, and the same quantity of pepper. Beat twelve eggs for four minutes in a bowl, pour them into the pan, and make an omelet as for No. 450; turn on a hot dish, and serve.

467. Omelet Raspail.—Chop one raw onion very fine, and put it in a saucepan with an ounce of butter. Take one ounce of small squares of salt pork, cook them slightly, adding an ounce of scraps of very finely minced, cooked roast beef, the same of ham, two finely chopped mushrooms, and a pinch of chopped parsley. Stir in well a tablespoonful of tomato sauce (No. 205) and a tablespoonful of grated bread-crumbs; season with a pinch of pepper and the third of a pinch of salt. Make a plain omelet with twelve eggs as for No. 450, fold up the opposite side, fill it with the preparation, fold the other side up, turn it on a hot dish, and serve.

468. Sardine Omelet.—Thoroughly skin eight fine sardines, place six of them in a frying-pan with an ounce of butter, cook for two minutes. Beat well twelve eggs in a bowl. Season with one pinch of salt and half a pinch of pepper, add them to the sardines in the pan; make an omelet as in No. 450, fold the opposite end up, place the two remaining sardines right in the centre, fold the other end up, turn it on a hot dish, and send to the table.

469. Cheese Omelet.—Put one ounce of butter in a frying-pan, heat it on the hot stove. Break twelve eggs into a bowl, beat them thoroughly for four minutes, adding two tablespoonfuls of grated Swiss cheese, half a pinch of salt, and half a pinch of pepper. Pour the whole into the frying-pan, and make an omelet as for No. 450; turn it on a hot dish, and besprinkle the top lightly with a very little Parmesan cheese; place in the oven for two seconds, then serve.

470. Omelet Régence.—Make an omelet with twelve eggs as for No. 450, and when nearly cooked, fold up the opposite side, then fill the centre with a quarter of a pint of hot Régence garnishing (No. 434), fold the other side up; turn on a hot dish, pour the sauce around, and serve hot.

471. Omelet à la Vanderbilt.—Take two fine, sound, green peppers, plunge them into hot fat for half a minute, then take them up and lay them on a dry cloth; skin them neatly, remove all the seeds from the insides, and when emptied cut them into small slices. Put these into a saucepan on the hot stove with two medium-sized fresh, sound, sliced tomatoes, twelve nicely shelled shrimps, and three tablespoonfuls of Madeira wine sauce (No. 185), then season with half a pinch of salt and a third of a pinch of pepper; cook slowly for fifteen minutes. Break twelve fresh eggs into a bowl, season them with half a pinch of salt and a third of a pinch of pepper, and beat well for five minutes. Put two ounces of good butter in a frying-pan, place it on the hot stove, and when the butter is melted drop in the eggs, and with a spoon or fork mix briskly for two minutes. Fold the opposite side up with a skimmer, lift up the thick part of the prepared sauce, and place it in the centre of the omelet, fold the other side either with a knife or fork, and let it cook for two minutes longer, then turn on a hot dish; pour the rest of the sauce in the saucepan around the omelet, and send to the table very hot.

472. Omelet à l'Espagnole.—Put in a stewpan on the stove one finely shred onion, one ounce of butter, a chopped green pepper, six minced mushrooms, and one large, finely cut-up tomato; season with half a pinch of pepper and one pinch of salt, adding a spoonful of tomato sauce (No. 205); let cook for fifteen minutes. Make a plain omelet with twelve eggs, as for No. 450, fold the opposite side, and put more than half of the stew inside of it, say three-quarters; fold the other side up, and turn it on a long dish, then pour the rest of the sauce around, and serve.

473. Omelet Mexicaine.—Have a pint of velouté sauce (No. 152) in a saucepan, place it on a moderate fire, add a piece of lobster butter (No. 149) about the size of an egg, twenty-four shelled and cooked shrimps, and season with half a pinch of salt and a very little pepper. Let cook for three minutes, stirring it lightly, then add half of a good-sized, empty and peeled green pepper, finely hashed; cook for two minutes longer, then let rest on the corner of the stove. Make an omelet with twelve eggs, as for No. 450, fold up the opposite side, pour half of the preparation in the centre, fold the other end up, turn the omelet on a hot dish, and garnish both sides with the rest of the shrimps, pouring the balance around the dish; then send to the table.

474. Omelet Soufflée, for Six Persons.—Have a deep, cold, silver dish ready, fifteen inches long by eleven wide. Put into a vessel four ounces of powdered sugar. Break twelve fresh eggs, drop the whites into a copper basin, and the yolks of five into the vessel containing the sugar, reserving the other seven yolks for other purposes. Add to the vessel containing the sugar and yolks a light teaspoonful of vanilla essence: now with the wooden spatula, begin to beat the yolks with the sugar as briskly as you possibly can for fifteen minutes. Lay it aside. Then with the aid of a pastry wire-whip, beat up to a very stiff froth the twelve egg whites in the copper basin, which will take from twelve to fifteen minutes. Remove the pastry wire-whip; take a skimmer in the right hand, and with the left take hold of the vessel containing the preparation of the yolks and sugar. Gradually pour it over the whites, and with the skimmer gently mix the whole together for two minutes. The preparation will now be of a light, firm consistency. Now, with the aid again of the skimmer, take up the preparation and drop it down in the centre of the cold dish, ready as above mentioned, taking special care to pile it as high as possible, so as to have it of a perfect dome-shape; a few incisions can be made all around, according to taste; immediately place it in a moderate oven to bake for fifteen minutes. Take it out of the oven, and, in order to avoid burning or soiling the table-cloth, lay the dish containing the omelet on another cold one, liberally sprinkle powdered sugar over it, and immediately send to the table.

N. B.—Special care should be taken when piling the preparation into the cold, silver dish; and the making of the incisions should be done as rapidly as possible, so that success will be certain. When desired, the vanilla essence can be substituted with the same quantity of orange-flower water.

475. Sweet Omelet.—Beat and sweeten with one ounce of sugar twelve eggs; make an omelet as for No. 450, using one ounce of fresh butter; turn it on a dish, and dredge another ounce of sugar over, then glaze it with a hot shovel or salamander, and serve very warm.

476. Omelet au Kirsch, or Rum.—Make a sweet omelet with twelve eggs as for the above (No. 475); when completed and glazed, throw around it a glassful of kirsch, and set the omelet on fire; serve it while burning. Rum omelet is prepared exactly the same way, substituting rum for kirsch.

477. Omelet Célestine.—Pulverize six macaroons, put them in a bowl, adding three tablespoonfuls of apple jelly (No. 1327) and one spoonful of whipped cream (No. 1254); mix well with the spatula. Make a sweet omelet as for No. 475, with twelve eggs; fold the opposite side up, pour the mixture into the centre, fold the other end up, turn it on a hot dish, and sprinkle the top with three tablespoonfuls of powdered sugar; glaze the omelet with a hot shovel or salamander, and decorate it with three lady-fingers (No. 1231) cut in two, also a cupful of whipped cream (No. 1254), the latter poured into a paper-funnel, and piped over in any design the fancy may dictate.

A pinch of salt represents 205 grains, or a tablespoonful.

Half a pinch of pepper represents 38 grains, or a teaspoonful.

A third of a pinch of nutmeg represents 13 grains, or half a teaspoonful.

BEEF.

478. Braised Beef à la Morlaisienne.—Procure a rump-piece of beef weighing three pounds, lard it with four large pieces of salt pork, seasoned with a pinch of chopped parsley and a crushed garlic. Lay the beef in a saucepan, with pieces of salt pork or fat at the bottom, add one sliced onion, the round slices of one carrot, one sprig of thyme, and a bay-leaf; season with a pinch of salt and half a pinch of pepper, then cover, and brown it well on both sides for ten minutes. Moisten with half a pint of white broth (No. 99) and half a pint of Espagnole sauce (No. 151), then cook for one hour. When finished, lay it on a dish, garnishing with six stuffed cabbages (No. 919). Skim off the fat, strain the gravy, and pour the sauce over, or else serve it in a separate sauce-bowl.

479. Braised Beef à la Mode.—Lard and prepare a piece of beef weighing three pounds as for the above (No. 478). Let it marinate for twelve hours in the juice of half a lemon, with one good pinch of salt, the same quantity of pepper, one sprig of thyme, two bay-leaves, and half a bunch of parsley-roots. Put the meat in a saucepan with half an ounce of butter, and let both sides brown well for ten minutes; take it out and lay it on a dish, then add to the gravy about two tablespoonfuls of flour, stirring it well, and moisten with one quart of broth (No. 99), mingling it carefully while the sauce is boiling. Replace the beef in the saucepan with two sliced carrots and twelve small glazed onions (No. 972), and cook for one hour, adding a strong bouquet (No. 254), a glassful of claret wine, if desired, and a little crushed garlic, also half a pinch of salt, and the third of a pinch of pepper. Serve on a hot dish, skim the fat off the gravy, straining it over. Arrange the carrots and onions in clusters around the dish, and serve.

All braised beef to be prepared exactly the same, only adding different garnishings.

480. Braised Beef à la Providence.—Braise a piece of beef of three pounds, as for No. 479, adding a quarter of a cooked cauliflower, half a cupful of flageolet-beans, and a cupful of cooked carrots cut with a vegetable-scoop five minutes before serving. Place the vegetables with the skimmed gravy in a pan, reduce for five minutes. Dress the beef on a hot dish, arrange the vegetables in four heaps, one at each end of the dish and one on each side of it. Pour the gravy over the beef, and serve.

481. Braised Beef à l'Orsini.—Braise a piece of beef as for No. 479, serve it on a dish garnished with rice, prepared as follows: with some cold risotto (No. 1017) form six balls the size of an egg; roll them in bread crumbs, then dip them in beaten eggs, lard them with half-inch slices of cooked, smoked tongue, and fry in hot fat for three minutes. Serve these round the beef, with its own gravy well skimmed and strained over.

482. Braised Beef à la Flamande.—Prepare the beef as for No. 479, and serve it decorated with clusters of a quarter of a cooked, red cabbage, two cooked carrots, and two turnips, all sliced. (Red cabbage, carrots, and turnips should always be cooked separately).

483. Braised Beef en Daube.—Add to a piece of braised beef, as for No. 479, one ounce of salt pork cut into small square pieces, the round slices of two carrots, and twelve glazed onions (No. 972), also one cut-up turnip. Put all these ingredients in the saucepan with the beef, three-quarters of an hour before serving.

484. Braised Beef à la Bignon.—Braise a piece of beef as for No. 479. Take six large potatoes and pare them as round as possible, scoop out the insides with a Parisian potato-spoon, being careful not to break them, parboil them slightly for three minutes on a quick fire, and then fill them with any kind of forcemeat handy; place them in the oven with two tablespoonfuls of clarified butter, and bake well for twenty minutes. Serve them around the beef, three on each side of the dish.

485. Braised Beef, Russian Sauce.—Cook a piece of braised beef as for No. 479, and serve it with a little of the gravy on the dish, and half a pint of Russian sauce (No. 211) separate.

486. Smoked Beef à la Crême.—Take one pound of very finely minced smoked beef, put it in a stewpan with half an ounce of butter, cook for two minutes, and moisten slightly with half a cupful of cream, adding two tablespoonfuls of béchamel (No. 154), and serve as soon as it boils. (Do not salt it).

487. Beefsteak Pie à l'Anglaise.—Slice two pounds of lean beef in half-inch-square slices, add two sliced onions, and stew together in a saucepan with one ounce of butter for ten minutes, stir in two tablespoonfuls of flour, and mix well; moisten with one quart of water or white broth (No. 99), still stirring. Season with a pinch each of salt and pepper, and add a bouquet (No. 254); let cook for twenty minutes, take out the bouquet, and fill a deep dish with the above preparation. Cut two hard-boiled eggs in slices, and lay them on top, cover with pie-crust (No. 1077), glaze the surface with egg yolk, and bake a light brown color for about eight minutes in the oven; then serve.

488. Beefsteak Pie à l'Américaine.—Proceed the same as for No. 487, but using in place of the eggs one pint of potatoes cut with a vegetable-scoop, also one ounce of lard, cut in small pieces, and cooking them with the beef the same length of time.

489. Corned Beef with Spinach.—Take three pounds of rump or brisket of corned beef, and put it into a saucepan, covering it with fresh water; boil briskly for an hour and a half, and serve with boiled spinach à l'Anglaise (No. 940).

490. Corned Beef with Kale-sprouts.—The same as for the above, only adding two quarts of kale-sprouts, half an hour before the beef is cooked, then arrange the cooked kale-sprouts on a dish, and put the corned beef over, and serve.

491. Sirloin Steak, or Entrecôte à la Bordelaise.—Procure two sirloin steaks of one pound each; season them with one pinch of salt and half a pinch of pepper. Baste on both sides with half a tablespoonful of oil, and put them on a broiler over a bright charcoal fire; broil them for six minutes on each side, and then place them on a hot serving-dish. Pour a pint of

Bordelaise sauce (No. 186) over the steaks, being careful to have the rounds of marrow on top of the steaks unbroken, and serve very hot. (Broiled sirloin steaks are all to be prepared as above, only adding different sauces or garnishings).

492. Sirloin Steak à la Béarnaise.—Prepare and broil two sirloin steaks as for No. 491, and when cooked, pour over half a pint of Béarnaise sauce (No. 166), and serve.

493. Sirloin Steak à la Moëlle.—Broil two sirloin steaks as for No. 491, take half a pint of Madeira sauce (No. 185), and to it add six drops of tarragon-vinegar, also the marrow of one marrow-bone cut in round slices. Boil once only, then pour the sauce over the steaks, and serve very hot.

494. Sirloin Steak Larded à la Duchesse.—Procure a piece of four pounds of tender sirloin, pare and trim it nicely, taking out the bones; lard it over the top with a small larding-needle, and season with half a pinch of salt and a third of a pinch of pepper. Line a baking-dish with some pork-skin, one medium-sized, sliced carrot, half a bunch of well-cleaned and pared parsley-roots, one peeled, sound, sliced onion, one sprig of thyme, and a bay-leaf. Place the sirloin on top, and put it in the oven to roast for thirty minutes. Take from out the oven, dress on a hot dish, leave it at the oven door; add half a pint of white broth (No. 99) or consommé (No. 100) to the gravy, boil it for two minutes, skim the fat off, strain the gravy into a sauce-bowl, and serve separate.

495. Sirloin Steaks à la Parisienne.—Broil two sirloin steaks as for No. 491, and serve surrounded with one pint of cooked Parisian potatoes (No. 986), and half a gill of maître d'hôtel butter (No. 145).

496. Sirloin Steaks aux Cêpes.—Lay two broiled sirloin steaks, as for No. 491, on a hot dish; cut six medium-sized cêpes into quarter pieces, put them in a frying-pan with one tablespoonful of oil, and fry for two minutes with one finely chopped shallot and a quarter of a clove of crushed garlic. Add these ingredients to half a pint of Madeira sauce (No. 185), and boil for two minutes longer, then pour over the steaks, besprinkle with a teaspoonful of chopped parsley, and serve.

497. Sirloin Steak, with Green Peppers.—Dish two broiled sirloin steaks (No. 491), and pour over them a sauce made as follows: empty three green peppers, mince them very fine, suppressing the seeds, and put them in a stewpan with a tablespoonful of oil. Cook for about three minutes, moistening with half a pint of Madeira sauce (No. 185); cook for five minutes longer, then pour the sauce over the steaks, and serve.

498. Sirloin Piqué à la Bordelaise.—Proceed the same as for No. 491, adding a pint of Bordelaise sauce (No. 186) separately.

499. Sirloin Piqué, Marrow sauce.—The same as for No. 491, only serving with a pint of hot marrow garnishing (No. 244) separately.

500. Minced Beef à la Provençale.—Cut into small slices a piece of beef weighing one pound and a half, put them in a saucepan with two tablespoonfuls of oil and two medium-sized, chopped onions; brown them together for five minutes, then add two tablespoonfuls of flour, and cover with a pint and a half of white broth (No. 99). Stir well and put in two cut-up tomatoes, two crushed cloves of garlic, and six finely shred mushrooms; season with a good pinch of salt and a pinch of pepper; place the lid on the pan. Let cook for twenty minutes, then dress on a hot dish. Arrange six heart-shaped croûtons (No. 133) around the dish, and serve.

501. Minced Beef à la Portugaise.—The same as for the above, only leaving out the mushrooms, and garnishing with six timbales prepared as follows: thoroughly clean the interiors of six small timbale-molds, then butter them well inside. Fill them up half their height with hot, boiled rice, well pressed down, so that when unmolding they will hold perfectly firm. Place them in the hot oven for two minutes. Unmold and arrange them around the dish at equal distances; dress six small, hot, roasted tomatoes (No. 1028), one on top of each column of rice, and then serve.

502. Minced Beef à la Catalan.—Proceed as for No. 500, browning the meat in oil, and adding two very finely chopped shallots, one onion, and a green pepper cut into pieces. When well browned, after five minutes, put in a pint of Espagnole sauce (No. 151), half a pinch of salt, and the same of pepper. Cook again for fifteen minutes and serve, with a teaspoonful of chopped parsley strewn over.

503. Broiled Tenderloin of Beef.—Procure two and a half pounds of tenderloin of beef; pare, cut it into three equal parts, flatten a little, then place them on a dish, and besprinkle with a pinch of salt, and the same of pepper. Baste them with one teaspoonful of sweet oil; roll them well, and put them on the broiler on a moderate fire; let cook for five minutes on each side; then place them on a hot dish, and use any kind of sauce or garnishing desired.

All broiled tenderloins are prepared the same way.

504. Broiled Tenderloin à la Chéron.—Broil three tenderloin steaks, as for No. 503; lay them on a dish on the top of a gill of hot Béarnaise sauce (No. 166), place on each steak one hot artichoke-bottom filled with hot Macédoine (No. 1032), pour just a little meat-glaze (No. 141) over, and serve.

505. Tenderloin à la Nivernaise.—Broil three tenderloin steaks, as for No. 503; put them on a hot dish, with half a pint of garnishing of mushroom sauce (No. 230); lay six poached eggs (No. 404) on top, and serve.

506. Tenderloin à la Florentin.—Prepare three fillets the same as for No. 503; pour a gill of hot Madeira sauce (No. 185) over the steaks, and garnish with three hot artichokes à la Florentin (No. 903), and serve.

507. Tenderloin à la Trianon.—Broil three fillets, as for No. 503; pour half a pint of Béarnaise sauce (No. 166) over, and garnish with four slices of truffles on each; also a little meat-glaze (No. 141), and serve.

508. Broiled Tenderloin aux Gourmets.—Have three tenderloin steaks prepared as for No. 503; when taken from the broiler, place them on a warm dish, and have already prepared the following garnishing: put in a saucepan one pint of Madeira sauce (No. 185); add to it two truffles cut into square pieces, four mushrooms, an artichoke-bottom, and a small blanched sweetbread, either from the throat or heart, all well minced together. Cook for ten minutes; then pour this over the hot serving-dish. Dress the fillets over, and serve.

509. Mignons Filets à la Pompadour.—After procuring two and a half pounds of fine, tender fillet of beef, pare it nicely all around; then cut it into six equal, small fillets. Flatten them slightly and equally. Place on a dish, season with a pinch of salt and half a pinch of pepper, evenly divided. Place them in a pan on the hot range, with half a gill of clarified butter, and cook them for four minutes on each side. Prepare a pint of Béarnaise sauce, as in No. 166. Dress three-quarters of it on a hot dish (reserving the other quarter for further action). Lay six round-shaped pieces of bread-croûtons, lightly fried in butter, over the Béarnaise sauce; dress the six fillets, one on top of each croûton; arrange then six warm artichoke-bottoms right in the centre of the fillets. Fill up the artichokes with a tablespoonful of hot Jardinière (No. 1033). Evenly divide the remaining quarter of a pint of hot Béarnaise sauce over the Jardinière. Cut into six even slices one good-sized, sound truffle; place one slice on the top of each, right in the centre of the Béarnaise sauce, and send to the table as hot as possible.

510. Mignons Filets à la Moëlle.—Prepare and fry six small fillets as for the above (No. 509) for three minutes on both sides; lay them on a dish, adding one pint of hot Madeira sauce (No. 185) with six drops of tarragon-vinegar and eighteen round slices of marrow. Let boil once only; then pour the sauce around the dish, dressing the marrow on top of the fillet, and serve.

511. Mignons Filets, Marinated, Russian Sauce.—Trim nicely and lard six fillets of beef—tail ends weighing each a quarter of a pound—steep them in a cooked marinade (No. 139) for twelve hours; then drain, and cook them in a sautoire, with one ounce of clarified butter, for three minutes on each side, and serve with one pint of Russian sauce (No. 211) on the dish, and the fillets on top.

512. Mignons Filets à la Bernardi.—Prepare six small fillets, as directed for No. 509; cook them for three minutes on each side; then lay them on a dish and pour over half a pint of hot Madeira sauce (No. 185). Serve with six small croûstades (No. 264), garnished with Macédoine (No. 1032), and six large game quenelles (No. 228).

513. Mignons Filets à la Bohémienne.—Lay on a dish six small fillets prepared the same as for No. 509. Pour over them half a pint of hot Madeira sauce (No. 185). Make six small croûstades (No. 264), fill them with a cooked macaroni à la creme (No. 954) cut into small pieces; also two tablespoonfuls of grated cheese. Cover them with a round slice of cooked smoked tongue, and garnish the steaks with these.

514. Mignons Filets à la Parisienne.—Pare nicely six small fillets; cook three minutes, as directed in No. 509; put half a pint of Madeira sauce (No. 185) in a saucepan, with two truffles and six mushrooms, all cut in slices. Let cook for ten minutes. Nicely arrange six small, round croûtons on the hot dish; dress the fillets over them, and pour the sauce around, but not over them; then serve.

515. Mignons Filets aux Pommes-de-terre Parisiennes.—When cooked the same as the above, for three minutes, pour over the fillets placed on a dish half a gill of good maître d'hôtel butter (No. 145) thickened with some meat-glaze (No. 141), and garnish with half a pint of Parisian potatoes (No. 986.)

516. Tenderloin Piqué à la Duchesse.—Procure four pounds of tenderloin; pare it well, and lard it, using a fine needle. Line the bottom of a roasting-pan with some pork-skin, one sliced onion, one sliced carrot, and half a bunch of well-washed parsley-roots. Place the tenderloin on top; add a pinch of salt, and roast it in a brisk oven for thirty-five minutes, basting it occasionally with its own juice. Dish it up, skim the fat off the gravy, then strain it over the fillet, and pour half a pint of good Madeira sauce (No. 185) over, and garnish with six potatoes Duchesse (No. 1006).

517. Tenderloin Piqué à la Portugaise.—Roast four pounds of tenderloin as in No. 516, lay it on a hot dish, arrange six stuffed tomatoes (No. 1023) around the tenderloin at equal distances. Put in a saucepan half a pint of tomato sauce (No. 205), and one gill of demi-glace (No. 185). Let boil for one minute, then pour it into a sauce-bowl and serve separate.

518. Tenderloin of Beef, Piqué à la Provençale.—Roast four pounds of tenderloin as for No. 516, slice half a pint of cêpes, and add them to half a pint of Madeira sauce (No. 185) with one crushed clove of garlic. Pour the sauce onto a dish, lay the tenderloin on top, and decorate with some twisted anchovies, and twelve stoned olives laid on each one; then serve.

519. Roast Tenderloin à la Hussard.—Procure four pounds of fillet of beef, pare it nicely, and season with one pinch each of salt and pepper; butter the surface lightly, and lay it in a roasting-pan, and put it to cook for ten minutes in a brisk oven, then set it aside to cool, and afterwards lay on it some very fine chicken forcemeat (No. 226), besprinkle with fresh bread-crumbs, and baste with three tablespoonfuls of clarified butter. Roast it again for thirty-five minutes, and serve with three-quarters of a pint of the following Hussard garnishing on the dish.

Put in a saucepan on the hot stove half a pint of Madeira sauce (No. 185), a gill of tomato sauce (No. 205), six good-sized, sound mushrooms, cut into small pieces, twelve godiveau quenelles (No. 221), and three ounces of cooked, smoked beef-tongue, cut in round pieces. Let all cook together for five minutes, and use when required.

520. Tenderloin Piqué à la Sevigne.—Roast a piece of tenderloin as for No. 519; when done and laid on a dish, pour over it half a pint of good Madeira sauce (No. 185), and decorate with six small bouchées filled with spinach (No. 588).

521. Tenderloin Piqué à l'Egyptienne.—Roast a piece of tenderloin as for No. 519, lay it on a dish, pouring over it half a pint of good Madeira sauce (No. 185). Garnish one side of the dish with three roots of boiled celery—the white part only—and the other side with eighteen cooked gumbos (No. 1030), then serve.

522. Tenderloin Piqué à la Richelieu.—Exactly the same as for No. 519, only adding one pint of hot Richelieu sauce under the fillet (No. 539), and serve.

523. Tenderloin Piqué à la Bernardi.—Take a four-pound piece of tenderloin, lard it—using a small larding needle—with very thin pieces of fresh ham and truffles, all cut the same size; put it into the oven to roast for thirty-five minutes, and then lay it on a dish, trimming the fillets carefully, the larded part being on the top. Pour over half a pint of good, hot Madeira sauce (No. 185), and garnish with three artichoke-bottoms, filled with hot Macédoine (No. 1032), three bouchées filled with spinach (No. 588), and three large game quenelles (No. 228). Arrange these to represent one single bouquet, and serve.

524. Porterhouse Steak.—Procure two porterhouse steaks of one and a half pounds each—see that they are cut from the short loin—flatten them well, pare and trim, and season with one pinch of salt and half a pinch of pepper. Put them on a dish with half a tablespoonful of oil; roll well, and put them on a moderate fire to broil seven minutes on each side. Lay them on a warm dish, pour one gill of maître d'hôtel butter (No. 145) over, and serve with a little watercress around the dish.

525. Double Porterhouse Steak.—Have a fine porterhouse steak of three pounds, and proceed as for No. 524. Broil on a rather slow charcoal fire, if possible, ten minutes on each side, then serve as for the above.

526. Hamburg Steak, Russian Sauce.—Take two pounds of lean beef—the hip part is preferable—remove all the fat, and put it in a Salisbury chopping machine; then lay it in a bowl, adding a very finely chopped shallot, one raw egg for each pound of beef, a good pinch of salt, half a pinch of pepper, and a third of a pinch of grated nutmeg. Mix well together, then form it into six flat balls the size of a small fillet. Roll them in fresh bread-crumbs, and fry them in the pan with two tablespoonfuls of clarified butter for two minutes on each side, turning them frequently and keeping them rare. Serve with half a pint of Russian sauce (No. 211) or any other desired.

527. Roast Beef.—In order to have a fine piece of beef cooked to perfection, and at the same time have it retain all its juices, purchase, from a first-class butcher only, a three-rib piece near the short loin part. Saw off the spine, also the bones of the three ribs to one inch from the meat, so as to have it as nearly a round shape as possible. Season with one and a quarter pinches of salt, divided equally all over, tie it together, and place it lengthwise in a roasting-pan. Pour a tablespoonful and a half of water into the pan so as to prevent its burning, then a few very small bits of butter can be distributed on top of the beef, if so desired. Set it in a rather moderate oven, and let roast for one hour and ten minutes, taking care to baste frequently with its own gravy. Remove it from the oven, untie, and dress it on a very hot dish, skim the fat from the gravy, and pour in two tablespoonfuls of broth, heat up a little, strain the gravy into a sauce-bowl, and send to the table.

The parings from the beef can be utilized for soup-stock; nothing need be wasted.

528. Corned Beef Hash à la Polonaise.—Brown in a saucepan two onions, with one ounce of butter; add one pound of cooked, well-chopped corned beef, and one pint of hashed potatoes. Moisten with a gill of broth, and a gill of Espagnole (No. 151). Season with half a pinch of pepper and a third of a pinch of nutmeg; stir well and let cook for fifteen minutes, then serve with six poached eggs on top (No. 404), and sprinkle over with a pinch of chopped parsley.

529. Corned Beef Hash au Gratin.—Make a hash as for the above, (No. 528), put it in a lightly buttered baking-dish, and besprinkle with rasped bread-crumbs. Moisten slightly with about one teaspoonful of clarified butter, and bake in the oven for fifteen minutes, or until it obtains a good brown color; then serve.

530. Corned Beef Hash à la Zingara.—The same as for No. 528, adding to the hash two good-sized, freshly peeled, and cut-up tomatoes (or half a pint of canned), one bruised clove of garlic, and one pinch of chopped parsley. Let all cook together for fifteen minutes; then serve.

531. Corned Beef Hash en Bordure.—Form a border around a baking-dish with mashed potatoes (No. 998), set it for two minutes in the oven, then fill the centre with hot corned beef hash (No. 528). Besprinkle the top with one pinch of chopped parsley, and serve.

532. Beef-Tongue à la Gendarme.—Boil a fresh beef-tongue in the soup-stock for one hour and a half. Skin it, then place it on a dish, adding one pint of Gendarme garnishing, made by pouring a pint of Madeira sauce (No. 185) into a saucepan. Put it on the hot stove, and add twelve small godiveau quenelles (No. 221). Cut up six small, sound pickles, four mushrooms, and two ounces of smoked beef-tongue; add these to the sauce, and let cook for five minutes, stirring it lightly, then serve.

533. Beef-Tongue, Sauce Piquante.—The same as for the above, No. 532. When the tongue is ready, decorate it with pickles, and serve with a pint of sauce piquante (No. 203) separate, instead of the other garnishing.

534. Beef-Tongue, Napolitaine.—The same as for No. 532, adding one pint of hot Napolitaine garnishing (No. 195), instead of the other garnishing.

535. Beef-Tongue à la Jardinière.—The same as for No. 532, adding one pint of hot Jardinière (No. 1033), in place of the other garnishing.

536. Beef-Tongue, with Spinach.—The same as for No. 532, substituting one pint of spinach with gravy (No. 943) for the other garnishing.

537. Beef-Tongue, au Risotto.—The same as for No. 532, only adding one pint of hot Risotto (No. 1017) for the other garnishing.

538. Beef-Tongue à la Milanaise.—The same as for No. 532, only substituting one pint of Milanaise garnishing (No. 251) for the other.

539. Roulade of Beef à l'Ecarlate.—Procure six pounds of fine brisket of prime beef; roll it up as close as possible, so as to have it very firm, then firmly tie it around. Put in a saucepan one sound, peeled onion, one well-washed and scraped, sound carrot, both cut into thin slices, one sprig of thyme, one bay-leaf, three cloves, and a few shreds of larding-pork. Place the roulade over all. Season with two pinches of salt and one pinch of pepper. Cover the pan very tightly to prevent steam from escaping. Should the lid be loose, place a weight on top of it. Place it on a moderate fire, and let gently simmer for twenty minutes in all. Remove the lid, add two glasses of white wine, and one gill of broth (No. 99). Cover very tightly again, place in the hot oven, and let braise for fully two hours. Remove from the oven, untie, dress on a hot dish. Skim the fat off the gravy, strain the gravy into a sautoire, and reduce it on the hot range to one-half. Cut up an ounce of cooked, smoked beef-tongue into cock's-comb shape, one good-sized, sound, sliced truffle, six godiveau quenelles (No. 221), and six mushrooms. Place all these in a sautoire on the fire, with half a wine-glassful of Madeira wine, letting boil for one minute. Strain the reduced gravy of the roulade over this; add half a gill of tomato sauce (No. 205), and half a gill of Espagnole sauce (No. 151). Cook again for five minutes, then pour it into a sauce-bowl and send to the table separate, very hot.

540. Stewed Beef à l'Egyptienne.—Cut two pounds of beef into small, square pieces, brown them in a stewpan with one ounce of butter, adding two onions, cut into square pieces. When well browned, for about ten minutes, add two tablespoonfuls of flour; stir briskly with a pint and a half of white broth (No. 99), also one gill of tomato sauce (No. 205). Season with one good pinch of salt and half a pinch of pepper, put in a bouquet (No. 254), one clove of crushed garlic, and let cook for twenty-five minutes. Dish up the beef with a bunch of eighteen cooked gumbos (No. 1030), also three stalks of white, cooked celery.

541. Stewed Beef à la Dufour.—Prepare two pounds of small, square cuts of beef, brown them with two onions cut in square pieces, adding two tablespoonfuls of flour, cooking for six minutes. Stir well, and moisten with one quart of broth (No. 99), and one gill of tomato sauce (No. 205.) Put in also one pint of raw potatoes, cut in quarters, and let cook thoroughly for twenty-five minutes, with a bouquet (No. 254), a good pinch of salt and half a pinch of pepper, also one crushed garlic; then serve.

542. Stewed Beef à la Turque.—Cook the beef as directed in No. 541, substituting a good teaspoonful of curry, and serve with six timbales filled with cooked rice (No. 501). Unmold them, and use them instead of the potatoes.

543. Stewed Beef à la Marseillaise.—Proceed the same as for No. 541, omitting the potatoes, but adding two tomatoes cut in pieces, six chopped mushrooms, and two crushed cloves of garlic, all cooked six minutes with the beef. Serve with a teaspoonful of chopped parsley strewn over.

544. Tripe à la Bordelaise.—Take a pound and a half of lozenge-shaped pieces of tripe, cut into twelve parts. Marinate them for two hours in one tablespoonful of oil, with a pinch of salt, half a pinch of pepper, one bay-leaf, one sprig of thyme, six whole peppers, the juice of one sound lemon, and one crushed clove of garlic. Drain, roll them in flour, then in beaten egg, and finally in fresh bread-crumbs. Fry in one ounce of clarified butter in a pan for five minutes on each side, and serve with a gill of maître d'hôtel butter (No. 145), adding to it a teaspoonful of meat-glaze (No. 141).

545. Tripe à la Créole.—Cut a pound and a half of tripe into small pieces, fry them in a pan with two ounces of butter, one chopped onion, and half a green pepper, also chopped. Brown them slightly for six minutes, then transfer them to a saucepan with one cut-up tomato and half a pint of Espagnole sauce (No. 151). Season with one pinch of salt and half a pinch of pepper, adding a bouquet (No. 254), also a crushed clove of garlic. Cook for ten minutes and serve with one teaspoonful of chopped parsley.

546. Tripe à la Poulette.—Shred one and a half pounds of tripe, brown it slightly for three minutes in a pan, with an ounce of butter, one pinch of salt, and half a pinch of pepper; then transfer it to a saucepan, with half a pint of good Allemande sauce (No. 210). Let cook five minutes longer, then squeeze in the juice of half a lemon, besprinkle with a pinch of chopped parsley, and serve.

547. Tripe à la Mode de Caën.—Take one raw, double tripe, one ox-foot, three calf's feet, all well-washed and cleansed several times in fresh water, cutting them in pieces two inches long by one square. Have an earthen pot, or a saucepan, put pieces of feet at the bottom, cover over with tripe, then a layer of sliced carrots and onions, and continue the same until the vessel is full, carefully seasoning each layer. Tie in a cloth a sprig of thyme, two bay-leaves, twelve whole peppers, and six cloves; put this in the middle of the pot, throw over a bottleful of cider or white wine, and a little brandy (say one pony); lay on the top the stalks of some green leeks, parsley-roots, and cabbage leaves; cover, and fasten it down with paste, so that the steam cannot escape, and leave it for about ten hours in a very slow oven. Take it from the oven and serve when required.

548. Tripe à la Lyonnaise.—Cut up a pound and a half of double tripe, also two onions, and brown them in the pan with one ounce of clarified butter until they assume a fine golden color. Drain them, put them back on the fire, add one tablespoonful of vinegar and a gill of good Espagnole (No. 157). Stew for two minutes longer, and serve with a pinch of chopped parsley sprinkled over.

A pinch of salt represents 205 grains, or a tablespoonful.

Half a pinch of pepper represents 38 grains, or a teaspoonful.

A third of a pinch of nutmeg represents 13 grains, or half a teaspoonful.

VEAL.

549. Blanquette of Veal.—Cut into two-inch-square pieces two and a half pounds of breast of veal. Soak it in fresh water for one hour; drain it well, then lay it in a saucepan; cover with fresh water; boil, and be very careful to skim off all the scum. Add a well-garnished bouquet (No. 254), six small, well-peeled, sound, white onions, two good pinches of salt and a pinch of white pepper. Cook for forty minutes. Melt about an ounce and a half of butter in another saucepan, add to it three tablespoonfuls of flour, stir well for three minutes; moisten with a pint of broth from the veal; boil for five minutes. Set it on the side of the stove. Beat up in a bowl three egg yolks, with the juice of a medium-sized, sound lemon and a very little grated nutmeg. Take the preparation in the saucepan, gradually add it to the egg yolks, &c., briskly mix with a wooden spoon meanwhile until all added. Throw this over the veal, lightly toss the whole, but be careful not to allow to boil again; then serve. All blanquettes are prepared the same way, adding different garnishings.

550. Blanquette of Veal à la Reine.—The same as for No. 549, adding six chopped mushrooms, and twelve godiveau quenelles (No. 221) two minutes before serving.

551. Blanquette of Veal With Peas.—The same as for No. 549, adding one pint of cooked, green, or canned blanched peas two minutes before serving.

552. Blanquette of Veal With Nouilles.—The same as for No. 549, adding a quarter of a pound of cooked nouilles (No. 1182) around the serving-dish as a border.

553. Blanquette of Veal à l'Ancienne.—The same as for No. 549, adding one ounce of salt pork cut into small pieces, and cooked with the meat from the commencement, and six sliced mushrooms two minutes before serving.

554. Brisotin of Veal.—Cut up six pieces of lean veal about a quarter of an inch thick, and of the length of the hand. Flatten them, and season with one pinch of salt and half a pinch of pepper. Lard the centres, using a small larding needle, with strips of larding-pork. Lay any kind of forcemeat at hand on them, roll well, and tie with a string. Put them into a deep sautoire with a very little fat, one sliced carrot, and one medium-sized, sliced onion. Cover the whole with a piece of buttered paper; set it on the fire, and let it take a good golden color for about five minutes. Moisten with half a pint of white broth (No. 99), then put the saucepan in the oven, and cook slowly for twenty minutes, basting it occasionally, and serve.

Brisotins are all prepared the same way, adding different garnishings.

555. Brisotin of Veal à l'Ecarlate.

—The same as for No. 554, adding half a pint of hot écarlate sauce (No. 539).

556. Brisotin of Veal, Nantaise.—The same as for No. 554, placing six stuffed lettuce-heads (No. 953) around the dish, and pouring one gill of hot Madeira sauce (No. 185) over it.

557. Calf's Brains with Black Butter.—Place three fine, fresh calf's brains in cold water, and then peel off the skins. Wash again in cold water; neatly drain; put them in a sautoire and cover with fresh water. Add two pinches of salt, half a cupful of vinegar, one medium-sized, sliced carrot, one sprig of thyme, one bay-leaf, and twelve whole peppers. Boil for five minutes, drain well, and cut each brain in two. Dress them on a dish, and serve with a gill of very hot black butter (No. 159).

Calf's brain is always prepared as above, adding any desired sauce.

558. Calf's Brains à la Vinaigrette.—Exactly the same as for No. 557, serving on a folded napkin on a dish, garnishing with a few green parsley-leaves, and a gill of vinaigrette sauce (No. 201), separately.

559. Fried Calf's Brains, Tartare Sauce.—Proceed as in No. 557, then dry the brains well in a napkin; bread them a à l'Anglaise (No. 301), and fry in hot grease for five minutes. Serve with half a pint of tartare sauce (No. 207), separately.

560. Veal Cutlets à la Pagasqui.—Chop well two or three times in the machine two pounds of lean veal, from the hip if possible; place the meat in a bowl with two ounces of finely chopped, raw veal-suet. Season with one good pinch of salt, half a pinch of pepper, and the third of a pinch of nutmeg. Add half a cupful of good cream, one chopped shallot and two raw eggs. Mix well together. Shape six pieces like chops, sprinkle them with bread-crumbs, and fry in a stewpan with two ounces of clarified butter for four minutes on each side. Serve with a gill of any kind of sauce.

561. Veal Cutlets à la St. Cloud.—Lard thoroughly six veal cutlets with two small truffles, cut julienne-shape, one ounce of cooked beef-tongue, and one ounce of larding-pork, both cut the same. Place them in a sautoire with a pinch of salt, one sliced carrot, and one sliced onion, and let them brown for ten minutes, being careful to keep the lid on the pan. Moisten with half a pint of broth, and put them in the oven to finish cooking for at least fifteen minutes. Serve with a hot salpicon sauce, the chicken cut in large pieces (No. 256), pouring the sauce on the dish, and lay the chops on top.

562. Veal Cutlets à la Maréchale.—Pare nicely six veal cutlets; season them with a tablespoonful of salt and a teaspoonful of pepper. Cook in a sautoire with two ounces of butter for five minutes on each side. Moisten with half a pint of Espagnole sauce (No. 151), adding four sliced mushrooms, twelve small godiveau quenelles (No. 221), and three chicken livers, blanched and cut into pieces. Cook for five minutes longer, and serve with six croûtons (No. 133).

563. Veal Cutlets à la Milanaise.—Pare nicely and season well with a tablespoonful of salt and a teaspoonful of pepper six veal cutlets. Dip them in beaten egg, then in grated Parmesan cheese, and finally in fresh bread-crumbs. Flatten them, and cook them in a sautoire with six ounces of clarified butter for five minutes on each side, and serve with half a pint of garnishing Milanaise (No. 251).

To prepare breaded veal cutlets with tomato sauce, bread six cutlets as for the above, omit the cheese, cook them as described, and serve with half a pint of tomato sauce (No. 205).

564. Broiled Veal Cutlets.—Cut six even veal cutlets from a fine piece of the loin of white veal, pare them and flatten them slightly; lay them on a dish, and season with a tablespoonful of salt, a teaspoonful of pepper, and one tablespoonful of sweet oil. Turn the cutlets around several times; then put them on the broiler to broil for eight minutes on each side. Remove them from the fire; arrange them on a hot dish, spread a little maître d'hôtel (No. 145) over them, and send to the table.

565. Veal Cutlets à la Philadelphia.—Pare and brown in a sautoire with two ounces of butter six veal cutlets. Season them with a pinch of salt and half a pinch of pepper, turning them carefully at times. Add two onions cut in thick slices, and place the lid on the sautoire. Stir the onions occasionally, and when of a golden brown color, moisten with half a pint of Espagnole sauce (No. 151). Cook for fifteen minutes, and serve with one teaspoonful of chopped parsley.

566. Veal Cutlets en Papillotes.—Pare nicely six veal cutlets; put them in a sautoire with one ounce of butter, and season with a tablespoonful of salt and a teaspoonful of pepper. Add half a chopped onion, and brown slightly. Cook for eight minutes with four finely chopped mushrooms, moistening with a gill of Espagnole sauce (No. 151). Cook for four minutes longer. Then take out the cutlets, drain them, and put them to cool. Add to the gravy a teaspoonful of chopped parsley and two tablespoonfuls of fresh bread-crumbs. Now take six pieces of oiled white paper cut heart-shaped, put a thin slice of cooked ham on one side of the paper; then lay on the ham a little of the stock, and on top of it a cutlet, and another layer of the stock, and over all a thin slice of cooked ham. Cover with the second part of the paper, close it by folding the two edges firmly together, and proceed the same with the other cutlets. Bake for a short time (at most five minutes) in the oven, rather slowly, and then serve.

567. Curry of Veal à l'Indienne.—Cut into pieces and blanch in salted water two pounds of any kind of lean, raw veal. Drain and wash them well. Put the pieces into a saucepan, and cover them with warm water; seasoning with two pinches of salt and one pinch of pepper, adding also a bouquet (No. 254), and six small whole onions. Cook for twenty-five minutes. Then make a gill of roux blanc (No. 135), in a saucepan, moistening it with the liquor from the veal; stir it well, and then add a tablespoonful of diluted curry-powder and three raw egg yolks, beating up as they are put in. Dress the veal on a hot dish; immediately strain the roux over it (as it must not cook again). Neatly arrange half a pint of hot, plain, boiled rice all around the dish, then serve.

568. Escalops of Veal, plain.—Pare and cut two pounds of veal (from the hip is preferable) into six even steak-form slices. Season with one pinch of salt and half a pinch of pepper. Then brown them in a sautoire on a very hot range, with one ounce of butter, for five minutes on each side; dress on a hot dish, and serve with any kind of sauce or garnishing desired.

569. Escalops of Veal à la Duxelle.—Prepare six escalops as for No. 568, adding a chopped shallot, six mushrooms shred as finely as possible, one crushed clove of garlic, and a teaspoonful of chopped parsley. Moisten with a gill of Espagnole sauce (No. 151), and half a glassful of white wine. Cook for five minutes longer, pour them on a hot dish, place the escalops over, and then serve.

570. Escalops of Veal with Stuffed Peppers.—Proceed exactly as for No. 568, adding the juice of half a medium-sized, sound lemon, and a gill of hot Madeira sauce (No. 185). Cook for three minutes longer, and decorate the dish with six stuffed green-peppers (No. 975) three minutes before serving.

571. Escalops of Veal à la Chicorée.—Prepare and proceed precisely the same as for No. 568. Cook for eight minutes. Then dress half a pint of chicorée au jus (No. 934) on the hot dish, and send to the table.

572. Escalops of Veal à l'Italienne.—The same as for No. 568, adding one medium-sized, chopped onion, six chopped mushrooms, one teaspoonful of parsley, and a crushed clove of garlic. Moisten with half a glassful of white wine, and cook for five minutes with a gill of Espagnole sauce (No. 151), and serve.

573. Escalops of Veal à la Provençale.—Prepare as for No. 568, replacing the butter by the same quantity of oil. Season well, and when browned on both sides add one shallot or a finely chopped onion. Let them color, and then moisten with a gill of broth. Add two tablespoonfuls of Espagnole sauce (No. 151), three chopped cêpes, two crushed cloves of garlic, and a teaspoonful of parsley. Boil once, and then serve with six croûtons of fried bread (No. 133).

574. Escalops of Sweetbreads à la Richelieu.—Take four blanched sweetbreads (No. 601); cut them into slices, and stew them in a saucepan, with an ounce of butter and half a glassful of white wine. Season with a tablespoonful of salt, a teaspoonful of pepper, and half a teaspoonful of nutmeg. Cook for six minutes, then moisten with a gill of thick Allemande sauce (No. 210), and add two sliced truffles and four sliced mushrooms. Fill six scallop-shells with the preparation; sprinkle the tops with fresh bread-crumbs; pour a few drops of clarified butter over all, and brown slightly in the oven for five minutes. Serve on a dish with a folded napkin.

575. Minced Veal à la Catalan.—Mince two pounds of lean veal, and brown it in a saucepan with three tablespoonfuls of sweet oil, one onion cut in quarters, and half a minced green-pepper. When a fine color, add two tablespoonfuls of flour, and mix thoroughly. Moisten with one pint of white broth (No. 99), and season with a heaped tablespoonful of salt, a teaspoonful of pepper; stir briskly, and add a bouquet (No. 254), three cloves of crushed garlic, and a gill of tomato sauce (No. 205). Cook well for twenty-five minutes; then serve, sprinkling a little chopped parsley over it.

576. Minced Veal à la Biscaënne.—Proceed as for No. 575, adding one pint of potatoes Parisiennes (No. 986), and two cut-up tomatoes, fifteen minutes before serving.

577. Fricandeau with Sorrel.—Cut a slice of three pounds from a leg of veal; remove the sinews, and lard the surface with a medium-sized larding needle. Place it in a sautoire in which there are already pieces of pork-skin, one sliced onion, one sliced carrot, and a bouquet (No. 254). Season with a tablespoonful of salt, cover with a buttered paper, and let it color slightly for five minutes on the stove. Then moisten with half a pint of white broth (No. 99), and cook one hour, basting it occasionally. Serve with half a pint of purée of sorrel (No. 974) on the dish, placing the veal on top.

All fricandeaus are prepared in the same way.

578. Fricandeau with Spinach.—The same as for No. 577, adding half a pint of hot spinach au gras (No. 943) instead of the sorrel.

579. Fricandeau à la Morlaisienne.—The same as for No. 577, serving it with a gill of hot Madeira sauce (No. 185), and garnishing with six small stuffed cabbages around the dish (No. 919).

580. Calf's Liver Stewed à l'Italienne.—Cut two pounds of fresh calf's liver into small pieces. Put them with one ounce of clarified butter into a pan on the hot range, with one peeled and finely chopped, sound onion, and a clove of crushed garlic. Season with one pinch of salt and half a pinch of pepper. Cook well for five minutes, shuffling the pan well meanwhile, then moisten with half a glassful of white wine and a gill of Espagnole sauce (No. 151). Add six chopped mushrooms, and cook once more for three minutes. Serve with a teaspoonful of finely chopped parsley.

581. Calf's Liver Sauté à la Provençale.—Proceed as for No. 580, adding two crushed cloves of garlic. Squeeze in the juice of half a lemon. Serve with a tablespoonful of chopped parsley.

582. Calf's Liver à l'Alsacienne.—Cut two pounds of calf's liver into square pieces, and put them in a sautoire with one ounce of clarified butter. Season with a tablespoonful of salt and a teaspoonful of pepper, and add two medium-sized, sliced onions. When well stewed for six minutes, pour in a teaspoonful of vinegar, and two tablespoonfuls of Espagnole sauce (No. 151), and let it just come to a boil. Serve with a little chopped parsley.

583. Calf's Liver Braised à la Bourgeoise.—Place a small calf's liver, larded thoroughly with pieces of larding pork, previously seasoned with a pinch of chopped parsley and a hashed clove of garlic, in a saucepan on the fire, with two tablespoonfuls of clarified butter, one sprig of thyme, two bay-leaves, half a sliced carrot, and half a sliced onion. Turn the liver over and moisten it with one gill of Espagnole sauce (No. 151), and a gill of white broth (No. 99). Season with a pinch of salt and half a pinch of pepper, and cook for forty-five minutes. Strain the sauce into another saucepan (meanwhile keeping the liver in a warm place), adding to the gravy two medium-sized, sound, well-scraped, sliced, raw carrots, and two ounces of salt pork cut into shreds. Stew well together for twenty-five minutes, and pour the garnishing over the liver just before serving, decorating with six small onions around the dish.

584. Calf's Liver Broiled with Bacon.—Take a nice, tender, fresh calf's liver weighing a pound and a half; pare and trim off the hard portions; cut it into six equal-sized slices, and put them on a dish. Season with a tablespoonful of salt, a teaspoonful of pepper, and one tablespoonful of sweet oil; mix well together. Broil for four minutes on each side. Arrange the slices on a hot serving-dish, and decorate with six thin and crisp slices of broiled bacon (No. 754). Spread a gill of maître d'hôtel butter (No. 145) over, and serve very hot.

585. Loin of Veal, Roasted.—Saw from a fine, white, fresh, and fat loin of veal with the kidney, the spine, and whatever hip-bone remains. Season the loin with a tablespoonful and a half of salt, and one heaped teaspoonful of pepper and roll the flank part neatly over the kidney, and tie it with a string.

Have ready a lightly buttered roasting-pan. Lay in it the loin; pour in half a glassful of water, and distribute a few bits of butter over the meat. Then cover its entire length with a piece of well-buttered paper. Place the pan in a moderate oven, and roast it for one hour and three-quarters, meanwhile basting it frequently with its own gravy. Take it out of the oven, untie it, and place it on a hot serving-dish. Add three tablespoonfuls of broth to the gravy in the pan, skim off the fat and reduce it to the consistency of a demi-glace sauce; then strain it through a colander, either over the roast or into a separate sauce-bowl, and send it to the table immediately.

Loin of lamb, roasted, is to be prepared exactly as above described, letting it cook fifty minutes instead of an hour and three-quarters.

Loin of mutton is also to be roasted and served in the same way, but one hour's cooking will be sufficient.

586. Grenadins of Veal, Purée of Peas.—Cut into six pieces two pounds of lean veal from off the leg; extract the sinews, and lard the veal nicely on one side, using a needle for the purpose. Lay the pieces in a sautoire, with one carrot, one onion, and some scraps of pork, and let them brown together for six minutes. Season with a tablespoonful of salt, and moisten with a gill of white broth (No. 99). Put the sautoire into the oven, covering it with a piece of buttered paper. After thirty minutes, or when of a good color, remove, and serve with half a pint of hot purée of peas (No. 49) on the dish, the grenadins on top, and the gravy strained over all.

587. Grenadins of Veal à la Chipolata.—The same as for No. 586, only adding half a pint of hot chipolata garnishing (No. 232) instead of the peas.

588. Grenadins of Veal à la Sevigné.—The same as for No. 586, only decorating the dish with six bouchées Sevigné, made by preparing six small bouchées (No. 270), and filling them with very finely chopped spinach au jus (No 943). Lay the covers on and serve very hot without any other garnishing.

589. Grenadins of Veal à l'Africaine.—Prepare the same as for No. 586, serving very hot, with three small, stuffed egg-plants (No. 909), and eighteen medium-sized, cooked gumbos (No. 1030).

590. Braised Noix of Veal à la Providence.—Lard thoroughly a knuckle of veal of three pounds, braise it nicely in a saucepan with an ounce of fresh salt pork, one tablespoonful of salt, and a teaspoonful of pepper. Cook for fifteen minutes, stirring occasionally, and moistening with half a pint of white broth (No. 99), and half a pint of Espagnole sauce (No. 151.) Add one pint of raw Jardinière (No. 1033) and a cupful of flageolets. Cook for forty-five minutes all together. Transfer the knuckle to a hot dish, pour the garnishing over, and serve.

591. Braised Noix of Veal en Daube.—Proceed the same as for braised beef en Daube (No. 483).

592. Panpiette of Veal à la Faubonne.—Cut two pounds of veal off the leg into six thin slices. Pare them to the size of the hand, and season with a tablespoonful of salt and a teaspoonful of pepper. Fill them with any kind of forcemeat, roll, and tie together with string. Put them in a sautoire with small scraps of pork, adding half a sliced carrot and half a sliced onion. Cover with a *barde* of larding pork on top, and brown for ten minutes. Moisten with a gill of white broth (No. 99); cover with buttered paper, and put in the oven to finish cooking for twenty-five minutes. Serve, with half a pint of purée of lentils (No. 46), mixed with two tablespoonfuls of cream, and a teaspoonful of chopped parsley.

593. Panpiette of Veal à l'Ecarlate.—The same as for No. 592, pouring half a pint of hot Ecarlate sauce (No. 247) over the panpiettes.

594. Panpiette of Veal, Purée of Chestnuts.—The same as for No. 592, adding half a pint of hot purée of chestnuts (No. 131).

595. Panpiette of Veal, Sauce Duxelle.—The same as for No. 592, putting half a pint of hot Duxelle sauce (No. 189) on the dish, and arranging the panpiettes over it.

596. Breast of Veal à la Milanaise.—Bone a breast of veal of two and a half pounds; season with one tablespoonful of salt and a teaspoonful of pepper. Stuff it in the usual way with forcemeat (No. 229). Roll and tie it, making a few incisions in the skin, and put it in a saucepan, with one sliced carrot and one sliced onion. Braise it for one hour and a half in the oven, basting it occasionally with its own gravy. Serve with half a pint of hot Milanaise garnishing (No. 251) on the dish, placing the meat on top, and straining the gravy over it.

597. Calf's Feet, Naturel.—Split each of three calf's feet in two; remove the large bone, and put them in fresh water for one hour. Wash thoroughly, drain, and place them in a saucepan, with two tablespoonfuls of flour and three quarts of cold water. Stir well; add a gill of vinegar, one onion, one carrot (all cut in shreds), twelve whole peppers, a handful of salt, and a bouquet (No. 254), and cook briskly for one hour and a half. Drain well, and serve with any kind of sauce required.

598. Calf's Feet à la Poulette.—The same as for No. 597, adding half a pint of hot poulette sauce, made by putting one pint of hot Allemande sauce (No. 210) into a saucepan, with one ounce of fresh butter, adding the juice of half a medium-sized lemon, and a teaspoonful of chopped parsley. Heat well on the hot stove until thoroughly melted and mixed, but do not let it boil. Keep the sauce warm, and serve for all sauce poulettes.

599. Calf's Feet, Sauce Piquante.—Same as for No. 597, adding half a pint of hot piquante sauce (No. 203).

600. Calf's Feet, Sauce Remoulade.—Same as for No. 597, adding half a pint of hot Remoulade sauce (No. 209).

601. How to Blanch Sweetbreads.—Clean and neatly trim three pairs of fine sweetbreads. Soak them for three hours in three different fresh waters, one hour in each water, with one pinch of salt in each water. Drain, place in cold water, and blanch them until they come to a boil. Then drain, and freshen them in cold water. Cover with a napkin, lay them aside in a cool place, and they will now be ready for general use. When they are to be used in molds, they should be gently pressed down with a pound weight.

602. Sweetbreads, Braised.—Take six blanched heart-sweetbreads as above, lard the upper parts slightly, and put them in a sautoire with some slices of pork-skin. Add half a sliced carrot, half a sliced onion, and a bouquet (No. 254). Sprinkle over them a pinch of salt, and cover them with a buttered paper. Reduce to a golden color, and moisten with half a pint of strong white broth (No. 99). Cook it in the oven for forty minutes, basting occasionally with the gravy, lifting the buttered paper, and replacing it each time in the same position. The sweetbreads will now be ready to serve with any kind of sauce or garnishing desired. Always place the sauce or garnishing on a hot serving-dish, and lay the sweetbreads over it, then send to the table.

603. Sweetbreads Braised à la Financière.—Prepare six sweetbreads, as in No. 602, and serve with half a pint of hot Financière sauce (No. 246).

604. Sweetbreads Braised with Sorrel.—The same as for No. 602, adding half a pint of hot purée of sorrel (No. 974).

605. Sweetbreads Braised au Salpicon.—The same as for No. 602, adding half a pint of hot salpicon (No. 256).

606. Sweetbreads à la Soubise.—The same as for No. 602, adding half a pint of hot soubise (No. 250).

607. Sweetbreads Braised, with Spinach.—The same as for No. 602, adding half a pint of hot spinach (No. 943).

608. Sweetbreads à la Sauce Duxelle.—The same as for No. 602, adding half a pint of hot duxelle sauce (No. 189).

609. Sweetbreads Braised, with Mushroom Sauce.—The same as for No. 602, adding half a pint of hot mushroom sauce (No. 230).

610. Sweetbreads Braised à la Sauce Béarnaise.—The same as for No. 602, adding half a pint of hot Béarnaise sauce (No. 166).

611. Sweetbreads Braised aux Cêpes.—The same as for No. 602, adding half a pint of hot cêpes.

612. Sweetbreads Braised aux Gourmets.—The same as for No. 602, adding half a pint of hot gourmet garnishing (No. 241).

613. Sweetbreads Braised à la Parisienne.—The same as for No. 602, adding half a pint of hot Parisienne garnishing (No. 240).

614. Sweetbreads Braised à la Godard.—The same as for No. 602, adding half a pint of hot Godard garnishing (No. 238).

615. Sweetbreads Braised à la Montglas.

—Place six braised sweetbreads, prepared as for No. 602, in six small, buttered paper-boxes, having cooked fine herbs (No. 143) strewn around the bottom. Heat in the oven for five minutes; then pour one tablespoonful of hot montglas sauce (No. 213) over each. Serve on a dish with a folded napkin.

616. Stewed Sweetbreads à la Catalan.—Cut four blanched sweetbreads (No. 601) into slices; put them in a sautoire with half a gill of sweet oil, one tablespoonful of salt, a teaspoonful of pepper, two well-hashed shallots, and half a sliced green pepper. Reduce to a good golden color for about six minutes, and add two peeled tomatoes cut into pieces, one gill of Espagnole sauce (No. 151), and a crushed clove of garlic. Cook for ten minutes; arrange on a hot dish, and serve.

617. Sweetbreads Broiled à la Colbert.—Cut in two each of three fine blanched sweetbreads as in No. 601. Season them with one pinch of salt and half a pinch of pepper, and pour one tablespoonful of sweet oil over them; mix them in well, and then broil them on a brisk fire for five minutes on each side. Dress on a hot dish, and serve with half a pint of hot Colbert sauce (No. 190).

618. Sweetbreads Braised à la Pompadour.—Braise the sweetbreads exactly as for No. 602. Serve with half a pint of hot Béarnaise sauce (No. 166), two truffles cut in small square pieces; arrange six artichoke-bottoms on the sauce, place a sweetbread on each artichoke, with a thin slice of truffle on top of each, and serve.

619. Sweetbread Croquettes, Périgueux Sauce.—Prepare six sweetbread croquettes (No. 276), and serve them on a dish with a folded napkin. Serve half a pint of Périgueux sauce (No. 191), separate.

620. Sweetbread Croquettes with Peas.—The same as for No. 619, adding half a pint of cooked peas, with a gill of Madeira sauce (No. 185), cooked together for two minutes. Pour it on the dish; place the croquettes over it, and serve.

621. Coquilles of Sweetbreads à la Dreux.—Cut four blanched sweetbreads (No. 601) into small slices, and stew them in a saucepan with half an ounce of good butter, half a glassful of white wine, and three tablespoonfuls of mushroom liquor. Reduce them for ten minutes, then add a gill of velouté sauce (No. 152), six minced mushrooms, and two truffles cut the same. Season with half a tablespoonful of salt, a scant teaspoonful of pepper, and half a teaspoonful of nutmeg, and finish by adding two tablespoonfuls of good cream, or half an ounce of good butter. Fill six silver table-shells with this; sprinkle them with fresh bread-crumbs; pour a few drops of clarified butter over them, and put them in the baking oven. Brown slightly for six minutes longer, and serve on a hot dish with a folded napkin.

622. Coquilles of Sweetbreads à la Cardinal.—The same as for No. 621, but instead of truffles use one ounce of smoked beef-tongue, and the same quantity of tomato sauce (No. 205), instead of the cream.

623. Coquilles of Sweetbreads à la Reine.—Cut four blanched sweetbreads (No. 601) in slices, and fry them in half an ounce of butter, half a glassful of white wine, and three tablespoonfuls of mushroom liquor. Season with half a tablespoonful of salt, a scant teaspoonful of pepper, and half a teaspoonful of nutmeg. Reduce for ten minutes, and moisten with one gill of Allemande sauce (No. 210), adding six sliced mushrooms, two sliced truffles, and twelve small quenelles of godiveau (No. 221). Finish the same as for No. 621.

624. Veal Stew, Marengo.—Cut three pounds of lean veal into pieces, and reduce them in a stewpan with one gill of oil, a cut-up onion or two shallots, and two ounces of salt pork, also cut up. Toss them occasionally, and when well browned after ten minutes, strew in two tablespoonfuls of flour, stirring well again. Moisten with one quart of white broth (No. 99), and one gill of tomato sauce (No. 205); season with a good tablespoonful of salt and a teaspoonful of pepper, adding a crushed clove of garlic, and a bouquet (No. 254). Cook for forty minutes, and serve with six croûtons (No. 133) around the dish, and a little chopped parsley sprinkled over it.

625. Veal Stew à la Provençale.—Cut three pounds of lean veal from the breast or shoulder into pieces, and place them in a stewpan with one ounce of butter, two tablespoonfuls of sweet oil, and one chopped onion. Cook them for ten minutes, stirring occasionally; add two tablespoonfuls of flour, stir again, and moisten with one quart of white broth (No. 99). Season with a heaped tablespoonful of salt and a teaspoonful of pepper, and add six minced mushrooms, three crushed cloves of garlic, and a bouquet (No. 254). Cook for forty minutes, and serve on a hot dish, sprinkling a little chopped parsley over it.

626. Veal Stew à la Grecque.—Place two pounds of lean veal cut in pieces in a stewpan, with two ounces of butter and one cut-up onion, and reduce for ten minutes, adding two tablespoonfuls of flour. Moisten with one quart of white broth (No. 99), and one gill of tomato sauce (No. 205).

Add a heaped tablespoonful of salt, a teaspoonful of pepper, and half a teaspoonful of nutmeg, a bouquet (No. 254), three white roots of table-celery, cut in two, and eighteen raw okras, pared whole. Cook for thirty minutes, and serve with the dish nicely decorated with the garnishing.

627. Veal, Stewed à la Portugaise.—The same as for No. 626, substituting three stuffed tomatoes (No. 987), or plain, roasted tomatoes, and three timbales of cooked rice (No. 501) for the other garnishing.

628. Veal, Stewed à la Solferino.—Reduce three pounds of pieces of veal cut from the breast or shoulder, in one ounce of butter, with six small onions. When cooked for ten minutes, add two tablespoonfuls of flour. Moisten with one quart of white broth (No. 99), and one gill of tomato sauce (No. 205), seasoning with one heaped tablespoonful of salt, and one teaspoonful of pepper. Stir well together until it reaches boiling-point; then add two carrots, and two turnips cut out with a vegetable-scoop, and a bouquet (No. 254). Cook again for forty minutes, and serve.

Any kind of vegetables in season can be added.

629. Veal, Stewed à la Bourgeoise.—Reduce in one ounce of butter three pounds of lean veal cut in pieces, with six small onions. After cooking ten minutes add two tablespoonfuls of flour, and moisten with one quart of white broth (No. 99). Stir well, and season with one heaped tablespoonful of salt, one teaspoonful of pepper, and half a glassful of red wine. Add two carrots cut in square pieces, one ounce of salt pork also cut in pieces, and a bouquet (No. 254). Cook for forty minutes longer, remove the bouquet, and serve.

630. Veal, Stewed with Oyster-plant.—The same as for No. 629, substituting for the garnishing one bunch of well-cleaned, raw oyster-plant cut into pieces, forty minutes before serving.

631. Veal, Stewed with Peas.—The same as for No. 629, substituting one pint of fresh peas for the oyster-plant thirty minutes before serving. Should green peas be out of season, use one pint of canned peas five minutes before serving.

632. Veal, Stewed à la Chasseur.—The same as for No. 629, substituting for the garnishing twelve minced mushrooms, sixteen quenelles de godiveau (No. 221), and one clove of garlic three minutes before serving. Serve with six croûtons (No. 133) around the dish.

633. Tendron of Veal à la Nantaise.—Pare nicely three pounds of the breast of veal; make a few incisions on the top, and tie it firmly together.

Lay it in a deep sautoire with a piece of pork-skin cut up, a carrot, and a cut-up onion. Cover with a buttered paper, and when it begins to color after five minutes, moisten it slightly with a pint of water or broth. Baste as frequently as possible, and let it cook one hour. Then put it on a dish, strain the sauce over it, garnish with six stuffed lettuce-heads (No. 953). Decorate with a tablespoonful of croûtons all around the dish, and serve.

634. Tendron of Veal with Sorrel.—The same as for No. 633, substituting one pint of cooked, hot sorrel (No. 974) on the dish, for the other garnishing.

635. Tendron of Veal à la Morlaisienne.—The same as for No. 633, substituting six small stuffed cabbages (No. 919) for the other garnishing.

636. Tendron of Veal à la Chipolata.—The same as for No. 633, pouring one pint of hot chipolata (No. 232) on the dish, and placing the tendron on top.

637. Calf's Head, plain.—Plunge a fine, fresh, white calf's head into hot water for one minute, lift it up, sharply rub it all over with a coarse towel, so as to remove all the remaining hairs. Carefully cut the flesh, starting from the centre of the head, right down to the nostrils. Then, with a very keen knife, bone it from the top to the base on both sides. Place in a saucepan two tablespoonfuls of flour, one gill of vinegar, one medium-sized, well-cleaned, sliced carrot, one sound peeled onion, eighteen whole peppers, and two pinches of salt. Pour in very gradually two quarts of cold water—briskly stirring meanwhile until all added. Cut up half of the head into six equal pieces; add them to the broth, as also the other whole half. Let all cook together on a moderate fire for one hour and a half. Lift up the pieces and half the head, place the six pieces on a dry napkin. Have ready a hot dish with a folded napkin over it, neatly dress the six pieces on it, decorate with parsley-greens, and serve with any desired sauce. Place the remaining whole half in a stone jar, strain the broth over it, and keep in a cool place for any purpose required.

For calf's brains, see No. 557.

638. Calf's Head à la Cavour.—Take half a boiled calf's head as for No. 637. Before serving pour a gill of hot tomato sauce (No. 205) over it, and surround it with twenty-four stoned and blanched olives, arranged in clusters, and six sippets of fried bread (No. 133).

639. Calf's Head à la Poulette.—The same as for No. 637, pouring half a pint of hot poulette sauce (No. 598) over it, and sprinkling it with half a tablespoonful of parsley.

640. Calf's Head à la Vinaigrette.—The same as for No. 637, laying a folded napkin on the dish, and arranging thereon the half of the head. Serve with parsley-leaves around the dish, and one pint of vinaigrette (No. 201), separately.

641. Calf's Head en Tortue.—Prepare and cut into six equal pieces, as for No. 637, half a calf's head. Place them on a hot dish, pour over it half a pint of hot tortue garnishing (No. 239), decorate with three pieces of heart-shaped, fried croûtons (No. 133), a little fried parsley, and send to the table very hot.

A pinch of salt represents 205 grains, or a tablespoonful.

Half a pinch of pepper represents 38 grains, or a teaspoonful.

A third of a pinch of nutmeg represents 13 grains, or half a teaspoonful.

MUTTON—LAMB.

642. Mutton Chops à la Provençale.—Flatten and pare neatly six fine, thick mutton chops, season them with a pinch of salt and half a pinch of pepper, oil them slightly with sweet oil, and then either broil or cook them in a sautoire for two minutes on one side only, and lay them aside to get cold. The chops should always be cooked for two minutes as above mentioned, after the garnishing has been prepared.

Garnishing à la Provençale.—Peel two small, sound, white onions, mince them very fine, place them in a pan with boiling water for five minutes to prevent them from getting brown, drain well, place them in a sautoire with one ounce of good butter, and cook for five minutes. Add a dash of white wine, a thin slice of garlic crushed with a spoon, half a spoonful of grated Parmesan cheese, and one gill of good béchamel sauce (No. 154). Season with half a pinch of salt and half a pinch of pepper. Stir all well until it comes to a boil, then put it away to cool. Divide the garnishing over the cooked side of the six chops about a quarter of an inch in thickness; besprinkle with fresh bread-crumbs mixed with a little grated Parmesan cheese. Carefully place the chops in a well-buttered pan, and pour a little clarified butter over them. Place in a very hot oven for five minutes, or until of a good color, and serve with half a pint of hot velouté (No. 152).

643. Mutton Chops, Breaded.—Flatten six fine, thick mutton chops, pare nicely, and season with one tablespoonful of salt and a teaspoonful of pepper. Dip them in beaten egg, roll in fresh bread-crumbs, and place in a sautoire with one ounce of clarified butter. Cook four minutes on each side, and serve with half a pint of any hot sauce or garnishing desired.

644. Mutton Chops, Bretonne.—Pare six nice mutton chops, season with a tablespoonful of salt and a teaspoonful of pepper, and pour a few drops of oil over each. Broil four minutes on each side. Arrange them on a dish, and serve with half a pint of purée of white beans (No. 92), mingled with two tablespoonfuls of good, hot meat-glaze (No. 141).

645. Mutton Chops à l'Africaine.—Broil six mutton chops as for No. 644, and serve with three stuffed egg-plants for garnishing (No. 909), and twelve sliced okras in clusters, in place of the other garnishing.

646. Mutton Chops à la Napolitaine.—The same as for No. 644, but substituting for the garnishing half a pint of hot Napolitaine (No. 195).

647. Chops Soyer, with Potatoes.—Take five pounds of saddle of mutton, cut and saw it into six pieces crosswise. Flatten, pare, and trim. Season with one tablespoonful of salt and a teaspoonful of pepper. Broil them for six minutes on each side, then place them on a hot dish, and serve with a garnishing of one pint, or the equivalent, of fried potatoes (No. 993) around the dish.

648. Leg of Mutton à la Portugaise.—Take a medium-sized leg of mutton, cut off the shank-bone, trim well, and make an incision on the first joint. Season with two pinches of salt and half a pinch of pepper, rub half an ounce of butter over it, and roast for one hour in a pan, basting occasionally with the gravy, and turning it once in a while. Remove from the oven; dress on a hot dish, and serve with three stuffed tomatoes (No. 1023), and three timbales of cooked rice (No. 501), straining the gravy over.

Plain roast leg of mutton is prepared the same, only served without any other garnishing than its own gravy.

649. Leg of Mutton à la Condé.—Roast a leg of mutton the same as for No. 648, and serve it with half a pint of cooked red beans (No. 951) added to the gravy, either on the same dish as the leg, or in a separate bowl.

650. Leg of Mutton, Bretonne.—Proceed the same as for No. 648, but using half a pint of cooked white beans instead of the other garnishing, and adding one teaspoonful of chopped parsley, also one hashed and browned onion.

651. Leg of Mutton, Caper Sauce.—Pare a nice leg of mutton as for No. 648, put it on to boil in a stock-pot, filled with slightly salted cold water, add a bouquet (No. 254), and one cut-up carrot. Boil one hour and a quarter, and serve with half a pint of hot caper sauce, made by putting a pint of hot Hollandaise sauce (No. 160) into a saucepan with a light handful of capers, and heating thoroughly for five minutes without boiling.

652. Mutton Hash à la Zingara.—Chop up two onions, and fry them in a saucepan with one ounce of butter for three minutes, adding one and a half pounds of cooked and hashed mutton, also one-fourth the quantity of hashed potatoes. Season with a good tablespoonful of salt, the same of pepper and half a saltspoonful of nutmeg. Also put in two cut-up, raw tomatoes, a tablespoonful of chopped parsley, and a crushed clove of garlic. Add a gill of Espagnole sauce (No. 151), and a gill of broth (No. 99). Mix all together, and cook twenty minutes, then serve with a pinch of chopped parsley sprinkled over the dish.

653. Mutton Hash au Gratin.—Proceed as for No. 652, omitting the tomatoes and garlic. Place the hash on a baking-dish, sprinkle a little fresh bread-crumbs over, spread a very little butter on top, and put into the oven until of a good golden color, for which it will require from eight to ten minutes.

654. Lamb's Feet à la Poulette.—The same as directed for calf's feet (No. 598), adding half a pint of hot poulette sauce (No. 598).

655. Mutton Stew, Fermière.—Put into a saucepan three pounds of breast or shoulder of mutton cut into square pieces, with one ounce of butter, and six small onions. Cook for ten minutes, or until of a good golden color. Add three tablespoonfuls of flour, mix well together, and moisten with three pints of light white broth or water, stirring continually while boiling. Season with a good tablespoonful of salt, a teaspoonful of pepper, and half a teaspoonful of nutmeg, adding two carrots and two turnips, cut in square pieces, a bouquet (No. 254), and one crushed clove of garlic. Cook on a moderate fire for thirty minutes; put in half a pint of lima beans, and let the whole cook again for fifteen minutes. Skim off the fat well, remove the bouquet and serve.

656. Mutton Stew, Solferino.—Proceed as directed for No. 655, adding half a pint of carrots and a like quantity of turnips, both cut with a vegetable-spoon; cook these thirty minutes with the stew, and ten minutes before serving add half a pint of stewed tomatoes (No. 1027) instead of the lima beans.

657. Mutton Stew à la Marseillaise.—The same as for No. 655, but instead of the other garnishings, add one pint of stewed tomatoes (No. 1027), four cloves of crushed garlic, two chopped onions, and twelve minced mushrooms. Let cook for thirty minutes, and serve with chopped parsley sprinkled over.

658. Mutton Stew, Portugaise.—Proceed the same as for No. 655, replacing the garnishing with three stuffed tomatoes (No. 1023), and three timbales of cooked rice (No. 501), nicely arranged around the dish.

659. Mutton Stew with Potatoes.—Exactly the same as for No. 655, replacing the garnishing with one pint of potatoes cut in quarters, (paring the edges a little), also six small onions. Let cook thirty minutes, and serve.

660. Irish Mutton Stew.—Cut in square pieces three pounds of mutton; wash well, drain, and put them in a saucepan, covering with fresh water. Let them come to a boil; then remove into another pan. Clean the pieces well again, return them to the saucepan and cover them with boiling water. Place on the fire, seasoning with two tablespoonfuls of salt, a teaspoonful of pepper, and half a teaspoonful of nutmeg. Add two carrots, two turnips, all cut up, six small onions, and a bouquet (No. 254). Let cook for twenty-five minutes, then add half a pint of potatoes cut in quarters. Dilute half a cupful of flour with half a pint of water, strain it into the stew, stirring thoroughly, and cook again for twenty-five minutes. Remove the bouquet, thoroughly skimming it before serving.

661. Mutton Kidneys en Brochette au Petit Salé.—Split twelve mutton kidneys in two, but do not separate the parts; remove the skin, place them in a deep plate, and season with a tablespoonful of salt, and a teaspoonful of pepper, adding two tablespoonfuls of sweet oil. Roll them well. Take six skewers, put a skewer through the two kidneys in the centre, and repeat the same for the others. Broil four minutes on each side. Arrange on a hot dish, pour a gill of maître d'hôtel butter (No. 145) over, and cover with six slices of broiled bacon (No. 754.)

662. Mutton Kidneys Sautés, Madeira Sauce.—Pare well twelve mutton kidneys and cut them into slices. Put into a frying-pan, with one ounce of butter, a tablespoonful of salt, and a teaspoonful of pepper. Toss them well for six minutes. Add half a pint of Madeira wine sauce (No. 185), squeeze in the juice of half a lemon, add another small piece of fresh butter, toss well again without boiling, and serve.

663. Mutton Kidneys Sautés à l'Italienne.—Proceed as for No. 662, adding one gill of cooked fine herbs (No. 143); toss well for one minute, being careful not to let it boil. Avoid boiling any kidneys when being prepared in this way. All stewed mutton kidneys are prepared the same, adding either six minced mushrooms one minute before serving, or if truffles are preferred, add three medium-sized, minced truffles.

664. Saddle of Mutton, Roasted, Plain.—Pare and trim a fine saddle of mutton, weighing about six pounds (if possible). Lift off the upper skin, make one slight incision in the middle, also three on each side; tie it firmly together with three strings, so that it retains its shape, season it with a good pinch of salt, and it will then be ready to roast. Place the saddle in a roasting-pan, adding a gill of cold water; put it in a moderate oven, and let cook for forty-five minutes. Baste it frequently with its own gravy, and serve on a very hot dish. Skim off all the fat, strain the gravy into a sauce-bowl, and serve separately.

N. B.—Should the saddle be of heavier weight, say twelve to fourteen pounds, one hour and a quarter will be necessary to cook it.

665. Saddle of Mutton, Sauce Colbert.—Proceed exactly the same as for No. 664, serving half a pint of Colbert sauce (No. 190) in a bowl.

666. Saddle of Mutton, Currant Jelly.—Same as directed for No. 664 serving with half a pint of hot jelly sauce (No. 884), or with a little currant jelly, separately.

667. Saddle of Mutton, Sauce Poivrade.—Proceed the same as for No. 664, serving with half a pint of poivrade sauce, separately (No. 194).

668. Saddle of Mutton, Londonderry Sauce.—The same as for No. 664, serving with half a pint of hot Londonderry sauce (No. 880).

669. Saddle of Mutton à la Sevigné.—Exactly the same as for No. 664, only serving with six boucheés à la Sevigné (No. 588).

670. Saddle of Mutton à la Duchesse.—Proceed as for No. 664, serving with six potatoes Duchesse (No. 1006).

671. Saddle of Mutton with Potatoes.—Served exactly the same as for No. 664, only adding one pint of potatoes château (No. 1009).

672. Lamb Fries à la Diable.—Skin well six medium-sized lamb fries; cut each into three slices and put them into a bowl. Season with a tablespoonful of salt, a very little cayenne pepper, the juice of half a lemon, one tablespoonful of sweet oil, and a teaspoonful of ground mustard diluted in a tablespoonful of Parisian sauce. Mix all well together, roll them in flour, and broil five minutes on each side. Arrange them on a hot dish garnished with six slices of lemon, and serve with a hot sauce à la Diable (No. 198), separately.

Lamb chops can be prepared the same way. Lamb fries, as above prepared, should be immediately served as soon as cooked.

673. Lamb Fries, Tomato Sauce.—Same as for No. 672, only dipping the slices in beaten egg instead of mustard, and then in rasped bread-crust. Fry them in hot fat for six minutes, and serve on a hot dish on a folded napkin, with half a pint of hot tomato sauce (No. 205), separately.

Lamb fries with Tartare sauce are prepared the same way, only serving with half a pint of Tartare sauce (No. 207), in a separate bowl.

674. Brochette of Lamb à la Dumas.—Take a raw leg of lamb weighing about three pounds; remove the bone and pare off the skin. Then cut into six square pieces of equal size. Put them in a vessel with two very finely chopped shallots, one teaspoonful of chopped chives, one teaspoonful of parsley, and a crushed clove of garlic. Add the juice of half a lemon, a tablespoonful of salt, a teaspoonful of pepper, and half a teaspoonful of nutmeg. Let them steep for about two hours, stirring at times; then take the pieces out, run a skewer through the centre of the six pieces, interlarding them with pieces of salt pork; dip them in bread-crumbs and broil for four minutes on each side. Serve with half a pint of hot Colbert sauce (No. 190), poured on the serving-dish, and place the brochettes over, arranging them nicely.

675. Ballotin of Lamb with Peas.—Bone a shoulder of spring lamb weighing about two and a half pounds. Let the end bone remain for a handle. Season with half a tablespoonful of salt, and the same quantity of pepper. Sew it up with a needle, fasten it firmly, and boil two or three minutes in the stock-pot. After letting it cool, lard the top with a larding needle as for a fricandeau, and place it in a saucepan with a piece of lard-skin, a carrot and an onion cut in slices. Brown slightly for six minutes; then moisten with a pint of broth (No. 99) and half a pint of Espagnole sauce (No. 157); cook in the oven forty-five minutes, take it out, and strain the sauce over a pint of hot, boiled, green peas (No. 978). Cook two minutes longer. Place the garnishing on a hot dish; remove the strings of the ballotin; lay it on the top of the garnishing, and serve.

676. Curry of Lamb, with Asparagus-tops.—Have three pounds of shoulder of lamb cut into pieces about two inches square. Wash well in fresh water, drain, put into a saucepan, and cover with fresh water. Let it come to a boil, then strain through a colander, and wash again in water. Place the pieces in a saucepan, covering them with boiling water; season with two tablespoonfuls of salt, one teaspoonful of pepper, six small onions, and a bouquet (No. 254). Put the lid on, and cook forty minutes. Then strain off the liquor into another saucepan containing half a pint of roux blanc (No. 135), stirring well until it boils, and then let it stand on the corner of the stove. Break into a separate bowl four egg yolks with the juice of half a lemon, beaten well together. Add this to the sauce, dropping it in little by little, and stirring continually. Pour all over the lamb, and add one pint of cooked asparagus-tops, but be careful not to let it boil again. Serve with a border of hot, boiled rice all around the dish.

677. Curry of Lamb à l'Indienne.—Proceed exactly as for No. 676, only adding three tablespoonfuls of curry diluted in half a cupful of water. Instead of the asparagus-tops, use a border of hot, cooked rice, carefully arranged around the dish. Lay the curry of lamb on top and serve.

678. Curry of Lamb à la Créole.—The same as for No. 676, adding, ten minutes before serving, one gill of tomatoes cut in pieces, and a green pepper cut into small pieces, serving with a border of hot, cooked rice around the dish.

679. Croquettes of Lamb à la Patti.—Prepare six lamb croquettes as for No. 276, adding half a pint of Patti garnishing (No. 245) laid on the dish, and arranging the croquettes on top. Pour over it a little meat-glaze (No. 141).

680. Croustades of Kidneys, with Mushrooms.—Prepare six croustades (No. 264), and fill them with kidneys sautés au Madère (No. 662).

681. Lamb Chops à la Signora.—Pare six fine lamb chops, and split them through the centre. Fill the insides with a very fine salpicon (No. 256); season with a pinch of salt and half a pinch of pepper. Close together, and dip in beaten egg, then in fresh bread-crumbs. Fry them for four minutes on each side in two ounces of clarified butter in a sautoire, and serve with a gill of hot Montglas sauce (No. 213) after arranging a curled paper at the end of each chop.

682. Lamb Chops à la Robinson.

—Pare six lamb chops, flatten nicely, and season with one pinch of salt and half a pinch of pepper. Place them in a sautoire with one ounce of butter, and fry for three minutes on each side. Serve with a pint of hot Robinson garnishing (No. 253) on the dish, and arrange the chops nicely over it, or any other garnishing desired.

683. Lamb Chops, Maison d'Or.—Pare neatly six lamb chops, make an incision in each one, and insert therein a slice of truffle. Season with a pinch of salt and half a pinch of pepper. Dip the chops in beaten egg and then in fresh bread-crumbs. Fry them in a sautoire with two ounces of clarified butter for four minutes on each side, and serve with six heart-shaped pieces of fried bread, each one covered with some pâté-de-foie-gras, and a gill of hot Madeira wine sauce (No. 185). Arrange a curled paper on the end of each chop.

684. Lamb Chops à la Clichy.—Pare nicely and flatten six lamb chops; season with one pinch of salt and half a pinch of pepper. Fry slightly in a sautoire with one ounce of butter for one minute on each side; then let them cool. Cover the surfaces with chicken forcemeat (No. 226), and wrap them in crepinette (a skin found in the stomach of the pig); dip in beaten egg, then in fresh bread-crumbs, and cook in a sautoire, with two ounces of butter for four minutes on each side. Arrange a nice paper curl at each end of the chops, and serve with half a pint of hot champagne sauce (No. 204) on the dish, and the chops over it.

685. Lamb Chops à la Maintenon.—Take six well-pared and flattened lamb chops. Season with a pinch of salt and half a pinch of pepper; put into a sautoire with one ounce of butter, and fry on one side only for one minute. Cover the cooked side with a mellow chicken croquette preparation (No. 276), also a little chicken forcemeat (No. 226) on top. Besprinkle with one very finely chopped truffle. Place the chops on a well-buttered baking-pan, and put them in a slow oven to cook for four minutes. Put a curled paper on the end of each chop, and serve with half a pint of hot, clear velouté (No. 152) on the dish, and the chops laid over it.

686. Lamb Chops à la Villeroi.—Pare neatly six chops, flatten them well, and season with a pinch of salt and half a pinch of pepper. Make an incision in each chop, and garnish the inside with a slice of truffle, previously dipped in demi-glace (No. 185); then dip the chops in beaten egg, roll them in fresh bread-crumbs, and put into a sautoire with two ounces of butter, and fry four minutes on each side. Pour half a pint of hot

Perigueux sauce (No. 191) on the dish, arrange the chops over, with curled paper on the ends, and serve.

687. Lamb Chops à la Masséna.—Trim neatly, flatten, and season with half a pinch each of salt and pepper, six lamb chops. Put them into a sautoire with one ounce of butter, and fry on one side only for one minute. Let them cool, and then fill the cooked centres with a little pâté-de-foie-gras. Take six pieces of fried bread the size of the chop, cut out the middles with a bread-cutter, fill in the space with pâté-de-foie-gras, and lay it on the cooked side of the chops. Garnish all around with chicken forcemeat à la crême (No. 225), forced through a paper cornet. Place them on a buttered baking-sheet, and put them into a slow oven. Cook for seven minutes. Prepare a pint of hot Madeira sauce (No. 185), pour it on a hot dish, arrange the chops nicely on top, with curled papers on the ends, and serve.

688. Minced Lamb à l'Anglaise.—Chop two onions fine, and fry in a saucepan with two ounces of butter for five minutes. Add two tablespoonfuls of flour, stirring well for two minutes. Moisten with a pint of broth (No. 99), and two tablespoonfuls of Parisian sauce, a bouquet (No. 254), and season with a tablespoonful of salt, a teaspoonful of pepper, and half a teaspoonful of nutmeg. Stir until it comes to a boil. Then cut two pounds of cooked lamb in small pieces, either from the shoulder or leg, mince finely, and add to the sauce. Cook twenty-five minutes, and serve with chopped parsley sprinkled over,

689. Epigrammes, of Lamb, Macédoine.—Take two breasts of lamb, tie them and put them on to boil in the soup-stock for forty-five minutes. Drain them well, then extract all the bones, and press down with a heavy weight on top. When thoroughly cold, cut each breast into three heart-shaped pieces, dip them in oil or fat, seasoning with a tablespoonful of salt and a teaspoonful of pepper. Roll in fresh bread-crumbs, and broil on a slow fire for four minutes on each side. Take six broiled, breaded lamb chops, prepared and cooked exactly the same, and serve with half a pint of hot Macédoine (No. 1032) or any other garnishing that may be required, arranging the breasts and chops over the garnishing.

690. Epigrammes of Lamb à la Chicorée.—Proceed exactly the same as for No. 689, only adding half a pint of hot chicory with a little gravy (No. 934), instead of the other garnishing, and serve the same.

691. Epigrammes of Lamb à la Louisiannaise.—The same as for No. 689, only serving with one pint of fried sweet potatoes (No. 993) around the dish, and a gill of hot Madeira wine sauce (No. 185).

692. Epigrammes of Lamb à la Soubise.—The same as for No. 689, serving with half a pint of hot Soubise (No. 250) and basting with a little meat-glaze (No. 141).

693. Shoulder of Lamb à l'Africaine.—Take a shoulder of lamb of about three pounds, season with one pinch of salt and one pinch of pepper, and tie it up well. Place in a saucepan with one sliced onion, and one sliced carrot, and brown for six minutes. Moisten with one pint of broth (No. 99), and a pint of Espagnole sauce (No. 151). Let cook for forty-five minutes. Skim all the fat from the gravy, and remove the shoulder to a hot dish and untie it. Garnish the dish with three stuffed egg-plants (No. 909), and half a pint of cooked gumbo (No. 1030). Strain the gravy over the shoulder, and serve.

694. Shoulder of Lamb, Purée Normande.—Proceed exactly the same as for No. 693, only substituting one pint of hot Normande (No. 175) for the other garnishing.

695. Shoulder of Lamb, with Stuffed Tomatoes.—The same as for No. 693, placing six stuffed tomatoes (No. 1023) around the dish before serving.

696. Shoulder of Lamb, Jardinière.—Proceed as directed in No. 693, only serving with one pint of hot Jardinière (No. 1033).

697. Shoulder of Lamb, Stuffed à la Macédoine.—Prepare a shoulder the same as for No. 693, but before tying it, fill the interior with American forcemeat (No. 229); let cook the same, and serve with one pint of hot Macédoine (No. 1032).

698. Shoulder of Lamb à la Rouennaise.—Braise a shoulder of lamb as for No. 693, cut three medium-sized turnips the shape of a large clove of garlic, and put them in a sautoire, with an ounce of butter, and a teaspoonful of powdered sugar on top. Place it in the oven, and leave it in until they become thoroughly brown, tossing the pan frequently to prevent burning. Pour the gravy from the meat over the turnips, dish up the shoulder, arrange the turnips around and serve.

699. Shoulder of Lamb à la Flamande.—The same as for No. 693, serving for garnishing half a pint of cooked carrots, half a pint of cooked turnips, and half a pint of cooked red cabbage, nicely arranged in clusters around the dish.

700. Hashed Lamb à la Polonaise.—Fry two chopped onions in a saucepan with an ounce of butter; add half a pound of cooked, hashed lamb to one pint of cooked, hashed potatoes (No. 1002). Season with a good tablespoonful of salt, a teaspoonful of pepper, and half a teaspoonful of nutmeg. Moisten with half a pint of broth, and cook for ten minutes. Place the hash on a hot dish, and arrange six poached eggs (No. 404) on top. Serve with chopped parsley sprinkled over.

701. Haricot or Ragout of Lamb à la Providence.—Take a fine breast or a shoulder of lamb weighing about three pounds, cut it into equal square pieces, and fry them in a saucepan with an ounce of butter or fat. Add six small, sound, peeled onions, and when browned, after about ten minutes, dredge in three tablespoonfuls of flour, stirring well for two minutes. Moisten with three pints of water or white broth; stir well, adding two pinches of salt, one pinch of pepper, two crushed cloves of sound garlic, and a bouquet (No. 254). Let cook for forty-five minutes. Two minutes after it begins to boil, thoroughly skim off the scum on the surface. Remove the bouquet and pour the ragout on a hot dish. Arrange half a pint of flageolets, plunged for half a minute into boiling water and well drained, or cooked lima beans, on one side of the dish, and the same quantity of cooked carrots, cut in quarters, on the other, and then serve.

702. Breast of Lamb, Jardinière.—Boil three medium-sized breasts of lamb for fifty minutes in the stock-pot, then the bones will be detached. Take them out, put the meat under a heavy weight, and let it thoroughly cool; then pare neatly. Cut each breast in two, and place on a dish. Season them with a good tablespoonful of salt, a teaspoonful of pepper, and immerse them in two tablespoonfuls of oil. Roll them in fresh bread-crumbs, and broil them for four minutes on each side. Serve them with one pint of hot Jardinière garnishing (No. 1033) on the dish, and the breasts nicely arranged over it.

703. Stewed Lamb and Oyster-plant.—As directed for ragout of lamb (No. 701); substituting for garnishing one bunch of thoroughly scraped and well-washed oyster-plant, cut into medium-sized pieces, and cooked with the stew.

704. Stewed Lamb à la Française.—The same as for No. 701; adding half a pint of carrots, half a pint of turnips, cooked with the lamb, and half an hour before serving putting in a pint of pared, small, whole, raw potatoes.

705. Stewed Lamb and Lima Beans.—Proceed as directed for No. 701, replacing the garnishing by one pint of cooked lima beans, added five minutes before serving.

706. Stewed Lamb, with Peas.—The same as for No. 701, only substituting for the garnishing one pint of green peas half an hour before the stew is ready or, if canned peas, five minutes before serving.

707. Stewed Lamb and Flageolets.—Proceed as directed for No. 701, only using instead of the garnishing a pint of well-soaked and drained flageolets, five minutes before serving.

708. Stewed Lamb à la Parisienne.—The same as for No. 701, using a garnishing of one pint of raw Parisian potatoes (No. 986) half an hour before serving.

709. Stewed Lamb and String Beans.—The same as for No. 701, only substituting for garnishing, one pint of pared and cleaned string-beans half an hour before serving.

710. Stewed Lamb Louisiannaise.—Proceed exactly as for No. 701, substituting for garnishing one pint of fried sweet potatoes, when serving, all around the dish.

711. Stewed Lamb à la Créole.—The same as for No. 701, adding for garnishing two cut-up tomatoes, one cut-up green pepper, and one chopped onion. Serve with a bouquet of cooked rice for a garnishing around the dish.

712. Lamb's Kidneys, Colbert Sauce.—Split open twelve kidneys, skin them well, and place on a dish with a tablespoonful of sweet oil. Season with a tablespoonful of salt, a teaspoonful of pepper, and half a teaspoonful of nutmeg. Take six silver skewers (if none on hand, use wooden ones), run each skewer through the centre of two kidneys (which should never become detached), roll them in fresh bread-crumbs, and put them to broil on a moderate fire for four minutes on each side. Place them on a very hot dish on which has been previously poured a pint of hot Colbert sauce (No. 190), and send to the table very hot.

713. Lamb's Kidneys, with Bacon.—Proceed as for No. 712, but do not roll them in bread-crumbs, and serve them with six slices of broiled bacon (No. 754) and a gill of maître d'hôtel butter (No. 145).

714. Stewed Kidneys With Cêpes.—Pare, trim, and skin well twelve kidneys. Cut them into slices, and cook for five minutes in a frying-pan with an ounce of clarified butter, a tablespoonful of salt, and a teaspoonful of pepper. Brown well; then add half a pint of Espagnole sauce (No. 151), also four cêpes cut into pieces. Warm without boiling, add the juice of half a lemon, and a teaspoonful of chopped parsley, and serve.

All stewed kidneys are prepared the same way, with any other garnishing required.

715. Lamb's Kidneys à la Diable.—Skin and pare well twelve kidneys, split them in two without separating the parts, and run the skewers through as for No. 712. Broil them slightly for one minute on each side. Mix together in a dish one teaspoonful of English mustard with two tablespoonfuls of Parisian sauce, the third of a teaspoonful of cayenne pepper, a teaspoonful of salt, and a like quantity of mignonette pepper. Roll the kidneys well in this, then in bread-crumbs, and finish by broiling them once more for three minutes on each side. Serve with a gill of maître d'hôtel butter (No. 145) poured over the kidneys.

716. Lamb Steak With Purée of Peas.—Cut and saw off six small steaks from a tender leg of lamb; pare and trim them nicely, flatten, and season with a good tablespoonful of salt sprinkled over, and a teaspoonful of pepper. Put a tablespoonful of sweet oil on a dish, roll the steaks well in it, then broil them for five minutes on each side. Place on a hot serving-dish half a pint of hot purée of peas (No. 49); arrange the steaks over, and serve.

The steaks can be served with any other garnishing required.

717. Lamb Steak, Sauce Piquante.—The same as for No. 716, serving for garnishing half a pint of hot piquante sauce (No. 203).

718. Lamb Steak à l'Américaine.—Proceed as for No. 716, and serve the lamb steaks with six small pieces of fried hominy (No. 1035), also one gill of hot Madeira sauce (No. 185) on the dish, and the steaks arranged over, with six slices of broiled bacon over them.

A pinch of salt represents 205 grains, or a tablespoonful.

Half a pinch of pepper represents 38 grains, or a teaspoonful.

A third of a pinch of nutmeg represents 13 grains, or half a teaspoonful.

PORK.

719. Black Sausage, Mashed Potatoes.—Take six black sausages (or blood pudding); make four light incisions on each side of them with a knife, then broil them for five minutes on each side. Neatly arrange a pint of mashed potatoes (No. 998) on a hot dish; nicely dress the sausages over, and serve. They also may be baked in a pan in the hot oven for ten minutes.

720. Suckling Pig, Apple Sauce.—Thoroughly clean the interior of a small, tender, suckling pig (reserving the liver); drain it well. Season the interior with two pinches of salt, one good pinch of pepper, and the third of a pinch of grated nutmeg. Chop up the liver very fine, and fry it in a saucepan, with half an ounce of butter, for five minutes. Stuff it with American forcemeat (No. 229), then sew up the aperture with a kitchen-needle. Have a roasting-pan ready, sprinkle into it half a cupful of cold water, then lay in the pig, so that it rests on its four legs. Completely cover all around with a buttered paper, then put it into a moderate oven, and let cook for two hours; baste it frequently, while cooking, with its own gravy. Remove it to a hot dish, untie, skim the fat from the gravy, and strain the lean part of it over the pig. Serve with a pint of hot apple sauce (No. 168) in a separate bowl.

721. Boiled Ham, plain.—Select a nice, small, lean ham of about seven pounds, and steep it in cold water during a whole night; take it out, lay it on a board or table, dry it thoroughly in a cloth, then put it in a saucepan and cover it with cold water. Let it boil for two hours, then remove it from its stock, lift off the upper skin, trim it neatly, and ornament artistically the large end bone with a pretty paper ruffle, then serve it with any kind of sauce required for garnishing.

722. Cold Boiled Ham, for family use.—Proceed the same as for No. 721, but let the ham be thoroughly cooled off before serving.

723. Roast Ham, Champagne Sauce.—Boil a ham exactly as directed for No. 721, making a few lengthwise incisions on the surface. Sprinkle the top with a little powdered sugar; arrange it in a roasting-pan, then place it in a slow oven for fifteen minutes. Serve with half a pint of champagne sauce (No. 204).

724. Roast Ham, with Corn à la Crême.

—The same as for No. 723, serving with it one pint of hot corn à la crême (No. 963).

725. Roast Ham, With Spinach.—Proceed as for No. 723, only serving with one pint of cooked hot spinach au jus (No. 943).

726. Pig's Cheek, With Spinach.—Take two lean, smoked pig's cheeks; let them soak in cold water over night, then drain them well, and put them in a saucepan, covering them with cold water. Let cook for one hour and three-quarters; then lay them on a dish, drain well again, and lift off the rind and skin which adheres to the tongue, then remove the bones, and place the cheeks on a hot serving-dish. Garnish with one pint of hot spinach au jus (No. 943); arrange the cheeks nicely on top, and serve.

727. Pig's Feet à la St. Hubert.—Split three good-sized, boiled pig's feet in two, place them on a deep dish, season with a pinch of salt, half a pinch of pepper, and one tablespoonful of oil. Roll them well together, and lay them in fresh bread-crumbs. Put them to broil for four minutes on each side, and then serve with half a pint of hot piquante sauce (No. 203), to which has been added a teaspoonful of diluted mustard. Pour the sauce on the dish, and arrange the feet nicely upon it.

728. Pig's Feet, Sauce Robert.—Exactly the same as for No. 727, serving with half a pint of hot Robert sauce (No. 192).

729. Pig's Feet, Sauce Piquante.—The same as for No. 727, serving with half a pint of hot piquante sauce (No. 203), omitting the mustard.

730. Pig's Feet, New York Style.—The same as for No. 727, serving them on six pieces of toast, with a gill of maître d'hôtel butter (No. 145) over the feet.

Boston Style.—Dip them in frying batter, then fry in a pan with two ounces of butter on a moderate fire for ten minutes. Dress them on a hot dish with a folded napkin, and serve with any sauce desired separately.

731. Pig's Feet à la Poulette.—Put three boiled pig's feet, cut in two, into a saucepan with half an ounce of butter, let simmer for five minutes, add a pint of poulette sauce (No. 598); heat without boiling for five minutes, then serve with a little chopped parsley sprinkled over.

732. Stuffed Pig's Feet à la Périgueux.—To one and a half pounds of boned turkey forcemeat (No. 813) add two minced truffles and half a glassful of Madeira wine; mix well together in a bowl. Spread six pieces of crépinette (a skin found in the stomach of the pig), the size of the hand, on the table. Lay on each one a piece of forcemeat the size of an egg; spread it well, and lay one-half of a boned pig's foot on top (No. 734). Cover with another light layer of forcemeat, and finish each with three thin slices of truffles. Cover the crépinettes so that they get the form of envelopes; fold them up, and dip one after the other in beaten egg, then in fresh bread-crumbs, and cook in a sautoire with two ounces of clarified butter. Place a heavy weight on top of the feet, let cook on a slow fire for twelve minutes on each side, and serve with half a pint of hot Périgueux sauce (No. 191) on the dish, and the pig's feet on top.

733. Stuffed Pig's Feet, Madeira Sauce.—Exactly the same as for the above, only serving with half a pint of hot Madeira sauce (No. 185) in place of the other.

734. Boned Pig's Feet.—Take three boiled feet, cut them in two, put them into boiling water for four minutes, then take them out. Drain well, bone them, then put the flesh into a dry, clean cloth, and wipe them thoroughly.

735. Sausages, with White Wine.—Brown a very finely chopped onion in a sautoire with one ounce of butter. Moisten with half a glassful of white wine, and add two country sausages; prick them slightly with a fork, then cover the pan, and let cook for five minutes. Put in half a pint of Espagnole sauce (No. 151), cook again for five minutes, and serve with a little chopped parsley sprinkled over.

736. Sausages à l'Anglaise.—Place twelve country sausages on a baking-tin; prick them a little, and separate them by twelve slices of bread cut the same height as the sausages. Bake in the oven for twelve minutes, baste them occasionally with their own juice, and serve with half a pint of hot Madeira sauce (No. 185) in a separate bowl.

737. Sausages à l'Italienne.—The same as for No. 735, adding six minced mushrooms to the sauce five minutes before serving.

738. Sausages à la Bourguignonne.—Take twelve country sausages, prick them with a fork, and place them in a baking-dish. Put them in the oven, and let cook for ten minutes; garnish a hot dish with a pint of hot purée of red beans (No. 951); and arrange the sausages on top, then serve.

739. Sausages, with Cabbage.—Procure a medium-sized white cabbage; remove all the green leaves, and cut it into four square parts, suppressing the centre stalks. Wash thoroughly in cold water, then drain well in a cloth; when finished cut them into small pieces, and put them into boiling, salted water for five minutes. Remove into cold water to let it cool off moderately;

take it out, drain in a colander, and put the cabbage into a saucepan with a gill of fat from the soup-stock, or an ounce of butter. Season with a good pinch of salt and half a pinch of pepper, also a whole medium-sized onion, and a carrot cut into four pieces. Put on the lid of the saucepan, remove to a moderate fire, and let cook for thirty minutes. Take twelve country sausages, prick them with a fork, add them to the cabbage, and let all cook together for twelve minutes. Dress the cabbage on a hot dish, and decorate with the sausages and carrots on top. Serve very hot.

740. Sausages au Gastronome.—Prick twelve nice, lean sausages with a fork; put them in a tin baking-dish, and cook them for six minutes in the oven. Add two raw eggs to a pint and a half of mashed potatoes, with three tablespoonfuls of grated Parmesan or Swiss cheese, mix well together, and lay it on a baking-dish. Place the sausages on top, put it in the oven, and let cook for six minutes. When finished take them out, and serve on a dish with half a gill of demi-glace (No. 185) thrown over.

741. Pork Tenderloin.—Procure three good-sized pork tenderloins, pare them neatly, remove the sinews, and cut each fillet lengthwise in two without detaching; place in a sautoire with a tablespoonful of butter. Season them one hour before cooking with two pinches of salt and one pinch of pepper, and let them cook on the stove for six minutes on each side. Arrange them on a hot serving-dish, and skim the fat from the surface of the gravy. Add to the lean part half a cupful of broth (No. 99), letting it come to a boil, and mixing well with a spoon. Strain the gravy over the fillets, and serve. Any sauce or garnishing desired may be added to the tenderloins.

742. Pork Andouillettes.—Procure one and a half pounds of andouillettes; cut them into six pieces, and make four slight incisions on each side. Place them in a tin baking-dish, and put them in the oven to cook for eight minutes. Remove them to a hot serving-dish, previously placing thereon a pint of mashed potatoes, or a pint of hot purée of peas, and place the andouillettes, nicely arranged, on top.

743. Pork Chops, Plain.—Take six thick pork chops, pare and flatten them nicely, then season with a pinch of salt and a pinch of pepper one hour before using them. Put them in a sautoire with one ounce of butter, and let cook on the stove for six minutes on each side. Arrange the chops on a hot dish, skim off the fat from the gravy, and add half a cupful of broth to the lean part. Let come to a boil, strain over the chops, and serve.

744. Pork Chops, Broiled.

—These are to be prepared exactly the same as for No. 743, only to the seasoning add one tablespoonful of sweet oil, and roll in the chops well. Put them to broil for six minutes on each side, then arrange them on a hot dish, and serve with a gill of hot maître d'hôtel butter (No. 145), well spread over the chops.

745. Pork Chops, Piquante Sauce.—Proceed exactly as for No. 743, serving with half a pint of hot piquante sauce over the chops (No. 203).

746. Pork Chops, Sauce Robert.—Same as for No. 743, sending them to the table with half a pint of hot Robert sauce (No. 192) poured over the chops.

747. Pork Chops à la Diable.—The same as for No. 743, but serving with half a pint of sauce à la Diable (No. 198) over the chops.

748. Pork Chops, Apple Sauce.—Proceed as for No. 743, serving with one pint of hot apple sauce (No. 168) in a separate bowl.

749. Pork Chops à la Purée de Pois.—The same as for No. 743, pouring half a pint of hot purée of peas on the dish, and placing the chops over.

750. Pork Chops with Purée of Potatoes.—Exactly the same as for No. 743, serving with a pint of purée of hot potatoes (No. 998) on the dish, and the chops nicely arranged over.

751. Roasted Fresh Pork.—Take three pounds of fresh loin of pork; season two hours before needed with two good pinches of salt and one good pinch of pepper, well distributed. Put it into a roasting-pan with half a cupful of water, place it in the oven, and let roast for fully one and a half hours, being careful to baste it frequently with its own gravy. Remove it to a hot dish, skim the fat from the gravy, strain the lean part over the roast, and serve.

752. Pork and Beans.—Take a pint of white dry beans, soak them in fresh water for six hours, then drain through a colander. Place them in a saucepan, or preferably an earthen dish; season with one small pinch of salt, half a pinch of pepper, one tablespoonful of either syrup or brown sugar, and one medium-sized carrot cut in two. Take a pound and a half of freshened salt pork (previously well-washed in fresh water), make four incisions on each side, and place it in the vessel with the beans; cover with the lid, and let cook all together, either on the stove or in the oven, for two hours and a half. If it should get too dry, moisten with a little broth. It will now be ready to serve. Place the garnishing on a hot dish, and arrange the pork on top; the whole can be returned again to the oven with a little powdered sugar sprinkled over the top, leaving it in five minutes to give it a golden color; then serve.

753. How to Prepare Ham for Broiling and Frying.—Procure a fine, sound, smoked ham, weighing about twelve to thirteen pounds, selecting it as lean as possible. With a sharp knife, begin cutting it carefully at the end of the shank bone, between the bone and the string used for hanging purposes, coming down on to the knuckle; follow the edge of the bone, until the small edge-bone is fully reached, then make a straight cross-cut from the bone, so as to separate it entirely. When this is accomplished, put the bone part aside for soup, garnishing, scrambled eggs, sauces, or any other needful purposes. Keep the ham hung up in a dry place in a moderate temperature.

For broiling and frying.—Cut from the boneless part the necessary number of slices desired to be used each time, as thin as possible, always beginning from the side of the edge-bone. Pare off the skin neatly from the slices, and arrange them on the broiler, then broil them for two minutes on each side; take from off the fire, dress them on a hot dish, and send to the table.

By preparing the ham as described in the above, it will always be crisp and enjoyable. When frying, four minutes will be sufficient in very hot fat.

754. How to Prepare English Breakfast Bacon.—Procure a fine, fresh English breakfast bacon, and with a keen knife cut the under bones off; pare both edges neatly, also the end (the opposite side to the string which hangs it up). With the use of the same sharp knife, cut the necessary number of slices desired for immediate use, and no more. Thin slices are always preferable, so that the bacon, whether broiled or fried, will be crispy and tasty. When cutting off the slices be careful to avoid detaching them from the skin, also cut them crosswise, but never lengthwise. Arrange the slices on the broiler, and broil on a moderate fire for two minutes on each side; dress the crispy slices on a hot dish, and serve immediately.

Four minutes will suffice for frying. See that the bacon is kept hanging by the string in a dry, cool place, but never put it on the ice.

A pinch of salt represents 205 grains, or a tablespoonful.

Half a pinch of pepper represents 38 grains, or a teaspoonful.

A third of a pinch of nutmeg represents 13 grains, or half a teaspoonful.

755. Chicken Roasted, Plain.—Singe, draw, wipe nicely, and truss a fine large chicken weighing three pounds. Cover it with a thin slice of salt fat pork, and place it in a roasting-pan with two tablespoonfuls of broth. Spread a very little butter over the breast, sprinkle on half a pinch of salt, and put it in the oven to cook for fifty minutes. Baste it frequently, and arrange it on a hot dish, untie, and decorate with a little watercress. Strain the gravy into a sauce-bowl, and send it to the table.

756. Chicken Broiled With Bacon.—Procure two very fine, tender, spring chickens, singe, draw, wipe neatly, and cut the heads off, then split them without separating. Place them on a dish, season with one pinch of salt, half a pinch of pepper, and one tablespoonful of sweet oil; turn them well in the seasoning. Put them to broil for nine minutes on each side. Prepare six small toasts on a hot dish, arrange the two broiled chickens over, spread half a gill of maître d'hôtel butter on top (No. 145), and decorate with six thin slices of broiled bacon (No. 754); then serve.

757. Chicken Pot-pie.—Take one fine Philadelphia chicken, from three and a half to four pounds, singe, draw, wipe well, and cut it into twelve even pieces. Put these in a saucepan, and cover them with cold water; leave them in for thirty minutes, then wash well, drain, and return them to the saucepan. Cover again with fresh water, season with two pinches of salt, one pinch of pepper, and a third of a pinch of nutmeg; add a bouquet (No. 254), six small onions, and four ounces of salt pork cut into square pieces. Cook for three-quarters of an hour, taking care to skim well, then add one pint of raw potatoes, Parisiennes (No. 986), and three tablespoonfuls of flour diluted with a cupful of cold water. Stir until it boils, then let cook for ten minutes. Remove the bouquet and transfer the whole to a deep earthen baking-dish; moisten the edges slightly with water, and cover the top with a good pie-crust (No. 1078). Egg the surface; make a few transverse lines on the paste with a fork, and cut a hole in the centre. Bake it in a brisk oven for fifteen minutes, then send to the table.

758. Chicken Croquettes à la Reine.—Make a croquette preparation as for No. 276, with chicken and mushrooms; roll it into six cork-shaped croquettes, dip each one separately in beaten egg, then in fresh or rasped bread-crumbs, fry them in very hot fat for four minutes, then drain them thoroughly, and place them on a hot dish over a folded napkin. Serve with half a pint of hot sauce à la Reine (No. 623) separately.

759. Chicken Croquettes à la Périgueux.—The same as for No. 758, serving with half a pint of hot Périgueux sauce (No. 191) separately.

760. Chicken Croquettes à l'Ecarlate.—Exactly the same as for No. 758, serving with half a pint of hot sauce Ecarlate (No. 247) separately.

761. Chicken Croquettes à la Périgourdin.—Prepare some forcemeat as for croquettes (No. 276), composed of chicken, mushrooms, two truffles cut into small square pieces, and bits of cooked smoked tongue, about one ounce. Fry them for four minutes, then serve the six croquettes with half a pint of hot Madeira sauce (No. 185). Add to it one chopped truffle and six chopped mushrooms; let cook five minutes, and serve in a separate bowl.

762. Croustade of Chicken à la Dreux.—Make six croustades (No. 264), each one four inches and a half long by three inches in diameter. Take three-quarters of a pound of white, boned, cooked chicken meat, cut in half-inch pieces; add to them half a pint of Duxelle sauce (No. 189), half a glassful of Madeira wine, and let cook together for four minutes. Fill the six croustades with this, arrange them nicely on a hot dish over a folded napkin, and serve.

763. Croustade of Chicken Livers, au Madère.—Prepare six croustades as for No. 762, fill them with chicken livers stewed in Madeira wine sauce (No. 767).

764. Cromesquis of Chicken à la Richelieu.—Make six cromesquis as for No. 268, and serve on a hot dish with a folded napkin, decorating with a little parsley-greens, and serving a pint of hot Richelieu sauce (No. 574) separately.

765. Cromesquis of Chicken à la Reine.—Exactly the same as for No. 764, serving with half a pint of hot sauce à la Reine (No. 623) separately, and garnishing the dish with parsley-greens.

766. Chicken Legs à la Diable.—Detach the legs from three medium-sized chickens; singe them slightly with a little alcohol lighted on a plate, then put them into the soup-pot and let boil for ten minutes. Remove them to a dish, cool them off thoroughly, then season with a good pinch of salt, half a pinch of pepper, and a very little cayenne pepper; add also two tablespoonfuls of Parisian sauce and half a teaspoonful of ground English mustard. Now roll them well together, and pass one after another into fresh bread-crumbs; put them to broil on a moderate fire for four minutes on each side, then arrange them on a hot serving-dish. Pour over one gill of hot sauce à la Diable (No. 198), sprinkle a little chopped parsley on top, and serve very hot. The legs can be served with any sauce or garnishing required.

Turkeys' legs are prepared exactly the same way, only they should be broiled six minutes on each side instead of four, and served with any desired sauce or garnishing.

767. Chicken Livers Stewed in Madeira Wine.—Cut away the gall from a pint of chicken livers, dry them well with a cloth, then fry them in a sautoire with one ounce of butter, on a brisk fire, for five minutes. Season with a pinch of salt, and half a pinch of pepper, add half a glass of Madeira wine, reduce for one minute, then moisten slightly with about half a pint of Espagnole sauce (No. 151). Cook again for three minutes, then add half an ounce of good butter, and the juice of half a lemon, tossing well without letting it boil; pour the whole on a hot serving-dish, and serve with six heart-shaped croûtons (No. 133).

768. Chicken Livers With Mushrooms.—Proceed the same as for No. 767, only adding six minced mushrooms three minutes before serving.

769. Chicken Livers en Brochette with Bacon.—Procure eighteen fresh chicken livers; cut away the gall, dry them well with a clean cloth, season with half a pinch each of salt and pepper, and cut each liver in two. Now prepare six slices of lean bacon (No. 754), broil them for one minute, then cut each slice into six pieces. Take six silver skewers, run a skewer through the centre of the liver, the same with a piece of bacon, and continue the same process until the six skewers are each one filled with a piece of liver and a piece of bacon. Roll them on a dish with one tablespoonful of good oil, dip them in fresh bread-crumbs, and put them on a moderate fire to broil for five minutes on each side. Arrange them on a hot dish, pour half a gill of maître d'hôtel butter (No. 145) over, and serve with a little watercress around the dish.

770. Chicken Livers Sautés à l'Italienne.—Proceed exactly as for No. 767, only adding half a gill of cooked fine herbs (No. 143) five minutes before serving.

771. Chicken Sauté à la Marengo.—Singe, draw, and cut into six pieces two small, tender chickens, each weighing a pound and a quarter. Lay them in an oiled sautoire, and brown slightly on both sides for five minutes, seasoning with a good pinch of salt and half a pinch of pepper; when a golden color, moisten with half a pint of Espagnole (No. 151), and half a cupful of mushroom liquor. Add twelve mushroom-buttons, and two truffles cut in thin slices, also half a glassful of Madeira wine. Let cook for twenty minutes, then serve with six fried eggs, as in No. 413, and six heart-shaped croûtons (No. 133). Adjust paper ruffles on the ends of the wings and legs of the chickens, and dress them nicely on the dish, decorating the borders with the fried eggs and sippets of bread, then serve.

772. Chicken Sauté à l'Hongroise.—Singe, draw, and cut into twelve pieces, two chickens of a pound and a quarter each; put them in a sautoire with an ounce of clarified butter, adding one finely chopped onion, half a pinch of salt, and half a pinch of pepper. Let cook slowly, without browning, for five minutes on each side, then moisten with half a pint of béchamel (No. 154), and half a cupful of cream. Let cook again for twenty minutes, skim the fat off, and serve with six pieces of fried bread croûtons (No. 133) around the dish.

773. Chicken Sauté à la Parmentier.—Singe, draw, and cut two chickens of a pound and a quarter each into twelve pieces; put them in a sautoire with one ounce of butter, season with a pinch of salt and half a pinch of pepper, and let cook on the stove for five minutes on each side, turning the pieces over with a fork. Moisten with half a pint of Espagnole sauce (No. 151), half a cupful of mushroom liquor, and add the juice of half a lemon. Let cook again for twenty minutes, then dress on a hot serving-dish, and decorate it with half a pint of potatoes château (No. 1009) in clusters.

774. Chicken Sauté with Tarragon.—Have two nice, tender young chickens of a pound and a quarter each; singe, draw, and cut each one into six pieces, and when well dried put them in a sautoire with one ounce of butter; season with a pinch of salt, and half a pinch of pepper, and let cook on a brisk stove for five minutes on each side. Moisten with half a pint of Espagnole sauce (No. 151), half a cupful of mushroom liquor, and half a glassful of sherry wine, and add a quarter of a bunch of well-washed, green tarragon-leaves. Let cook for twenty minutes, then dress nicely on a hot serving-dish, and decorate with six heart-shaped croûtons (No. 133).

775. Chicken Sauté à la Chasseur.—Prepare two chickens exactly as for the above (No. 774), moistening with half a pint of Espagnole sauce (No. 151), and half a cupful of mushroom liquor; add six finely minced mushrooms, half a glassful of sherry or Madeira wine, the zest of half a sound lemon, and one chopped shallot. Let cook for twenty minutes, and serve with six pieces of fried bread, cut heart-shaped, croûtons (No. 133).

776. Chicken Sauté à la Bordelaise.—Singe, draw, and cut up two chickens, each weighing a pound and a quarter, into twelve pieces; put them in a sautoire with two tablespoonfuls of oil and one chopped shallot. Let brown well for five minutes, then moisten with half a glassful of white wine, adding three artichoke-bottoms, each one cut into four pieces. Season with a pinch of salt, and half a pinch of pepper, then put the lid on and let simmer slowly for fifteen minutes; when ready to serve, add a little meat-glaze, a teaspoonful (No. 141), the juice of half a lemon, and a teaspoonful of chopped parsley. Dish up the pieces, crown-shaped, with paper ruffles nicely arranged, and garnish with the artichoke-bottoms in clusters, and twelve cooked potatoes château (No. 1009).

777. Chicken Sauté à la Régence.—Singe, draw, and dry well two tender chickens of a pound and a quarter each; cut them into twelve pieces, and put them in a sautoire with one ounce of butter. Season with a good pinch of salt and half a pinch of pepper, add half a glassful of Madeira wine, reduce for one minute, then put the lid on, and let simmer for six minutes. Moisten with half a pint of velouté (No. 152), and half a cupful of mushroom liquor. Let cook for ten minutes, then put in two truffles cut into small pieces, six mushrooms, a small sweetbread, and one ounce of cooked, smoked beef-tongue, all finely chopped. Finish cooking for ten minutes longer, then take from off the fire and incorporate therein two raw egg yolks diluted in the juice of half a lemon; while adding the egg yolks gently shuffle the pan, thicken well the sauce, then serve with paper ruffles neatly arranged at the ends of the wings and legs of the chickens.

778. Chicken Sauté à la Bohémienne.—Prepare two chickens as for the above (No. 777); put them in a sautoire with one ounce of butter, seasoning with a good pinch of salt and half a pinch of pepper. Cook on a brisk fire for six minutes, turning the pieces of chicken frequently with a fork; moisten with half a wine-glassful of Madeira wine, reduce for one minute, then add half a pint of Espagnole sauce (No. 151). Cook for ten minutes; add half a pint of cooked macaroni cut in small pieces. Cook again for ten minutes. Nicely arrange the chicken on a hot dish, pour the gravy over, and fill six bouchées (No. 270) with the macaroni taken from the stew, also a little grated Parmesan cheese sprinkled over. Garnish the dish all around with the bouchées, adjust paper ruffles at the end of the chicken legs, and serve hot.

779. Chicken Boiled à la Providence.—Singe, draw, and wipe well two chickens of a pound and a quarter each; truss them from the wing to the leg with a needle, and boil them in good broth for three-quarters of an hour. Prepare a pint of Allemande sauce (No. 210) with the broth of the chickens, adding a gill of small cuts of boiled carrots, the same of cooked Lima beans or flageolets, and let all cook together for three minutes. Dish up the chickens, untruss them, and pour the sauce over, arranging the vegetables on each side. Serve with chopped parsley strewn over.

780. Chicken Fricassé à la Reine.—Cut up two fine, tender, raw chickens into twelve even pieces. Place them in a large sautoire, with one quart of cold water, on a brisk fire; as soon as it comes to a boil, thoroughly skim. Season with one and a half pinches of salt, half a pinch of pepper, two cloves, and one bay-leaf, also a light bouquet (No. 254). Let boil slowly for twenty-five minutes. Place in another saucepan one and a half ounces of butter, which you melt on the hot range, add to it three tablespoonfuls of flour, thoroughly mix with a wooden spoon, while slowly cooking without browning, as the above, under no circumstances, should be allowed to get brown. Strain the broth into a bowl through a sieve. Return the pieces of chicken to the sautoire (but only the chicken), leaving it at the oven door till further action. Now add, little by little, the broth to the flour, being careful to stir continually until all added. Let boil for two minutes. Have three egg yolks in a bowl with a tablespoonful of good butter, half a gill of cold milk, and just a little cayenne pepper—*no more than a third of a saltspoonful*—squeezing in also the juice of half a medium-sized sound lemon. Mix all well together; and then add it to the sauce; stirring continually till all added. Heat up well, but do not allow to boil. Strain it through a sieve over the chicken. Mix well together, adding two truffles, and four mushrooms cut into small dice-shaped pieces. Dress the whole on a hot dish, arrange paper ruffles at the end of the legs, and serve with heart-shaped croûtons (No. 133) around the dish.

781. Chicken Fricassé à l'Américaine.—Boil two chickens as for No. 779; cut them into twelve pieces, and put them into a sautoire with eight minced mushrooms, an ounce of cooked salt pork cut into small squares, and half a pint of Allemande sauce (No. 210). Warm thoroughly without boiling, and serve with six heart-shaped pieces of fried bread (No. 133).

782. Pillau of Chicken à la Turque.—Take a fine tender chicken weighing two pounds, singe, draw, and wipe it well, then cut it into twelve even pieces. Brown them in a stewpan with an ounce of butter, one chopped onion, and one chopped green pepper. Let cook for six minutes, stirring lightly with a wooden spoon, then moisten with a pint of good broth (No. 99), and a gill of tomato sauce (No. 205). Add two ounces of dried mushrooms which have been soaking in water for several hours, or twelve canned mushrooms; season with a good pinch of salt, half a pinch of pepper, and half a teaspoonful of diluted saffron. Now add half a pint of well-washed, raw rice (if using Italian rice, only pick it) and three tablespoonfuls of grated Parmesan cheese; cook for twenty minutes longer, dress neatly on a hot dish, and serve.

783. Chicken Pillau à la Créole.—Exactly the same as for No. 782, adding three medium-sized, cut-up, fresh tomatoes, or half a pint of canned tomatoes with the other garnishings.

784. Chicken with Rice.—Singe, draw, and wipe well, a tender fowl of three pounds; truss it from the wing to the leg, then put it into a saucepan covering it with water; add two pinches of salt, half a pinch of pepper, one carrot cut into four pieces, one whole onion stuck with three cloves, and a bouquet (No. 254). Cook for about twenty-five minutes, or until half done, then add half a pint of well-picked, raw rice; cook again for twenty minutes, and when finished, dish up the chicken, suppressing the bouquet, onion, and carrot; arrange the rice nicely around it, and serve.

785. Chicken à la Maryland.—Procure two small, tender spring chickens, leave the half of one aside for other use, and detach the legs and the wings; lay them on a plate, season with a good pinch of salt and half a pinch of pepper, then dip them in beaten egg, and afterward roll them in fresh bread-crumbs. Place them in a buttered pan, pour an ounce of clarified butter over, and roast in the oven for eighteen minutes. Pour half a pint of cream sauce. (No. 181) onto a hot serving-dish, arrange the chicken nicely on top, and decorate with six thin slices of broiled bacon (No. 754), also six small corn-fritters (No. 965). Serve as hot as possible.

786. Suprême of Chicken à la Toulouse.—Singe, draw, and wipe neatly three fine, tender spring chickens. Remove the skin from the breasts. Make an incision on top of the breast-bone from end to end, then with a small sharp knife, carefully cut off the entire breast on each side, including the small wing-bone, which should not be separated from the breast, and seeing that the entire breasts are cleverly cut away, without a particle of it on the carcasses.

Under each breast will be found a small fillet, which you carefully remove, and place on a dish for further action. With a small sharp knife make an incision in each breast—at their thinner side—three inches in length by one inch in depth. Season the inside of each breast with a pinch of salt and half a pinch of pepper, equally divided. Stuff the breasts with two ounces of chicken forcemeat (No. 226), mixed with two fine, sound truffles finely sliced, and four mushrooms, also finely sliced. Butter well *a well-tinned* copper sautoire. Gently lay in the six breasts; then take each small fillet, press gently with the fingers, and give each a boatlike shape. Make six slanting, small incisions on top of each, insert in each incision a small slice of truffle, cut with a tube half an inch in diameter. Slightly wet the top of each breast with water; carefully arrange one fillet on top of each breast lengthwise. Sprinkle a little clarified butter over all with a feather brush. Pour into the pan, *but not over the suprême,* a quarter of a glassful of Madeira wine and two tablespoonfuls of mushroom liquor; tightly cover the pan with the lid, then place in the hot oven for ten minutes. Pour on a hot serving-dish one pint of hot Toulouse garnishing (No. 176). Remove the suprêmes from the oven, neatly dress them over the garnishing, adjust paper ruffles on each wing-bone, and immediately send to the table.

787. Suprême of Chicken à la Bayard.—Proceed as for No. 786, only serving with one pint of garnishing Bayard (No. 231).

788. Suprême of Chicken à la Reine.—Exactly the same as for No. 786, only substituting one pint of hot sauce à la reine (No. 780) for the other garnishing.

789. Suprême of Chicken à la Patti.—Prepare the suprême the same as for No. 786, then have a purée of rice with cream à la Patti (No. 245), garnish the dish with this, and lay the suprême on top. Decorate the rice with two thinly sliced truffles, pour a gill of good sauce Périgueux (No. 191) over, and serve with paper ruffles.

790. Suprême of Chicken à la Rothschild.—Have six chicken suprêmes prepared exactly the same as in No. 786, but stuffing them with purée of chestnuts instead of the chicken forcemeat. Mince very fine two sound truffles, then mix them with a pint of hot purée of chestnuts (No. 131); then arrange the purée on a hot dish, place six round-shaped croûtons (No. 133), instead of heart-shaped, nicely dress the suprêmes over the croûtons, decorate the top of each suprême, *right in the centre,* with one mushroom-head.

791. Turban of Chicken à la Cleveland.—Select two very tender chickens, singe, draw, and wipe them well; bone them and cut them into quarters, then put them into a sautoire with one ounce of butter, a good pinch of salt and half a pinch of pepper; add half a glassful of Madeira wine, and let parboil very slowly for ten minutes. Take half a pint of chicken forcemeat (No. 226), add to it one chopped truffle, three chopped mushrooms, and half an ounce of cooked minced tongue. Stir well together; put this forcemeat on a silver dish, lay the pieces of chicken on top, crown-shaped, and decorate with twelve whole mushrooms and two thinly sliced truffles. To the gravy in which the chickens were cooked add half a pint of Espagnole sauce (No. 151), a teaspoonful of chopped chives, and a small pat of fresh butter. Pour this immediately over the chickens, put the dish in the oven, and let cook very slowly for ten minutes. Squeeze the juice of half a lemon over, and serve with six heart-shaped pieces of fried bread (No. 133).

792. Chicken Curry à l'Indienne.—Take a good, tender three-pound chicken, singe, draw neatly, and cut it into square pieces. Put them in cold water for five minutes, wash them well, then drain, and put them in a saucepan, covering it to the surface with hot water; season with two good pinches of salt, one pinch of pepper, and the third of a pinch of nutmeg. Add a bouquet (No. 254), and six small onions; let cook on a moderate stove for forty-five minutes, skimming it well. Take another saucepan, in it place one and a half gills of white roux (No. 135), moisten it with all of the broth from the chicken, and mix well together. Prepare a tablespoonful of diluted curry with four egg yolks, and the juice of half a lemon, beat all this well together, pour it into the sauce a little at a time, stirring continually and not allowing it to boil. Pour the sauce over the chicken, which remains in the saucepan, and dress immediately on a hot dish, decorated with boiled rice all around as a border, and serve.

793. Chicken Curry à l'Espagnole.—The same as for No. 792, adding two cut-up tomatoes and one green pepper, cooking them ten minutes with the chicken.

794. Chicken Curry à la Créole.—The same as for No. 792, adding one green pepper cut very fine, also one chopped onion, and half a clove of garlic, cooking them twenty minutes with the chicken.

795. Boiled Turkey à l'Anglaise.—Take a very fine, tender turkey of about five pounds, singe, draw, and truss well with a needle from the wing to the leg. Put it into the soup-pot, and let cook for one hour; remove to a hot serving-dish. Decorate the dish with a pint of cooked Spinach à l'Anglaise (No. 940), and six slices of hot, cooked, lean ham. Serve with half a cupful of hot broth poured over the turkey so as to keep it moist.

796. Boiled Turkey, Celery Sauce.—Exactly the same as for No. 795, substituting for garnishing one pint of hot celery sauce (No. 200), served separately.

797. Boiled Turkey, Oyster Sauce.—Proceed as for No. 795, serving with one pint of hot oyster sauce (No. 173), separately.

798. Boiled Turkey, Egg Sauce.—The same as for No. 795, serving with one pint of hot egg sauce (No. 161), separately.

799. Boiled Turkey à la Baltimore.—Serve a boiled turkey as for No. 795, garnishing it with half a head of cooked and hot cauliflower, one good-sized cooked carrot, cut in slices, and six cooked small onions, all neatly arranged around the dish, with half a pint of hot Allemande sauce (No. 210), served separately.

800. Roast Turkey, Stuffed with Chestnuts.—Singe, draw, wash well, and neatly dry a fine, tender turkey, weighing five to six pounds; fill the inside with the chestnut stuffing described below, then nicely truss the turkey from the wing to the leg; season with a heavy pinch of salt, well sprinkled over. Cover the breast with thin slices of larding pork. Put it to roast in a roasting-pan in a moderate oven for one hour and a half, basting it occasionally with its own gravy. Take from out the oven, untruss, dress it on a hot dish, skim the fat off the gravy, add a gill of broth (No. 99) or consommé (No. 100) to the gravy, let it just come to a boil, strain into a bowl, and send to the table separately.

Plain roast turkey is prepared the same, suppressing the stuffing, and roasting it only one hour and fifteen minutes.

Chestnut Stuffing.—Peel a good-sized, sound shallot, chop it up very fine, place in a saucepan on the hot range with one tablespoonful of butter, and let heat for three minutes without browning, then add a quarter of a pound of sausage meat. Cook five minutes longer, then add ten finely chopped mushrooms, twelve well-pounded, cooked, peeled chestnuts; mix all well together. Season with one pinch of salt, half a pinch of pepper, half a saltspoonful of powdered thyme, and a teaspoonful of finely chopped parsley. Let just come to a boil, then add half an ounce of fresh bread-crumbs, and twenty-four whole cooked and shelled French chestnuts; mix all well together, being careful not to break the chestnuts. Let cool off, and then stuff the turkey with it.

801. Hashed Turkey à la Royale.—Take a pound and a half of dice-shaped pieces of cooked turkey; place them in a saucepan with a pint of béchamel (No. 154), three tablespoonfuls of mushroom liquor, and two truffles cut in square pieces. Season with one pinch of salt, half a pinch of pepper, and the third of a pinch of nutmeg. Let all heat together for ten minutes, then serve with six heart-shaped pieces of bread (No. 133), lightly covered with pâté-de-foie-gras neatly arranged around the dish.

802. Hashed Turkey à la Béchamel.—The same as for No. 801, omitting the truffle and bread croûtons, and serving with chopped parsley strewn over.

803. Hashed Turkey à la Polonaise.—The same as for No. 801, only serving with six poached eggs (No. 404), and six heart-shaped croûtons (No. 133), instead of the truffles and pâté-de-foie-gras.

804. Hashed Turkey à la Crême.—Exactly the same as for No. 801, substituting one pint of cold, fresh cream, and a tablespoonful of fresh butter for the béchamel, also omitting the truffles and pâté-de-foie-gras; reducing the cream with the hash to one half, which will take from four to five minutes. Pour on a hot dish and serve.

805. Hashed Turkey en Bordure.—Decorate the border of a baking-dish with a potato croquette preparation (No. 997), place it in the oven for six minutes, then fill the centre with hashed turkey à la béchamel (No. 802), and put it in the oven again for five minutes before serving.

806. Turkey Breasts à la Chipolata.—Singe, draw, and wipe neatly a fine young turkey of six pounds. Detach the two legs entirely from the turkey. Place in a saucepan any piece of pork-skin that is on hand, adding one cut-up carrot, one onion, also cut up, and a bouquet (No. 254). Lay the breasts of the turkey over the garnishing, season with one pinch of salt and half a pinch of pepper, then put on the lid and let get a golden color for about ten minutes. Moisten with one pint of broth (No. 99), and put it into the oven without the lid, letting it cook for forty minutes, basting it frequently with its own gravy. Arrange on a hot dish, and serve with a pint of hot chipolata (No. 232). The stock remaining in the pan can be used for preparing Espagnole sauce.

807. Turkey Breasts à la Robinson.—Proceed exactly as for No. 806, but after cooking for twenty minutes, take it off and place it in another saucepan. Baste it with its own gravy, adding half a pint of Espagnole sauce (No. 151). Blanch half a pint of chicken or turkey livers, cut them into two or three pieces according to their size, and put them with the turkey, adding half a glassful of Madeira wine. Let cook for twenty minute more, and serve with the livers around the breasts, and the gravy thrown over.

808. Roast Goose, Stuffed with Chestnuts, Apple Sauce.—Have a fine, tender goose of four pounds, singe, draw, wash well, and thoroughly wipe the interior with a cloth; then fill it with some stuffing as for the turkey (No. 800). Close both ends, truss well, sprinkle a pinch of salt over, envelop in buttered paper and put it into a roasting-pan. Cook it for one hour and a half in a moderate oven, basting it occasionally with the dripping. Remove from the oven, dress on a hot serving-dish, untruss, skim off the fat from the gravy, add to it a gill of white broth (No. 99), let come to a boil, then strain the gravy into a sauce-bowl and serve separately.

809. Timbale of Foie-Gras Lagardère.—Butter lightly six timbale molds; decorate the inside according to taste with pieces of truffle and smoked beef-tongue; fill them half full with cream forcemeat (No. 225), leaving an empty space in the centre, filling this in with a reduced salpicon (No. 256). Cover the salpicon with a very little pâté-de-foie-gras, and finish filling with the cream forcemeat. Put the molds in a sautoire holding hot water to half their height; boil gently, and then place them in a slow oven for ten minutes. Unmold on a hot dish, and serve with half a pint of hot sauce Périgueux (No. 191) separately. Place on top of each timbale a small, round croquette of foie-gras, then serve.

810. Vol-au-Vent à la Financière.—Fill six vol-au-vents made with feuilletage paste (No. 1076) with a quart of financière garnishing (No. 246), and serve them on a dish with a folded napkin.

811. Vol-au-Vent à la Toulouse.—Fill six vol-au-vents (No. 1076) with a quart of hot Toulouse garnishing (No. 176), and serve the same as for the above.

812. Vol-au-Vent à la Reine.—Fill six vol-au-vents (No. 1076) with a quart of hot Reine garnishing (No. 623), and serve as for No. 810.

813. Boned Turkey à la Prosperity of America.—Procure a fine, tender, young Rhode Island turkey, weighing eight pounds. Singe, draw, and neatly wipe the interior. Make an incision right along the back. Begin boning from the neck down toward the breast, on both sides, being very careful not to make any holes in the skin, as it should remain perfectly intact. Make an incision from the first joint, then bone both legs. Cut away also, very carefully, the two wing bones. Season the inside with one pinch of salt and half a pinch of pepper, evenly divided. Place it on a dish, and lay it in the ice-box until needed. Take two pounds of lean, raw veal, three pounds of fresh pork, and half a pound of larding pork, all cut up into small dice-shaped pieces. Season with two pinches of salt, one pinch of white pepper, the third of a saltspoonful of grated nutmeg, and the same quantity of thyme. Mix all well together. Place all in the chopping machine, and chop it exceedingly fine, repeating the process, if necessary, until it is chopped to perfection. Should there be any sinews among the ingredients, remove them all. Place on a cold dish, and put away in the ice-box to cool until the following is prepared. Have ready a quarter of a pound of the end (red) part of a cooked smoked beef-tongue, eighteen medium-sized, sound truffles, both tongue and truffles cut in dice-shaped pieces half an inch square. Take the forcemeat from the ice-box, and thoroughly mix the tongue and truffles with it, pouring in also a wine-glassful of Madeira wine. Half a cup of well-peeled pistache can be added, if at hand. Take the turkey from the ice-box, spread it on a clean table (skin-side downward). Then, with a keen knife, cut away even slices from the breasts, arrange them on the thin, so that the turkey should have an equal thickness all over. Place the forcemeat right in the centre of the turkey, column shaped, leaving a clear space of two inches at each end, and of four inches at each side. Spread on a table a strong, clean napkin, sprinkling over it a little cold water. Fold up first both ends of the turkey, then both sides, so that the four ends should be enveloped; gently lift, and lay it right in the centre of the napkin. Roll it carefully in the napkin. Tightly tie one end first, then the other, as firmly as possible, taking in the slack of the napkin. Place it in a large saucepan on the hot range, with the carcass, and whatever bones and débris pertain to it, completely cover with cold water, place the lid on, and when coming to a boil thoroughly skim it, then add one medium-sized, sound, scraped carrot, and one well-peeled onion with three cloves stuck in. Season with one pinch of salt, and then let boil on a moderate fire for fully two and a half hours. Remove the galantine with a skimmer; let cool enough so that it can be easily handled. Cut the strings at both ends; roll it over again as before, and tightly tie both ends exactly as before. Lay it in a flat tin pan, placing on top of it a board the size of the boned turkey, and on top of it a weight of seven pounds, leaving the weight on until the galantine is thoroughly cold, which will take a whole night; but avoid placing it in the ice-box until thoroughly cold. Two days after the preparation it will be ready for use; keeping it in the ice-box in the same napkin in which it was cooked.

814. Jelly for Boned Turkey.

—Strain the broth in which the galantine was cooked into another saucepan, thoroughly skim all the fat off, add one ounce of clarified gelatine. Boil for five minutes. Crack into another saucepan the whites of two raw eggs, and the shells as well, squeeze in the juice of half a sound lemon, adding half a glassful of Madeira wine, and a small piece of ice, the size of an egg, finely cracked. Beat all sharply together with a wire whip. Place the broth on the table at hand near the eggs, &c., and with a soup-ladle in the left hand, a wire whip in the right, add a ladleful of broth, little by little, to the eggs, carefully and sharply stirring with the whip until all the broth has been added. Place it then on a very moderate fire, and let gently come to a boil. Immediately strain through a flannel bag or a napkin into a clean bowl and let cool, and it will be ready for use.

815. Pigeon Cutlets à la Victoria.—Singe, draw, and bone three fine pigeons, leaving on the legs; cut them in two, and stuff lightly with chicken forcemeat (No. 226), immerse then in beaten egg and fresh bread-crumbs, then cook in a sautoire with half an ounce of clarified butter, for four minutes on each side, and serve with half a pint of hot Victoria sauce (No. 208) on the warm dish, and the cutlets on top, with paper ruffles nicely arranged.

816. Squabs Roasted Plain.—Singe, draw, cut off the necks, wipe neatly, and truss six fine, small squabs; put them in a roasting-pan with half a pinch of salt, evenly divided, and a very little butter spread over. Put the pan into a brisk oven to cook for twelve minutes; then remove from the oven, untruss, and dress them on a hot dish, on which you previously have placed six small canapés, prepared as in No. 832, one on each canapé; neatly decorate the dish with fresh watercress; skim the fat from off the gravy, add to it a gill of white broth (No. 99); let it just come to a boil, strain it into a sauce-bowl, and send to the table separately.

817. Squabs Broiled on Toast, with Bacon.—Singe, draw, cut the necks off, and wipe nicely three very good-sized squabs; split them without detaching the parts, then lay them on a dish, and season with a pinch of salt, half a pinch of pepper, and a tablespoonful of sweet oil; roll them in well, and put them to broil for six minutes on each side. Prepare a dish with six toasts, arrange the squabs over, and spread a gill of maître d'hôtel butter (No. 145) on top. Decorate the dish with six slices of broiled bacon (No. 754), and serve.

818. Ballotin of Squab à l'Italienne.

—Singe, draw, and bone six tender squabs; stuff them with a good chicken forcemeat (No. 226), and leave on one leg, to decorate later with a ruffle. Form them into a circle, arranging each squab so it assumes a round shape; place them in a buttered sautoire; season with a good pinch of salt and half a pinch of pepper, and cover with a piece of buttered paper. Put it in the oven for fifteen minutes, and when cooked serve with half a pint of hot Italian sauce (No. 188), the squabs laid on top, with a paper ruffle fastened on to each leg.

819. Squabs à la Crapaudine.—Singe, draw, then split six squabs through the back without entirely dividing the parts; break the bones of the legs and wings, flatten them well, and lay them on a dish to season with a good pinch of salt, one pinch of pepper, and two tablespoonfuls of oil, roll them in well, then dip them in fresh bread-crumbs, and broil them slowly for seven minutes on each side. Arrange them on a hot dish, and serve with half a pint of hot Robert sauce (No. 192), to which add three chopped mushrooms. Serve the sauce on a dish, and the squabs on top.

820. Squabs à l'Américaine.—Singe, draw, and truss nicely six fine, fat squabs; stuff them with American forcemeat (No. 229), and place them in a roasting-pan with a pinch of salt, evenly distributed, and half an ounce of butter well spread over the squabs. Place them in the hot oven, and roast for eighteen minutes. Take from out the oven, dress them on a hot dish; untruss; skim the fat off the gravy, add to it one gill of broth (No. 99), let come to a boil, strain into a sauce-bowl, decorate the dish with a little fresh watercress. Arrange a slice of broiled bacon (No. 754) over each bird, and send to the table.

821. Squabs à la Chipolata.—Prepare and roast six squabs same as for No. 816, and serve them with a pint of hot chipolata garnishing (No. 232) on a hot dish, and the squabs arranged over.

822. Squabs en Compote.—Singe, draw, and truss with their legs thrust inside, six fine, fat squabs; lay them in a saucepan with half an ounce of butter, one cut-up onion, and one carrot cut the same. Season with a pinch of salt, then put the lid on the pan, and cook on a good fire for ten minutes. Put in a saucepan six small glazed onions (No. 967), one medium-sized carrot, cut with a vegetable-scoop (blanching the latter for two minutes), one ounce of salt pork cut into small pieces, and six cut-up mushrooms; moisten them with a pint of Espagnole sauce (No. 151), and let cook together for thirty minutes. Transfer the squabs to this preparation, and let cook again for five minutes; dress the garnishing on a hot dish, arrange the squabs on top, and serve.

823. Roast Duck à l'Américaine.—Select a fine young duck, weighing three and a half pounds; singe, draw, and wipe it well, then stuff it with American forcemeat (No. 229), and place it in a roasting-pan with half an ounce of butter, and besprinkle with a pinch of salt, then roast it in the oven for forty minutes, basting it occasionally. Lay it on a dish, untruss, skim the fat off, add a gill of white broth (No. 99), let it come to a boil, then strain the lean part of the gravy over, and garnish with six pieces of fried hominy (No. 1035).

824. Roast Duck, Apple Sauce.—Have a fine, tender duckling of three and a half pounds; singe, draw, wipe neatly, and truss. Place it in a roasting-pan, spread half an ounce of butter over, and a pinch of salt. Place it in a brisk oven, and let cook for thirty minutes, not failing to baste it occasionally with its own gravy. Dress it on a hot dish, untie the string, skim the fat off the gravy, add a gill of broth (No. 99), let it come to a boil, then strain the lean part over the duck, decorate with a little watercress, and serve with half a pint of hot apple sauce separately (No. 168).

825. Duckling à la Rouennaise.—Take two fine ducklings of one and a half pounds each, singe, draw, and truss them with the legs thrust inside; lay them in a roasting-pan, and cover them with half an ounce of butter, seasoning with a pinch of salt; put them in the oven for ten minutes. Cut four medium-sized turnips into small dice-shaped pieces, put them in a saucepan with half an ounce of butter and half a teaspoonful of powdered sugar; let cook for ten minutes, then moisten with a pint of Espagnole sauce (No. 151). Lay the ducks in the saucepan with the turnips, and let cook again all together for twenty-five minutes; arrange the ducks on a hot dish, untruss, and decorate the dish with the turnips. Pour the sauce over all, and serve.

826. Salmi of Duck à l'Américaine.—Procure two fine ducks; singe, draw, wipe neatly, and cut off the wings, legs, and breasts; put the two carcasses in a saucepan, sprinkle a little salt over, and put it in the oven to cook for six minutes; remove them, and hash them up. Put them back into a saucepan with a pint of white broth (No. 99), and a small bouquet (No. 254), and let cook on a moderate fire for fifteen minutes. Put an ounce of butter in a sautoire, lay in the wings, legs, and breasts, then season with a pinch of salt and half a pinch of pepper; cook on a very brisk fire for three minutes on each side, then add half a glassful of Madeira wine, half a pint of Espagnole sauce (No. 151), and the zest of a lemon; strain the gravy of the carcasses over, and let all cook again for fifteen minutes. Dress nicely on a hot dish, and decorate with six heart-shaped croûtons of fried hominy, and serve (No. 1035).

827. Salmi of Duck, with Olives.—Prepare the salmi of ducks as for the above (No. 826), adding half a pint of parboiled and stoned olives to the sauce. Use six heart-shaped fried croûtons of bread (No. 133) instead of the hominy, and serve.

828. Salmi of Duck à la Chasseur.—Make a salmi the same as for No. 826, adding twelve sliced mushrooms, and serve with six heart-shaped croûtons (No. 133).

829. Salmi of Duck à la Bourgeoise.—Prepare two fine ducks as for No. 826, and add twelve glazed onions (No. 967), and two raw carrots cut clove-garlic-shaped, letting them cook in salted water for ten minutes previous to adding them to the salmi, also half an ounce of salt pork, cut in square pieces, and let cook together with the ducks for fifteen minutes more; then serve.

830. Salmi of Duck à la Montglas.—Singe, draw, and wipe two fine, tender ducks; cut away the wings, legs, and breasts, then put the carcasses in a roasting-pan; sprinkle a little salt over, spread on each bird a very little butter, and place them in the oven for six minutes; remove them, and hash them up. Lay them in a saucepan, moistened with a pint of white broth (No. 99); add a small bouquet (No. 254), and let cook on the stove for fifteen minutes. Put an ounce of butter in a sautoire, add the wings, legs, and breasts, previously laid aside; season with a pinch of salt, half a pinch of pepper, and the third of a pinch of nutmeg, and let cook on a brisk fire for three minutes on each side. Add half a glassful of good sherry, half a pint of Espagnole sauce (No. 151), half a pint of tomato sauce (No. 205), two thin slices of smoked beef-tongue cut into Julienne-shaped pieces, two cut-up truffles, six fine mushrooms, also cut up; then strain the gravy of the carcasses over this; let cook all together for fifteen minutes more, then artistically dress the salmi on a hot dish, decorate with six heart-shaped bread croûtons (No. 133), adjust paper ruffles to the end of the wings and legs, and serve.

831. Salmi of Duck à la Maréchale.—Proceed exactly the same as for "Salmi à l'Américaine" (No. 826), adding twelve small godiveau quenelles

(No. 221), and twelve mushrooms cut in two. Let heat well for five minutes, then serve with six fried bread croûtons (No. 133).

A pinch of salt represents 205 grains, or a tablespoonful.

Half a pinch of pepper represents 38 grains, or a teaspoonful.

A third of a pinch of nutmeg represents 13 grains, or half a teaspoonful.

———

GAME.

832. Canapés for Game.—Cut out the desired number of canapés from a loaf of American bread (a stale one is preferable) one and a half inches thick. Trim neatly, pare off the crusts; then cut out a piece in the centre of each, from end to end, so that the cavity will hold the bird easily when sending to the table. Spread a little butter over them, place on a tin plate; then brown in the hot oven until they obtain a good golden color. Remove from out the oven, arrange them on a hot dish, and they will be ready to serve.

833. Croquettes of Game à la Périgueux.—Make six game croquettes exactly the same as the chicken croquettes (No. 758)—the mushrooms can be omitted—and serve with half a pint of hot sauce périgueux (No. 191), separately.

834. Quails Roasted, Plain.—Pick six fine, tender, fat quails, singe, draw, and wipe them well; truss them, laying a thin layer of lard on the breasts. Put them in a roasting-pan, spreading a very little butter on top of each quail; then pour half a cupful of water in the pan. Season with a pinch of salt, and let cook in the oven for eighteen minutes. Place on a hot dish six heart-shaped pieces of toast; untruss the quails, and arrange them on top, decorating with a little watercress. Strain the gravy into a sauce-bowl, and serve it separately.

835. Quails Broiled With Bacon.—Have six fine fat quails. Singe, draw, and wipe them well. Split them through the back without separating the parts, and break the two leg bones. Put them on a dish; season with a pinch of salt, half a pinch of pepper, and a tablespoonful of sweet oil, mixing them in well, and put them to broil on a moderate fire for six minutes on each side. Arrange six toasts on a hot dish, lay the quails on top, and pour a gill of maître d'hôtel butter (No. 145) over, decorating with six slices of broiled bacon (No. 754), and serve.

836. Braised Quails, Celery Sauce.—Take six nice fat quails, singe, draw, and wipe them well. Truss, and cover the breasts with a thin layer of lard. Place them in a sautoire with a piece of pork rind, half a carrot, and half an onion, both cut-up, and let them get a good golden color on the fire. Moisten with half a cupful of water, then put them in the oven, and let cook for twenty minutes. Serve with a pint of celery sauce (No. 200), and a little meat-glaze (No. 141) thrown over.

837. Quails à la Financière.—Braise six quails the same as for the above (No. 836), and serve them with a pint of hot financière garnishing (No. 246) in place of the celery sauce.

838. Doe-birds, Roasted, Plain.—Singe, draw, and truss six fine, fat doe-birds. Put them in a roasting-pan with half a cupful of water, seasoning with a pinch of salt. Spread a very little butter over the birds, and put them in a hot oven for twelve minutes. Dress them on a hot dish with six small canapés (No. 832). Decorate the dish with a little watercress, and serve.

839. Broiled Doe-birds.—Singe, draw, and wipe well six fine doe-birds; split them through the back without detaching the parts, and lay them on a dish. Season with a good pinch of salt, half a pinch of pepper, and one tablespoonful of oil. Roll them in well, and broil for four minutes on each side. Prepare a hot dish with six toasts; arrange the doe-birds on top, and serve with a gill of maître d'hôtel butter (No. 145) well spread over. Decorate the dish with a little watercress.

840. Roasted Doe-birds à l'Américaine.—Proceed exactly as for No. 838, replacing the canapés of bread with six canapés of fried hominy (No. 1035), or corn fritters, arranging six slices of broiled bacon over each bird, and serve the same.

841. Roasted Doe-birds à l'Africaine.—Exactly as for No. 838, only serving with six stuffed egg-plants (No. 909) instead of the canapés.

842. Salmi of Doe-birds à la Gastronome.—Make a salmi as for salmi of snipe (No. 870), and serve with six small potato croquettes (No. 997).

843. Roast Partridge, Bread Sauce.—Singe, draw, and wipe two fine, young partridges; truss them neatly, and cover the breasts with a layer of thin lard, tying it twice around. Lay them on a roasting-pan, spreading a little butter over each, and moistening with half a cupful of water. Put the pan in a brisk oven for twenty-five minutes, basting the birds occasionally.

Dress each one on a bread canapé (No. 832), removing the strings. Decorate the dish with a little watercress. Strain the gravy into a sauce-bowl, and serve it separately; also serving half a pint of hot bread-sauce (No. 162) in another bowl.

844. Partridge Broiled à l'Américaine.—Singe, draw, and wipe neatly three tender partridges; cut them in halves, lay them on a dish, and season with a good pinch of salt, half a pinch of pepper, and a tablespoonful of oil. Roll them in well, then put them to broil for seven minutes on each side. Prepare six slices of fried hominy (No. 1035). Arrange them on a hot dish; place the partridges over, and pour a gill of maître d'hôtel butter on top (No. 145). Place six slices of broiled bacon (No. 754) over the birds, and serve.

845. Partridge and Cabbage.—Select a fine, tender cabbage, clean it thoroughly, cut it into four parts; wash well in cold water, remove the root, and put into salted boiling water for five minutes. Remove, and drain well, then return it to the saucepan with one carrot cut in four pieces, one whole onion stuck with four cloves, a quarter of a pound of salt pork, in one piece, a bouquet (No. 254), one pint of white broth (No. 99), and one pint of lean stock. Season with a good pinch of salt and a pinch of pepper. Take (in preference) two old partridges; singe, draw, and wipe them well; truss them with their wings turned inside, and put them on a roasting-pan with half a pinch of salt, and a little butter well spread over their breasts, and put them to roast for six minutes. Make a hollow space in the centre of the cabbage, place therein the two partridges and cover them over, laying a piece of buttered paper on top to prevent the air from escaping; put the lid on and cook in the oven for one hour. Now lift off the lid, remove the paper, skim off any fat adhering to the surface, and dress the cabbage neatly on a hot dish; untruss, and arrange the partridges, decorating the dish artistically with the carrots and salt pork, cut into six slices. Take away the onion and bouquet, and serve.

846. Partridge à la Financière.—Singe, draw, wipe, and truss two partridges with their wings inside. Lay a piece of pork-rind in a saucepan, adding one carrot and one onion, both cut in slices, two bay-leaves, one sprig of thyme, and the two partridges. Season with one pinch of salt and half a pinch of pepper. When they have assumed a good golden color on the hot stove, moisten with half a pint of white broth (No. 99), then put the saucepan in the oven and let cook for twenty minutes. Dress them on a serving-dish, untruss, pour half a pint of hot sauce financière (No. 246) over, and serve. The gravy from the partridges can be utilized for making the financière sauce.

847. Partridge Braised with Celery Sauce.—Proceed exactly the same as for the above (No. 846), replacing the financière by a pint of hot celery sauce (No. 200).

848. Partridge Sauté à la Chasseur.—Singe, draw, and wipe two fine, tender partridges, cut them into twelve pieces, and place them in a sautoire with an ounce of butter, seasoning well with a good pinch of salt and half a pinch of pepper. Brown well for three minutes on each side; then add a finely chopped shallot, half a glassful of Madeira wine, half a pint of Espagnole sauce (No. 151), and twelve whole mushrooms. Finish cooking for fifteen minutes, then serve with six bread croûtons (No. 133) around the dish.

849. Chartreuse of Partridge.—Prepare the partridges as for No. 845. Take a Charlotte-mold, which will hold three pints, butter lightly, and decorate with small pieces of cooked carrot and turnip, cut very evenly with a vegetable-tube. When ready, fill the bottom with a layer of cooked cabbage; cut the partridges into pieces, put a layer of them on the cabbage, covering the hollow spaces with more cabbage; lay on top six slices of salt pork, add the rest of the partridges, and finish by covering the surface with cabbage, pressing it down carefully. Place the mold on a tin baking-dish, and put it in a moderate oven for fifteen minutes, leaving the oven-door open during the whole time. Have a hot dish ready, turn the mold upside down on it, and draw off carefully. Serve with a little demi-glace (No. 185).

850. Suprême of Partridge, Sauce Périgueux.—Singe, draw, wipe neatly, and remove the skin from the breasts of three partridges. Make an incision on top of each breast-bone, from end to end, then with a keen knife carefully cut off the entire breast on both sides of the partridges, including the small wing-bone, which should not be separated from the breasts, and seeing that the entire breasts are cleverly cut away, without leaving a particle of it on the carcasses. Under each breast will be found a small fillet, which you carefully remove, and place on a dish for further action. With a small, sharp knife, make an incision in each breast, at their thinner side, three inches in length by one inch in depth. Season the inside of each breast with a pinch of salt, and half a pinch of pepper, equally divided. Stuff the breasts with two ounces of chicken forcemeat (No. 226), mixed with two fine, sound, finely sliced truffles, and four finely sliced mushrooms. Butter well a *well-tinned* copper sautoire; gently lay in the six breasts; take each small fillet, press them gently with the fingers, giving them a boatlike form. Make six slanting, small incisions on top of each, insert in each incision a small slice of truffle, cut with a tube half an inch in diameter. Lightly wet the top of each breast with water, then neatly lay one fillet on top of each breast lengthwise. Sprinkle a little clarified butter over all with a feather brush. Pour into the pan (not over the suprêmes) a quarter of a glassful of Madeira wine and two tablespoonfuls of mushroom liquor, tightly cover the pan with a lid, then place in the hot oven for ten minutes. Pour on a hot dish one pint of hot Toulouse garnishing (No. 176). Remove the suprêmes from the oven, neatly dress them over the garnishing, adjust paper ruffles on each wing bone, and immediately send to the table.

851. Suprême of Partridge à la Godard.—The same as for the above (No. 850), but serving with half a pint of Allemande sauce (No. 210), adding two sliced truffles, six sliced mushrooms, six blanched cock's combs, and six blanched cock's kidneys, in place of the Périgueux sauce. Heat up well on the corner of the stove for four minutes, but do not allow it to boil, and pour the garnishing over the hot dish, dressing the suprêmes over it; serve very hot.

852. Grouse, Roasted Plain.—Singe, draw, wipe, and truss two fine fat grouse. Place them in a roasting-pan with half a cupful of water, spread a little butter over each, and season with a pinch of salt. Put them into a brisk oven, and let cook for eighteen minutes, taking care to baste frequently with their own gravy; then untruss. Have a hot serving-dish ready; place two bread canapés (No. 832) on it; arrange the grouse over, and decorate the dish with a little watercress. Strain the gravy into a sauce-bowl, and serve it separately.

853. Grouse, Roasted à la Sam Ward.—Take two fine fat grouse; pick, singe, draw, and dry them well; then truss them nicely. Place them in a roasting-pan, putting inside of each bird a piece of broiled toast four inches long and two wide. Drip in on each toast, with a spoon, a small glassful of good Madeira wine or sherry; season the grouse with a pinch of salt; spread a little butter over. Put them in a brisk oven, and let cook for eighteen minutes, taking care to baste them frequently. Lay them on a hot dish, untruss, strain the gravy over, and decorate with a little watercress. Serve with a little red currant jelly separately.

854. Grouse, Broiled with Bacon.

—Singe, draw, and wipe nicely two fat grouse. Split them in two through the back without separating the parts; lay them on a dish, and season with a pinch of salt, half a pinch of pepper, and a tablespoonful of sweet oil. Roll them in well; then put them to broil on a brisk fire for seven minutes on each side. Prepare a hot dish with six small toasts, arrange the grouse over, spread a gill of maître d'hôtel butter (No. 145) on top, and garnish with six thin slices of broiled bacon (No. 754), then serve.

855. Salmi of Grouse à la Parisienne.—Singe, draw, wipe, and truss two fine fat grouse; season with a pinch of salt, spread a few small bits of butter on the birds, then place them in a roasting-pan, and put them in a brisk oven to cook for eight minutes. Untruss and cut away the wings, legs, and breasts. Put an ounce of good butter into a saucepan with half a medium-sized carrot, cut in very small pieces, half an onion cut the same, a sprig of thyme, two bay-leaves, and six whole peppers. Reduce to a good golden color for about five minutes, then hash the bodies of the two grouse, and add them to the other ingredients. Moisten with a pint of Espagnole sauce (No. 151), half a glassful of good sherry wine, half a cupful of mushroom liquor, and the zest of a lemon; season with half a pinch of salt, half a pinch of pepper, and a third of a pinch of nutmeg; let cook for twenty minutes. Now put the wings, legs, and breasts into a separate saucepan, and strain the above sauce over the parts, adding six minced mushrooms and two minced truffles. Let cook for three minutes, then dress neatly on a hot dish, and serve with six croûtons (No. 133) on top, and paper ruffles nicely arranged.

856. Salmi of Grouse à la Walter Scott.—Proceed exactly the same as for the above (No. 855), omitting the mushrooms and truffles, and serving with half a pint of bread sauce (No. 162) separately.

857. Salmi of Grouse à la Florentine.—The same as for No. 855, only serving the salmi with a garnishing of six hot artichokes à la Florentine (No. 903) in place of the other garnishing.

858. Suprême of Grouse à la Richelieu.—Proceed the same as for the suprême of partridge (No. 850), but substituting tongue for truffles, and serving with a gill of hot sauce Périgueux (No. 191), mingled with a gill of tomato sauce (No. 205), boiled together for three minutes.

859. Teal Duck, Roasted Plain.—Pick, singe, draw, wipe, and truss three fine teal ducks; place them in a roasting-pan. Season with a pinch of salt; put them in a brisk oven to roast for fourteen minutes, then untruss.

Arrange on a hot serving-dish, and decorate with six slices of fried hominy (No. 1035) and a little watercress.

860. Teal Duck, Broiled.—Have three fine, fat teal ducks; pick, singe, and dry them neatly; cut the heads off, and split the birds in two without separating the parts. Lay them on a dish, and season them with a pinch of salt, half a pinch of pepper, and a tablespoonful of sweet oil. Roll them in well, and put them to broil on a moderate fire for seven minutes on each side. Have a hot dish with six toasts ready, lay the ducks on top, spread a gill of maître d'hôtel butter (No. 145) over, decorate with a little watercress, and serve.

861. Salmi of Teal Duck à la Régence.—Prepare the salmi of teal duck as for the salmi of duck à l'Américaine (No. 826), adding half a pint of hot Régence garnishing (No. 235) four minutes before serving.

862. Ptarmigan, Roasted Plain.—Proceed exactly the same as for roasted teal ducks, No. 859.

863. Ptarmigan, Broiled Plain.—Prepared the same as for teal ducks broiled, No. 860.

864. Salmi of Ptarmigan à la Chasseur.—To be prepared exactly as salmi of duck à l'Américaine (No. 826), adding twelve mushrooms, cut in two, four minutes before serving, and decorating with six heart-shaped croûtons (No. 133).

865. Plovers, Roasted Plain.—Pick, singe, draw, and wipe neatly six fine, fat, tender plovers; pick out the eyes, truss the legs together, skewer the head under one leg, and lay a thin slice of larding pork on each bird; tie securely, then place them in a roasting-pan. Season with a pinch of salt evenly divided over each; spread also a very little butter over. Put them in the hot oven, and roast for ten minutes. Remove from the oven, arrange six small canapés (No. 832) on a hot dish, dress the birds on the canapés, decorate with a little watercress, and serve.

866. Plovers Broiled.—Pick, singe, draw, and wipe six fine, fat plovers; pick out the eyes, split them through the back without separating the parts, and place them on a dish. Season with one pinch of salt, half a pinch of pepper, and a tablespoonful of sweet oil. Roll them in well, and put them on a broiler to cook for four minutes on each side. Dress them on a hot dish with six pieces of toast, spread a gill of maître d'hôtel butter (No. 145) over, decorate with a little watercress, and serve.

867. Salmi of Plover à la Maison d'Or.

—Proceed exactly the same as for salmi of woodcock (No. 873), adding, on the serving-dish, six heart-shaped bread croûtons (No. 133), covered with pâté-de-foie-gras.

868. English Snipe, Roasted.—Procure six fine English snipe; pick, singe, draw, and wipe them (reserve the hearts and livers for further use); pick out the eyes, remove the skin from the heads, truss the legs, skewer them with the bills; tie a thin slice of larding pork around each bird, and put them in a roasting-pan, sprinkling a pinch of salt over. Set them in the oven to roast for eight minutes. Hash up very fine the hearts and livers, with a teaspoonful of chives and a teaspoonful of good butter, seasoning with half a pinch of salt and the third of a pinch of pepper. Cover six bread canapés (No. 832) with this, sprinkling a little fresh bread-crumbs on top. Spread a very little butter over all, and put them on a tin plate in the oven for two minutes. Arrange the canapés on a hot dish, dress the snipe nicely over, decorate with a little watercress, and strain the gravy into a sauce-bowl, serving it separately.

869. English Snipe, Broiled.—Pick, singe, draw, and dry well six fine English snipe; remove the skin from the heads, split them in two without detaching the parts, and put them on a dish. Season with a pinch of salt, half a pinch of pepper, and a tablespoonful of oil. Roll them in well, then put them to broil (with the bills stuck into the breasts), and let them cook for four minutes on each side. Prepare a hot dish with six toasts, arrange the snipe over, spread a gill of maître d'hôtel butter (No. 145) on top, decorate the dish with a little watercress, and serve.

870. Salmi of Snipe à la Moderne.—Singe, draw, and neatly wipe six fine, fat snipe. Chop off the legs, and then stuff the inside with a little game forcemeat (No. 228) through a paper cornet; fill the cavity of the eyes with a little more of the game forcemeat (No. 228), and covering each eye right over the game forcemeat with a small bit of truffle, cut with a tube. Insert the bills in the breasts, and then lay them on a roasting-pan, with a little butter; place in the hot oven to roast for six minutes. Take from out the oven, lay each one on a square piece of bread, fried in a little clarified butter, pour one pint of hot salmi sauce (No. 193) over, to which have been added twelve whole mushrooms, and serve.

871. Woodcock, Roasted Plain.—Procure six fine, fat woodcocks, pick, singe, and draw them, putting the hearts and livers on a plate for further use. Take out the eyes, and remove the skin from the heads; truss up the feet, skewer them with the bill, and tie a *barde* of fat pork around the breasts; then chop up all the hearts and livers very fine, with one teaspoonful of chives, half a pinch of salt, a third of a pinch of pepper, and a teaspoonful of butter. Prepare six bread canapés (No. 832), two and a half inches long, by one and a half wide; fry them for two minutes in very hot fat, drain them thoroughly, and cover each canapé with some of the above mixture, spreading a little fresh bread-crumbs and a very little butter over; place them in a small baking-pan and lay aside. Now put the woodcocks in a roasting-pan with a little butter well spread over the birds, and roast them in a brisk oven for ten minutes. Two minutes before they are done, put the canapés in the oven, then take both out, and lay the canapés on a hot dish; untie the birds, and arrange them over the canapés, decorating the dish with a little watercress. Strain the gravy into a sauce-bowl, and serve it separately.

872. Woodcock, Broiled With Bacon.—Pick, singe, draw, pick out the eyes, and remove the skin from the heads of six fine woodcocks; wipe them neatly, and split them through the back without separating the parts. Put them on a dish to season with a pinch of salt, half a pinch of pepper, and one tablespoonful of sweet oil. Roll them in well, then put them on to broil with the bills stuck into the breasts. Let broil for four minutes on each side, then arrange them on a dish with six pieces of heart-shaped fried bread, covered with the hashed hearts and livers as in No. 871, spread a gill of maître-d'hôtel butter (No. 145) over, and decorate with six slices of broiled bacon (No. 754), then serve.

873. Salmi of Woodcock à la Chasseur.—Pick, singe, draw, pick out the eyes, and remove the skin from the heads of six fine woodcocks; wipe them neatly, and put them in a roasting-pan with half a pinch of salt. Cook for four minutes in the oven; then cut off the legs and necks, but preserve the heads. Put an ounce of butter into a saucepan, with half a raw carrot and half a raw onion, all cut in pieces, a small bouquet (No. 254), and six whole peppers. Cook for five minutes on the stove, then moisten with half a pint of Espagnole sauce (No. 151), half a glassful of sherry wine, and three tablespoonfuls of mushroom liquor. Season with half a pinch of salt and half a pinch of pepper, and let cook for fifteen minutes more. Stick a good-sized, fine mushroom in the bill of each head, run the bill into the breast of each woodcock, and put them in a sautoire; strain the sauce over, add twelve mushrooms cut in two, and the zest of one lemon. Let cook for six minutes more, then arrange nicely on a dish, decorating it with six bread croûtons (No. 133); pour the sauce over, and serve.

874. Canvas-back Ducks, Roasted.—Procure two fine, fat canvas-back ducks, pick, singe, draw well, and wipe neatly; throw a light pinch of salt inside, run in the head from the end of the neck to the back, truss nicely, and place in a roasting-pan. Sprinkle a little salt over, put them in a brisk oven, and let cook for eighteen minutes; arrange on a very hot dish, untruss, throw two tablespoonfuls of white broth (No. 99) into each duck, and serve with six slices of fried hominy (No. 1035), and currant jelly.

875. Canvas-back Ducks, Broiled.—Take two fine, fat canvas-back ducks; pick, singe, draw, and wipe them thoroughly. Split them through the back without detaching them, and lay them on a dish to season with a good pinch of salt, half a pinch of pepper, and a tablespoonful of oil. Roll them in well, and put them to broil for seven minutes on each side. Dress them on a hot dish, spread a gill of maître-d'hôtel butter over (No. 145), decorate with a little watercress, and serve.

876. Red-head Ducks, roasted—Broiled.—Red-head ducks roasted are prepared exactly the same as canvas-back ducks roasted (No. 874).

Red-head ducks broiled are prepared exactly the same as for canvas-back ducks broiled (No. 875).

877. Reed-birds, Roasted.—Procure twelve freshly killed, fine, fat reed-birds; cut off their legs and wings, pick the eyes out, and remove the skin from the heads, clean and wipe them neatly, and with a skewer remove the gizzards from the sides, then cover their breasts lightly with thin slices of bacon; arrange them on three kidney-skewers, four on each, and lay them in a roasting-pan; season with a pinch of salt, spread a very little butter over, and set them in the oven to roast for seven minutes; remove them to a hot dish with six hot toasts; garnish with watercress and send to the table immediately.

878. Saddle of Venison, Jelly Sauce.—Procure a saddle of a small venison, weighing about five pounds; pare it neatly, remove the sinews from the surface, and lard it with a larding-needle as finely as possible; tie it three times around. Put into the roasting-pan one sliced onion and one sliced carrot; lay in the saddle, seasoning with one pinch of salt; spread half an ounce of butter over, and put it in a brisk oven to roast for forty minutes, basting it frequently with its own gravy. Untie before lifting it from the pan, arrange neatly on a hot dish; pour into the pan half a glassful of Madeira wine and a gill of white broth (No. 99); let come to a boil on the stove. Skim the fat off the gravy, straining the lean part over the saddle. Serve with half a pint of hot currant-jelly sauce (No. 884) separately.

All saddles of venison are prepared the same way, only with different sauces and garnishings.

879. Venison Steak, Broiled.—Procure from a freshly killed deer a fine leg of about five pounds weight; remove the noix, cut it into six steaks; pare and flatten them nicely. Put them on a plate to season with a good pinch of salt, a pinch of pepper, the third of a pinch of nutmeg, and one tablespoonful of oil. Roll them in well, and put them to broil for five minutes on each side. Dress on a hot dish, and spread a gill of maître-d'hôtel butter (No. 145) over; decorate the dish with a little watercress, and serve.

All venison steaks are prepared the same way, only served with different sauces and garnishings.

880. Venison Steak, Londonderry Sauce.—To be prepared the same as for the above (No. 879). Cut into Julienne-shaped pieces half an ounce of citron, also the zest of half a small, sound lemon cut in the same way. Place them in a saucepan with a glassful of good port wine; cook for two or three minutes at most. Add now a gill of currant jelly, stir all well together until the jelly is thoroughly dissolved, add just a little Cayenne pepper, but no more than the equivalent of the third of a saltspoonful. Allow to come to a boil. Pour the sauce on the hot serving-dish, place the steaks one overlapping another, and serve very hot.

881. Venison Steak, Colbert Sauce.—Proceed the same as for No. 879, serving with half a pint of hot Colbert sauce (No. 190).

882. Venison Steak, Purée of Chestnuts.—The same as for No. 879, serving with half a pint of purée of chestnuts (No. 131).

883. Venison Steak, Mashed Potatoes.—The same as for No. 879, serving with a pint of mashed potatoes and a little gravy (No. 998).

884. Venison Steaks, Currant-Jelly Sauce.—The same as in No. 879, serving with the following sauce: put in a saucepan on a hot range a wine-glassful of good port wine, let it come to a boil; then add half a pint of currant jelly (No. 1326), thoroughly stir until the jelly is well dissolved, pour in a gill of sauce Espagnole (No. 151); let again come to a boil, then pour the sauce on a hot dish; dress the steaks over it, one overlapping another, and send to the table hot.

885. Venison Chops, Chestnut Purée.—Have six fine venison chops; pare, flatten a little, and place them on a plate with a good pinch of salt, half a pinch of pepper, and a tablespoonful of oil. Roll them in well, and put them to broil for four minutes on each side; arrange half a pint of hot purée of chestnuts (No. 131) on a dish. Place the chops over, and serve with a good gravy thrown over all.

886. Civet of Venison, Poivrade Sauce.—Procure two and a half pounds of venison, the lower part if possible (for the lean parts are preferable), cut it into small square pieces, and lay them in an earthen jar, with one sliced onion, half a bunch of parsley-roots, a sprig of thyme, two bay-leaves, twelve whole peppers, two pinches of salt, half a pinch of pepper, and half a glassful of vinegar. Let them marinate for twelve hours. Drain off the juice, and put the venison in a sautoire with an ounce of clarified butter; let cook for ten minutes, then add three tablespoonfuls of flour, stirring well. Moisten with one and a half pints of broth (No. 99), also the marinade-liquor (or juice), well strained. Season with a pinch of salt and half a pinch of pepper, and let cook again for forty minutes. Arrange the civet nicely on a hot dish, sprinkle a little chopped parsley over, and serve.

887. Civet of Venison à la Française.—Prepare the venison exactly the same as for No. 886, and after marinating it twelve hours, drain it well from the marinade-juice, and place it in a saucepan with an ounce of clarified butter, and let brown for ten minutes on a moderate fire; then add three tablespoonfuls of flour, constantly stirring while adding it. Moisten with one and a half glassfuls of red wine, also a pint of hot white broth (No. 99). Season with half a pinch of salt and half a pinch of pepper, then stir well again until boiling, and add twelve well-peeled, small, sound onions, and one ounce of salt pork cut into small, square pieces, also a bouquet (No. 254). Let cook all together for forty minutes; and four minutes before serving add twelve whole mushrooms. Dress on a hot dish, suppress the bouquet, decorate with bread croûtons as in No. 133, all round the dish, and serve.

888. Civet of Venison à la Parisienne.—The same as for the above (No. 887), omitting the salt pork, and substituting for it eighteen small mushrooms instead of twelve.

889. Venison Pie à l'Américaine.—Have three pounds of venison cut into small, square pieces (the parings are preferable); place them in a saucepan with an ounce of butter, and brown them well for six minutes, then add one tablespoonful of flour; stir well, and moisten with a quart of white broth (No. 99); throw in six small, glazed, white onions, a bouquet (No. 254), two pinches of salt, one pinch of pepper, and the third of a pinch of nutmeg. Let cook on the stove for forty-five minutes with the lid on, and when done, lay the stew into a deep dish; cover with a good pie-crust (No. 1077), carefully wetting the edges; egg the surface with beaten egg, make two incisions on each side and a small hole in the centre, then bake in the oven for forty minutes. Prepare a dish with a folded napkin, lay upon this the dish containing the pie, and serve.

890. Antelope Steak, Russian Sauce.—Prepared exactly the same as Venison steak (No. 879), and served with half a pint of hot Russian sauce (No. 211) on the dish, and the steak over it.

891. Antelope Chops, Port Wine Sauce.—Broil six fine antelope chops exactly the same as in No. 885. Heat a glassful of port wine in a saucepan, add two cloves, one bay-leaf, eighteen whole peppers, a gill of currant jelly (No. 1326), thoroughly stir until the jelly is completely dissolved, then thicken with half a gill of sauce Espagnole (No. 151), lightly heat again; then strain on a hot serving-dish, neatly dress the chops over it, and send to the table very hot.

892. Hare, Roasted, Stuffed.—Procure two fine hares, cut them in half, that is, separating the fore-quarters from the hind-quarters. Bone the saddles down to the legs, but not the legs; place them on a deep earthen dish, pour in a wine-glassful of white wine, adding one medium-sized, sound, sliced lemon, one peeled and sliced onion, one sprig of thyme; seasoning with a pinch and a half of salt, a pinch of pepper, and two cloves. Roll the saddles well several times in the seasoning, and put aside to steep for at least twelve hours.

Stuffing.—Place in a saucepan on the hot range half a good-sized, sound, chopped onion with a tablespoonful of butter; cook for one minute, then add two ounces of sausage-meat, six chopped mushrooms, a teaspoonful of chopped parsley, season with half a pinch of salt and the third of a pinch of pepper. Cook all together for six minutes. Let cool, until needed.

Peel four fine, sound apples, cut each into six equal parts, remove the cores; place them in a pan on the fire with half a glassful of white wine or good cider. Boil for four minutes, then place this with the above forcemeat, and mix all well together.

Take the marinated hares, stuff the saddles (which were boned) with the above stuffing evenly, give them a nice round shape, and tie so as to hold them firm; arrange a piece of larding pork over each saddle, then lay them in a roasting-pan, with one carrot and one onion cut into slices and placed at the bottom of the pan; pour one pint of white broth (No. 99) right over the hares. Place in the hot oven, and roast for forty-five minutes, taking care to baste frequently with its own gravy. Remove from the oven, untie, dress on a hot dish, strain the gravy over the saddles, nicely decorate the dish with heart-shaped croûtons (No. 133) all around, and serve.

The fore-quarters can be utilized for Civet, etc., as desired.

893. Civet of Hare à la Française.—Remove the entire skin from a good-sized, tender hare, neatly draw it, preserving the blood, if there is any, and also the liver, the gall being carefully removed. Place the blood and liver on the same dish, and proceed to cut the hare into twelve pieces. Put them into a stone jar, seasoning with one and a half good pinches of salt, a good pinch of pepper, a third of a pinch of nutmeg, one sliced onion, one sprig of thyme, two bay-leaves, and half a glassful of white wine. Mix all well together, and steep well for six hours. Lift out the pieces of hare, and put them in a saucepan with one ounce of butter, adding twelve glazed, small onions, and one ounce of salt pork, cut into small pieces; let cook on a brisk fire for ten minutes, then add three tablespoonfuls of flour, stir well, and moisten with a glassful of red wine, also half a pint of white broth (No. 99). Stir until it boils, then season again with half a pinch of salt and half a pinch of pepper; cook for one hour longer, and fifteen minutes before it is done put in the blood, heart, and liver, finely chopped and all well mixed together. Serve on a dish with six croûtons (No. 133).

894. Gibelotte of Hare.—Proceed exactly the same as for the above (No. 893), replacing the glassful of red wine by a full pint of white broth (No. 99), and adding twelve whole mushrooms four minutes before serving.

895. Fillets of Hare, Sauce Poivrade.—Have two fine English or American hares; clean them neatly as for No. 893, cut them off from the end of the rack, remove the skin from the fillets, and lard the surface with a small needle. Put them on a dish, and season with a pinch and a half of salt, half a pinch of pepper, and the third of a pinch of nutmeg; add one onion, and one carrot cut in pieces, also three tablespoonfuls of white wine. Let all souse together for two hours, then transfer the whole to a roasting-pan, with any scraps of pork-rind, one sliced carrot, and a sliced onion at the bottom of the pan; put it in the oven, and let cook for thirty minutes. Place the fillets on a dish, add to the pan one gill of hot broth (No. 99), let come to a boil, and then strain the gravy over, and serve with half a pint of poivrade sauce (No. 194) separately.

A pinch of salt represents 205 grains, or a tablespoonful.

Half a pinch of pepper represents 38 grains, or a teaspoonful.

A third of a pinch of nutmeg represents 13 grains, or half a teaspoonful.

VEGETABLES.

896. Artichokes à la Barigoul—Lean.—Take three large, fine, sound French artichokes, parboil them for three minutes, drain, and pare the tips as well as the bottoms. Remove the chokes with a vegetable-scoop. Place them in a saucepan, with a medium-sized, sliced carrot, one sound, sliced onion, and a tablespoonful of good butter. Season the artichokes with a pinch of salt only. Cut up very fine one peeled, sound shallot, and place it in a separate pan with a tablespoonful of butter, and cook it for three minutes, being careful not to let it get brown. Add ten chopped mushrooms, a tablespoonful of chopped parsley, and a teaspoonful of finely chopped chervil. Season with a pinch of salt and half a pinch of pepper. Cook for five minutes, stirring occasionally meanwhile. Then stuff the artichokes with the preparation, placing on top of each, one whole mushroom. Place them in the hot oven, with a wine-glassful of white wine and a gill of white broth (No. 99); put the lid on the pan, and cook for forty minutes. Remove, and dress them on a hot dish. Add a gill of good Allemande sauce (No. 210) to the sauce of the artichokes, heat up a little, but do not boil; strain it into a bowl, and serve separately.

The Same, Fat.—Pare the tips, as also the bottoms, of three fine, fresh, large French artichokes. Remove the chokes with a vegetable-scoop. Place them in a saucepan with half an ounce of butter, one sliced carrot, two cloves, one bay-leaf, and one sprig of thyme. Cut up very fine one sound, peeled shallot, place it in a saucepan, with one medium-sized green pepper cut up in small dice-shaped pieces, and a tablespoonful of sweet oil. Cook three minutes. Add a quarter of an ounce of minced cooked ham, eight chopped mushrooms, and one tablespoonful of well-cleaned rice. Let cook for three minutes. Season with a pinch of salt and half a pinch of pepper; add a glassful of white wine, cook for five minutes longer. Add half a gill of tomato sauce (No. 205), and let cook for five minutes more. Stuff the artichokes with the above; arrange a thin slice of larding pork on top of each, place them on the hot stove, with half a glassful of white wine; boil for two minutes, then add half a gill of white broth (No. 99); cover the pan, place in the hot oven, and let cook for forty minutes. Remove from the oven; dress the artichokes on a hot dish, add a gill of Madeira sauce (No.

185) to the gravy. Reduce it for three minutes; strain it into a bowl, and serve separately, very hot.

897. Artichokes Sautés.—Cut six fine, solid, green artichokes into quarters, and remove the choke entirely. Trim the leaves neatly, and parboil them for five minutes in salted and acidulated water. Remove, and drain them thoroughly. Lay them in a sautoire; season with a pinch of salt, a pinch of pepper, and add two ounces of good butter. Cover the pan with the lid, and set to cook in a moderate oven for twenty-five minutes. Take it out, place the artichokes in a deep dish, and serve with any desired sauce.

898. Artichokes à la Duxelle.—Chop up finely, and brown for ten minutes in an ounce of butter, six mushrooms, two fine, sound shallots, a quarter of a bunch of parsley, and a clove of garlic. Pare six small or three large artichokes; remove the choke with a spoon, and fry the tops of the leaves in boiling fat for two minutes, being careful to fry only the leaves. Place them in a sautoire, covering each artichoke with a thin slice of salt pork, and laying a buttered paper on top. Moisten with half a pint of hot consommé (No. 100) and half a glassful of white wine. Then place them in a moderate oven to braise for thirty-five minutes. When done, put the prepared gravy into a gill of Italian sauce (No. 188); place the artichokes in a hot dish, pour the sauce over them, and serve.

899. Fried Artichokes.—Take three fine, large French artichokes; remove the first three or four rows of leaves; cut each artichoke into six pieces; remove the choke with a spoon; pare the tips of the remaining leaves, and lay the pieces in a bowl, with two tablespoonfuls of oil, a good pinch of salt, half a pinch of pepper, a third of a pinch of nutmeg, and a tablespoonful of vinegar. Stir all well together. Make a batter as for No. 1186, dip the artichokes in it, and mix well. Have some fat boiling in a deep pan; lift up the pieces with a skimmer and lay them in one by one, putting in as many as the pan will hold. Stir well, detach those pieces which adhere to the others, and after twelve minutes, or when they are of a golden color, take them out with a strainer. Throw a good handful of parsley-greens into the pan, and as the fat ceases to crackle, after three minutes, take it up; drain through a napkin sprinkled with a little salt. Pile the artichokes on a dish, dome-shaped, garnish with fried parsley, and serve.

900. Artichokes, with Sauce.—Trim neatly six small raw artichokes; pare the under parts, lay them in a saucepan, and cover them partially with boiling water, adding a handful of salt and one tablespoonful of vinegar. Let them cook for about forty minutes, then draw out a leaf, and if it detaches easily, the artichokes are sufficiently done. Take them from the water, and put them to drain upside down. Arrange them on a dish with a folded napkin, and serve. Artichokes prepared in this way can be eaten with white, blonde, Hollandaise, or any kind of sauce. To keep the artichokes green, tie a piece of charred wood about the size of an egg in a linen cloth, and pour over it the water to be used for boiling the artichokes.

901. Stuffed Artichokes à la Barigoul.—Pare three fine, large, French artichokes; cut the under leaves straight, then parboil them sufficiently to remove the choke. After laying them in cold water for five minutes, and draining them thoroughly, fill the empty space with a forcemeat made of half an ounce of hashed salt pork, six minced mushrooms, a teaspoonful of chopped parsley, and two hashed shallots, and seasoning with half a pinch of pepper and a third of a pinch of nutmeg, mixing all well together. Tie them up with a string. Heat three tablespoonfuls of olive oil in a pan, and in it brown well the artichokes for three minutes on each side. Place them in a sautoire, and put on top of each artichoke a small slice of fresh pork or veal, or some butter, adding a glassful of broth (No. 99). Cook them in the oven for forty minutes, place the artichokes in a hot dish, pour the sauce over and serve.

902. Artichokes à la Vinaigrette.—Prepare and cook three large or six small, fine artichokes the same as for No. 900. The large ones are to be eaten boiled, cooled, and served with the following sauce in a sauce-bowl: pound the yolk of a hard-boiled egg in a bowl, dilute it with two spoonfuls of vinegar, season with a pinch of salt, and half a pinch of pepper, a finely chopped shallot, and three tablespoonfuls of good oil. Mix well together, and serve.

The small artichokes may be served in the same way, or they can be eaten raw (as they frequently are in Europe), with the choke removed. Dress the artichokes on a dish with a folded napkin, and serve the sauce in a separate bowl.

903. Artichokes à la Florentine.—Fill six parboiled fresh or conserved artichoke-bottoms with a preparation made of fresh sliced mushrooms, if at hand, a small, cooked cauliflower, weighing half a pound when pared, and stewed in half a pint of béchamel (No. 154), with two tablespoonfuls of grated cheese, seasoned with half a pinch of pepper, and the third of a pinch of nutmeg. Sprinkle with fresh bread-crumbs, and pour over them a little clarified butter; brown in the oven for ten minutes; place the artichokes in a hot dish, pour a gill of hot Madeira sauce (No. 185) over them, and serve.

904. Asparagus, Sauce Hollandaise.—Scrape nicely and wash carefully two bunches of fine asparagus; tie them into six equal bunches, arranging the heads all one way, and chop off the ends evenly. Boil them until they are done in salted water, or from twenty to twenty-two minutes; lift them out, drain them thoroughly on a cloth, and lay them nicely on a dish with a folded napkin. Untie, and serve with half a pint of hot Hollandaise sauce (No. 160), in a separate bowl.

Asparagus with drawn butter is prepared in exactly the same way, and is served with a gill of drawn butter (No. 157).

905. Asparagus à la Vinaigrette.—Prepare two bunches of sound asparagus as in No. 904, and serve with half a pint of sauce vinaigrette (No. 902), after the asparagus has been thoroughly cooled. Asparagus can be served in this way either hot or cold.

906. Asparagus à la Tessinoise.—Boil for only twelve minutes two bunches of fine fresh asparagus as for No. 904, place them on a dish in layers, with grated Swiss or Parmesan cheese between. Lightly brown a third of a medium-sized, sound, chopped onion in one ounce of butter, and pour over the whole; sprinkle the top with a little cheese and fresh bread-crumbs, and cook in a moderate oven for fifteen minutes.

Take out of the oven, and send to the table in the same dish.

907. Fried Egg-plant.—Peel one medium-sized egg-plant, cut it into six round slices, about half an inch in thickness, and season with half a teaspoonful of salt and a teaspoonful of pepper. Dip the pieces in beaten egg and in fresh bread-crumbs, and fry them in hot fat for five minutes. Remove, salt slightly again, and drain them well; serve on a hot dish over a folded napkin.

908. Broiled Egg-plant.—Peel neatly a sound, medium-sized egg-plant, and cut it into six even slices half an inch thick, in such a way that one egg-plant will be sufficient. Place the slices in a dish; season them with a pinch of salt and half a pinch of pepper, and throw over them a tablespoonful of sweet oil. Mix well together; then arrange the slices on the broiler, and broil them for five minutes on each side. Remove them from the fire, place them in a hot dish, spread a gill of maître d'hôtel (No. 145) over them, and send them to the table.

909. Stuffed Egg-plant.

—Cut a good-sized egg-plant into six parts, so that the peel remains intact on one side. Make four incisions inside of each piece, and fry them for one minute in boiling fat; dig out the fleshy part of the egg-plant with a potato-scoop, and fill it with any forcemeat at hand. Sprinkle the top with bread-crumbs and a little clarified butter; brown well in the oven for ten minutes, and serve.

910. Beet-roots, Boiled Plain.—Wash a quart of sound, young beet-roots thoroughly in cold water. Place them in a saucepan, covering them with cold water; season with a handful of salt and two tablespoonfuls of vinegar; put on the lid and cook for one hour and ten minutes. Take them from the fire; lift them from the water, and peel them while they are warm. When done, put them in a stone jar; strain over them the liquor in which they were boiled; spread two tablespoonfuls of powdered sugar on top; cover them, and put them away in a cool place for use when required.

Beet-roots are generally served as a salad, a hors-d'œuvre, or a garnishing for salad.

911. Beet-roots Sautées au Beurre.—With the same quantity of beet-roots proceed as in No. 910; when cooked and peeled, cut them up in clove-shaped pieces; then put them in a sautoire with one ounce of butter, seasoning with a pinch of pepper, and sprinkling a very little powdered sugar over them. Let them cook on the stove for six minutes, carefully tossing them from time to time; then arrange them in a hot vegetable-dish, and serve.

912. Beet-roots Sautées à la Crême.—Proceed the same as in No. 911, adding half a pint of hot béchamel (No. 154) three minutes before serving.

913. Mushrooms Sautées à la Bordelaise.—Select a pound of the largest, driest, thickest, and firmest mushrooms procurable; pare neatly, wash them well, drain, and cut lozenge-shaped. Place them in an earthen dish, sprinkle them with a tablespoonful of good oil, a pinch of salt, and twelve whole peppers, and leave them in the marinade for two hours. Take them out and stew them for six minutes; when done, place them on the serving-dish, and cover them with the following sauce: Place in a sautoire three tablespoonfuls of oil, a teaspoonful of parsley, the same of chives, and a clove of crushed garlic, all well chopped. Heat for five minutes; then add them to the mushrooms, which are ready to serve.

914. Mushrooms Sautés on Toast.—Choose a pound of fine, sound, large, fresh mushrooms, neatly pare off the ends, clean, and wash them well. Drain, and place them in a sautoire with an ounce of good butter. Season with a pinch of salt and half a pinch of pepper. Cover, and let them cook for ten minutes, tossing them well meanwhile. Squeeze in the juice of half a medium-sized sound lemon; add a pinch of chopped parsley, nicely sprinkled over. Place six pieces of toasted bread on a hot dish, dress the mushrooms over the toasts, and serve.

915. Mushrooms Sautés à la Crême.—Prepare a pound of fine, fresh mushrooms exactly the same as above (No. 914), and if very large cut them in two. Place them in a sautoire with an ounce of good butter. Season with a pinch of salt and half a pinch of pepper, then put the lid on, and cook on a moderate fire for six minutes; then add two tablespoonfuls of velouté sauce (No. 152), and half a cupful of sweet cream. Cook again for four minutes, and serve them in a very hot dish with six heart-shaped bread croûtons (No. 133) around it.

916. Mushrooms Broiled on Toast.—Pare neatly, wash well, and dry thoroughly one pound of fine, large mushrooms. Lay them on a dish, season with a pinch of salt, half a pinch of pepper, and a tablespoonful of sweet oil. Roll them in well; then put them on to broil for four minutes on each side; arrange them on a hot dish with six slices of toast; pour a gill of maître d'hôtel butter (No. 145) over the mushrooms, and serve.

917. Blanched Cabbage.—Pare off the outer leaves from a medium-sized cabbage; cut it into four square pieces, wash thoroughly, dry, and put it in a saucepan covering it with salted hot water. Cook for ten minutes, drain, and put it into cold water to cool off; remove from the water, and drain again.

All cabbages are blanched before using them, with the exception of stuffed cabbage, which must be left whole.

918. Cabbage with Cream.—Drain, and let cool a well-blanched cabbage (No. 917); chop it up, and place it in a saucepan with two ounces of butter, seasoning with a good pinch of salt, half a pinch of pepper, and the third of a pinch of grated nutmeg; add a tablespoonful of flour, stir well, and moisten with a cupful of cream. Reduce until the cabbage and gravy are well incorporated, which will take about forty-five minutes. Arrange on a hot dish, and serve.

919. Stuffed Cabbage.—Cut out the root and heart from a medium-sized cabbage-head, and pick off several of the outer leaves; parboil the rest as for No. 917. After removing it from the fire, open the leaves carefully, so as not to break them; then season the cabbage with a pinch of salt and half a pinch of pepper, and fill the inside of the leaves with a good sausage forcemeat (No. 220). Close them up, and tie the cabbage so that none of the stuffing escapes; then lay it in a sautoire containing one cut-up carrot, one cut-up onion, a piece of lard skin, and half a pint of white broth (No. 99). Cover with a little fat from the soup-stock; lay a buttered paper on top, and let cook for one hour in the oven, basting it occasionally with its own juice; untie, and serve with half a pint of Madeira sauce (No. 185).

920. Cabbage for Garnishing.—Prepare a cabbage exactly the same as for No. 919; divide it into six parts, stuff each one with sausage forcemeat (No. 220), wrap them up, and tie, rolling them well. Put them in a sautoire garnished the same as for the stuffed cabbage, and cook for forty minutes in the oven; untie, and serve when needed.

921. Pork and Cabbage.—Pare neatly, and divide a medium-sized cabbage into four pieces; wash them well, parboil for ten minutes, and then put them into any kind of vessel with a pound of salt pork, well washed, three cervelas, a branch of celery, one onion, two large carrots, a blade each of bay-leaf and thyme, half a pinch of pepper, but no salt, and cover with a buttered paper. Let simmer on a gentle fire for one hour and a half; then place the cabbage in a dish, using a skimmer; also the pork and sausages, laying them on top; decorate the dish with the rest of the vegetables, and serve.

922. Brussels Sprouts, Sautés au Beurre.—Pare neatly, and pick off the outer dead leaves of one pound of imported Brussels sprouts, or one and a half pounds of domestic sprouts; wash them thoroughly, drain, and cook them in boiling salted water for seven minutes. Drain, and let cool in cold water; drain them once more, then throw the sprouts into a sautoire containing two ounces of butter. Season with half a pinch each of salt and pepper, adding a teaspoonful of chopped parsley; cook slightly for five minutes; then serve.

923. Brussels Sprouts, Sautés à la Crême.—Pare, pick, and blanch one pound of sprouts as in No. 922. When well drained, put them in a sautoire with two tablespoonfuls of velouté (No. 152); season with half a pinch of salt, and the third of a pinch each of pepper and nutmeg. Add half a cupful of sweet cream. Let them heat, but not boil, for five minutes, tossing them frequently; dress on a hot dish, and serve.

924. Sourkrout.

—After washing three pints of imported sourkrout in several waters, drain it well, and put it in a saucepan with a large piece of well-washed salt pork, three cervelas, two carrots, two whole onions, half a cupful of roast meat-fat, six juniper berries, a glassful of good white wine, and a pint of white broth (No. 99). Let it cook slowly for three hours; then drain the sourkrout, dish it up with the pork on top, which can either be served in one piece, or divided into six slices, arranging the cervelas around, nicely dressed.

925. Cauliflower, Boiled with Butter.—Take one large or two small cauliflowers; pare, pick, and examine them well to see if anything adheres which should be removed; wash them thoroughly in fresh water, and then put in a saucepan, covering with cold water; season with a handful of salt and half a pinch of pepper, and add an ounce of kneaded butter. After cooking about thirty minutes, drain them through a colander, and lay them on a dish, pouring over them a sauce made of one ounce of good butter, a third of a pinch of salt, the same of pepper, and a tablespoonful of vinegar, then serve.

Cauliflowers prepared the same way can be served with a white sauce or Hollandaise sauce. They are also eaten as a salad when cold.

926. Cauliflower au Gratin.—Pare, pick, cook, and drain one large or two medium-sized cauliflowers as for No. 925. Cut off the roots; then place them on a buttered baking-dish, covering them with a pint of good béchamel (No. 154), to which three tablespoonfuls of grated Parmesan cheese have been added. Sprinkle the top with three more tablespoonfuls of grated cheese and a little fresh bread-crumbs. Place the dish in the oven and let it get a golden brown color. It will require about twenty minutes' cooking, but care must be taken to turn the dish frequently, so that the cauliflower will be equally well browned all over.

927. Carrots Sautées à la Crême.—Pare off the ends of six good-sized carrots, scrape them neatly, wash thoroughly, and cut them in rounds half an inch thick. Cook them in white broth (No. 99), (salted water will answer as well); cover the saucepan, and let them cook for thirty minutes. Remove, drain, and place them in a sautoire, with three tablespoonfuls of béchamel (No. 154), and a cupful of cream or milk. Season with a pinch of salt, half a pinch of pepper, and the third of a pinch of nutmeg. After ten minutes, place them in a hot dish, sprinkle a good pinch of chopped parsley over, and serve.

928. Celery, with Gravy à la Bonne Femme.

—Procure two bunches of fine Kalamazoo celery. If there should be four heads in each bunch, reserve two for table celery, as hors-d'œvres. Pare the outer branches, and clean thoroughly, cutting off the hard and green leaves. Cut them into equal lengths, and blanch them in boiling water for five minutes; drain, and add half a pint of broth (No. 99) to the water. Put the celery into a gill of white roux (No. 135) in a sautoire, and season with a pinch of salt, twelve whole peppers, and a third of a pinch of nutmeg. When the celery is sufficiently cooked, or after twenty-five minutes, finish the sauce with a gill of clear gravy or half an ounce of butter. Place the celery in a hot dish, pour the sauce over and serve.

929. Celery with Cream.—Pare nicely four heads of fine celery, and cut it into pieces two inches in length; wash thoroughly; remove from the water with the hands, and lay it on a napkin. By so doing no sand will adhere to the celery. Blanch it in boiling salted water for five minutes; remove, drain, and put it in a sautoire with two ounces of butter and one tablespoonful of fecula; stir all well together, and moisten with half a pint of consommé (No. 100). Cook and reduce the whole for twenty minutes; when done, thicken with two beaten egg yolks diluted in three tablespoonfuls of cream, and add the third of a pinch of grated nutmeg. Serve garnished with six croûtons (No. 133).

930. Celery à la Moëlle de Bœuf.—Take six heads of fine celery, cut off the green leaves, pare neatly, wash thoroughly, drain, and tie each head near the end where the green part has been cut away. Blanch them in salted boiling water for ten minutes, then remove, drain, and put them in a sautoire, with a pint of Madeira sauce (No. 185). Cook for fifteen minutes. Arrange the heads on a hot dish; remove the strings, and add to the sauce in the sautoire eighteen slices of marrow half an inch thick. Cook for one minute, being careful not to break the pieces of marrow; pour the sauce over the celery, and serve.

931. Cardons à la Moëlle.—Prepared exactly the same as in No. 930.

932. Chicory, with Cream or White Sauce.—Clean and pick three large heads of chicory; throw away all the outer green leaves; wash them in two waters, drain, and blanch them in boiling, salted water. Remove them after ten minutes, and cool them in fresh water. Take them out, and press out the water thoroughly; then chop up the chicory, and place it with four ounces of butter in a saucepan, and cook a quarter of an hour, or until dry. Pour over it two glassfuls of cream or milk, a very little at a time, reduce, and grate in a third of a pinch of nutmeg; add a pinch of salt and half a pinch of pepper; stir well together, leave it on for five minutes, and serve with six heart-shaped croûtons (No. 133) around the dish.

933. Chicory, with Gravy.—Take six large, fine, fresh heads of chicory, pare any outer leaves that may be damaged, leaving the root intact; wash well in two waters, remove, and put them to blanch for ten minutes in salted boiling water. Take them out, put them back into cold water, and let them cool off thoroughly. Drain neatly, and cut them in halves. Put a piece of lard skin at the bottom of a sautoire, add one carrot, one onion, both cut up, and a bouquet (No. 254). Place the chicory on top, season with half a pinch of salt, half a pinch of pepper, and a third of a pinch of nutmeg, and cover with a buttered paper. Place the sautoire on the stove, and when the chicory is a golden color (not letting it take longer than ten minutes), moisten with half a pint of white broth (No. 99). Put it in the oven for thirty minutes; arrange the chicory on a hot dish, strain the sauce over, and serve.

934. Chicory for Garnishing.—Prepare exactly as for No. 933, using it when needed.

935. Cucumbers à la Poulette.—Peel three fine, large cucumbers, blanch them in salted boiling water for five minutes, drain, and cut them into pieces one inch thick. Place them in a sautoire with one ounce of butter, strew over them a pinch of very fine flour, stir well, and moisten with half a pint of white broth (No. 99), seasoning with half a pinch of salt, and the same of pepper. Stir well until it boils, and reduce the whole for fifteen minutes, adding a teaspoonful of chopped parsley, a third of a pinch of nutmeg, two beaten egg yolks, and two tablespoonfuls of sweet cream. Cook again, without letting it come to a boil, for three minutes, and serve.

936. Cucumbers à la Béchamel.—Peel, pare nicely, and blanch six small, fine cucumbers in salted boiling water for five minutes. Remove, drain, and place them in a sautoire with half a pint of good béchamel sauce (No. 154), half an ounce of butter, the third of a pinch of nutmeg, and three tablespoonfuls of milk. Cook all together for fifteen minutes, and pour the whole on a hot dish, and serve.

937. Stuffed Cucumbers.—Peel six small cucumbers, pare them carefully and shapely; cut off the lower ends, and with a vegetable-spoon empty them, after extracting all the seeds. Place them in slightly acidulated water; rinse them well, and parboil them in boiling water for three minutes. Remove them, and put in cold water to cool. Drain them, and fill the insides with a cooked forcemeat made of the breasts of chickens (No. 226). Line a sautoire with slices of pork-skin; add the cucumbers, season with a pinch of salt and half a pinch of pepper, a bouquet (No. 254), a glassful of white wine, two cloves, and a spoonful of dripping from any kind of roast. Cover with a piece of buttered paper, and place it in a slow oven to cook gently for twenty minutes. When done, transfer them carefully to a hot dish; free them entirely from any fat, pour half a pint of Madeira sauce (No. 185) over them, and serve.

938. Stewed Cucumbers for Garnishing.—-Peel and slice three large, fine cucumbers; marinate them with a pinch of salt, half a pinch of pepper, a tablespoonful of vinegar, and one sliced onion. Leave them in for one hour; strain, and put the whole into a saucepan with a pint of Espagnole sauce (No. 151). Cook for twenty minutes; strain through a fine sieve, and use for any garnishing required.

939. Spinach Blanched au Naturel.—Take a peck of fresh, sound spinach, cut off the stalks, pare neatly, wash it twice in plenty of water, lifting it out with the hands. Place it in boiling salted water, and boil it for fifteen minutes. Remove, and drain it thoroughly; place it in cold water again, and let it cool. Lift and drain, pressing it well; lay it on a wooden board, and hash it very fine.

940. Spinach à l'Anglaise.—Proceed exactly the same as for No. 939, but the spinach must not be hashed; when well drained put it into a saucepan with one ounce of butter; mix well for five minutes, and it will be ready for any use desired.

941. Spinach à la Vieille Mode.—After the spinach is blanched and well chopped, as for No. 939, put it in a saucepan with an ounce of butter and the third of a pinch of grated nutmeg. Stir with a wooden spoon, and cook for five minutes, adding an ounce of butter kneaded with two tablespoonfuls of flour, two tablespoonfuls of powdered sugar, and half a pint of milk. Stir frequently, and cook for ten minutes; then serve, garnished with six sippets of bread fried in butter.

942. Spinach à la Maître d'hôtel.—After blanching the spinach as for No. 939, and chopping it very fine, put it dry into a saucepan. Place it to simmer on a moderate fire, seasoning with a pinch of salt, half a pinch of pepper, and the third of a pinch of grated nutmeg. When warm, add an ounce and a half of butter; stir well, and let it heat for fifteen minutes. Lay it on a hot dish, and decorate it with six bread croûtons (No. 133); then serve.

943. Spinach, with Gravy.—When the spinach is blanched and well drained (No. 939), put it in a saucepan with half a cupful of veal-stock (either the reduced gravy of a fricandeau, or a glaze), cook for ten minutes, and when ready to serve, add a good ounce of butter; melt well together, and serve with six pieces of fried bread.

944. Spinach, with Sugar.—Season the blanched spinach (No. 939) with a very little salt, three lumps of sugar, a little crushed lemon-peel, and two pulverized macaroons. Cook slowly all together for ten minutes, and serve surrounded by six lady-fingers (No. 1231).

945. String Beans, Blanched.—Take two quarts of fresh, tender string beans; break off the tops and bottoms carefully; string both sides, and pare both edges neatly; wash them well in cold water, lift them, and drain. Place them in boiling salted water, and cook for twenty-five minutes. Drain again, and return them to cold water, letting them get thoroughly cool. Lift them out, and dry. They are now ready to use when required, for salads or any other purpose.

946. String Beans, with Cream.—Place the blanched beans (No. 945) in a saucepan with an ounce of butter, and cook on the stove for five minutes, tossing them well. Season with half a pinch of salt, the same of pepper, and add half a bunch of chives and two sprigs of parsley tied together. Pour in half a cupful of fresh cream or milk, diluted with two egg yolks. Heat well, without boiling, for five minutes. Then serve as a *hors-d'œuvre or entremet*. Sugar may be added with advantage, if desired.

947. String Beans au Blanc.—String the fresh string beans (No. 945); if too large, cut them lengthwise, and cook them in water with salt and butter; drain, and place them in a saucepan with one ounce of butter; add a teaspoonful of parsley and the same of chopped chives. Cook for five minutes, and when done, thicken the gravy with half a cupful of cream, two egg yolks, and the juice of a lemon. Mix well together for two minutes, and serve.

948. String Beans à l'Anglaise.—Blanch and cook the beans as for No. 945, keep them warm, and of a light green color; place them in a hot dish, pour over them a gill of good melted butter, sprinkle a little chopped parsley on top, and serve very hot.

949. String Beans à la Bretonne.—Cut a medium-sized onion in dice-shaped pieces, and place them in a saucepan with an ounce and a half of butter; let it get a good golden color on the stove for five minutes; then add a tablespoonful of flour. Stir well, and moisten it with a pint of white broth (No. 99). Stir well again, until it comes to a boil; season with half a pinch each of salt and pepper. Add the cooked string beans, with a clove of crushed garlic, to the sauce; cook for ten minutes; place in a hot dish; sprinkle a teaspoonful of chopped parsley over it, and serve.

950. Beans Panachées.—Place half a pint of cooked string beans (No. 945) and the same quantity of flageolets or Lima beans in a sautoire with an ounce and a half of good butter; season with half a pinch each of salt and pepper; toss them well while cooking for five minutes. Place them in a hot dish; sprinkle a light pinch of chopped parsley over them, and send to the table.

951. Red Beans à la Bourguignonne.—Take a quart of sound red beans; pick out all the small stones that are likely to be mixed with them; wash them thoroughly, lay them in plenty of cold water, and let them soak for six hours. Drain, and put them in a saucepan, covering them with fresh water, adding an ounce of butter, a bouquet (No. 254), and a medium-sized onion with two cloves stuck in. Boil for twenty minutes, stirring in a good glassful of red wine; season with a pinch of salt and half a pinch of pepper, and let it cook again for forty-five minutes. Remove, take out the bouquet and onion, and place the beans in a hot, deep dish; decorate with six small glazed onions (No. 972) around the dish, and serve.

Dried red beans, white beans, Lima beans, split dried peas, lentils, or any other kind of dried beans, should always be soaked six hours in fresh water before using them.

952. Fresh Lima Beans.—Take a quart of fresh, shelled Lima beans, or three quarts of unshelled; parboil them in salted water for about twenty minutes, then take them from the fire, drain, and let cool in fresh water. Drain again, and place them in a sautoire with an ounce and a half of good butter, seasoning with half a pinch each of salt and pepper, and the third of a pinch of nutmeg. Cook for five minutes, tossing well; then moisten with two tablespoonfuls of cream, adding a pinch of chopped parsley; mix well together, and serve.

953. Stuffed Lettuce.—Pick, clean, pare nicely, and wash thoroughly six lettuce-heads; parboil them for five minutes, drain them well, and fill the insides with godiveau (No. 221) or sausage forcemeat (No. 220). Tie each head, and put them in a sautoire, laying them down carefully, and adding a gill of Madeira sauce (No. 185), and a gill of white broth (No. 99). Season with half a pinch each of salt and pepper, cover with buttered paper, and cook in the oven for fifteen minutes. Arrange on a hot dish, untie, pour the sauce over, and serve.

954. Macaroni à la Crême.—Boil for three-quarters of an hour three-quarters of a pound of Italian macaroni in plenty of salted water, adding a small piece of butter (half an ounce), and an onion stuck with two cloves. Drain well, and put it back into a saucepan with a third of a pound of butter, a third of a pound of grated Swiss cheese, the same quantity of grated Parmesan cheese, a third of a pinch of nutmeg, and a pinch of pepper. Moisten with half a pint of white broth (No. 99) and four tablespoonfuls of cream. Cook all together for five minutes, stirring well, and when the macaroni becomes ropy, dish it up, and serve.

955. Macaroni au Gratin.—After the macaroni is prepared as for No. 954, place it in a baking-dish, sprinkle over it a little bread-crumbs and grated cheese; pour over it a little clarified butter, and place it in the baking oven for ten minutes, or until it assumes a golden color; then serve.

956. Macaroni à l'Italienne.—Prepare three-quarters of a pound of sound Italian macaroni as for No. 954; place it in a saucepan with a gill of tomato sauce (No. 205), a gill of Madeira sauce (No. 185), and a quarter of a pound of grated Parmesan cheese; season with half a pinch of pepper and the third of a pinch of nutmeg; then let cook slowly for ten minutes, tossing frequently. Arrange on a hot dish, and serve with some grated cheese, separately.

957. Macaroni à la Napolitaine.—Boil the macaroni in salt and water as for No. 954; drain, place it in a saucepan, and add half a pint of good Espagnole sauce (No. 151), half a pint of tomato sauce (No. 205), a quarter of a pound of grated cheese, two truffles, six mushrooms, and half an ounce of cooked, smoked beef-tongue, all cut up in dice-shaped pieces. Cook together on a brisk stove for ten minutes, tossing them well meanwhile, and serve.

958. Macaroni à la Milanaise.—Prepare exactly the same as for No. 957, cutting the truffles, mushrooms, and beef-tongue julienne-shaped.

959. Spaghetti à la Napolitaine.—Boil three-quarters of a pound of sound, fine spaghetti as for the macaroni in No. 954; drain,and put it back into a saucepan with half a pint of tomato sauce (No. 205), half a pint of Espagnole (No. 151), six mushrooms, two truffles, and a small piece of cooked, smoked, red beef-tongue, all cut up dice-shaped. Season with half a pinch of pepper and the third of a pinch of nutmeg, adding a quarter of a pound of grated Parmesan cheese. Cook for ten minutes, tossing well, and serve with a little cheese, separately.

960. Spaghetti à l'Italienne.—Place the spaghetti in a saucepan as for No. 959; add a pint of tomato sauce (No. 205), and a quarter of a pound of grated Parmesan cheese; season with half a pinch of pepper and a third of a pinch of nutmeg, and cook for ten minutes, tossing well, and serving as in No. 959.

961. Spaghetti au Gratin.—Prepare three-quarters of a pound of boiled spaghetti as in No. 959, place it in a saucepan, moistening with half a pint of Allemande sauce (No. 210), and half a pint of béchamel sauce (No. 154). Season with one pinch of pepper, and the third of a pinch of nutmeg, adding a quarter of a pound of grated cheese. Toss well, put it in a baking-dish, sprinkle the top with grated cheese and fresh bread-crumbs; pour over it a very little clarified butter, and place it in the oven. When of a fine golden color, after about fifteen minutes, take from the oven, and serve.

962. Boiled Green Corn.—Pare off the outer leaves and silk of six young and tender ears of corn, and place them in a saucepan, covering them with water. Add half a cupful of milk, half an ounce of butter, and a handful of salt. Cook for twenty minutes, and serve on a folded napkin.

963. Corn Sauté à la Crême.—Take six ears of cooked green corn, prepared as for No. 962, drain, cut off the corn from the cobs with a sharp knife, being very careful that none of the cob adheres to the corn. Place it in a sautoire with a gill of hot béchamel sauce (No. 154), half a cupful of cream, and half an ounce of butter; season with half a pinch each of salt and pepper, and the third of a pinch of nutmeg. Cook gently on the stove for five minutes, place in a hot dish, and serve.

964. Corn Sauté au Beurre.—Proceed as for No. 963, adding one ounce of butter, but suppressing the other ingredients. Season the same, but cook only for eight minutes, tossing it well. Place in a hot dish, and serve.

965. Corn Fritters.—Prepare four young, tender, good-sized, fresh ears of green corn exactly as for No. 963; after draining it carefully, place it in a china bowl; season with a pinch of salt and half a pinch of pepper, and add two fresh eggs, a quarter of a pound of well-sifted flour, and half a pint of cold milk. Do not beat the mixture, but stir it vigorously with a wooden spoon for five minutes, and it will be sufficiently firm. Butter well a frying-pan, take a kitchen ladle that contains the equivalent of a gill, and with this put the preparation into the pan in twelve parts; be careful they do not touch one another, and let them get a good golden color on each side for four minutes. Dress them on a folded napkin, and serve.

966. Barley Fritters.—The same as in No. 965, substituting boiled barley for corn.

967. Glazed Turnips, with Gravy.—Pare, and cut pear-shaped, twelve equal-sized, small white turnips; parboil them for five minutes, and drain them when done. Butter the bottom of a sautoire capable of holding them, one beside the other, and let them get a golden color, adding half a pint of powdered sugar. Moisten with half a pint of white broth (No. 99), half a pinch of salt, and add a very small stick of cinnamon. Cover with a buttered paper cut the shape of the sautoire, and place it in the oven to cook for twenty minutes. When the turnips are cooked, lift off the paper. Place the turnips on a hot dish, and reduce the gravy to a glaze for six minutes. Arrange them nicely on a dish, pour half a gill of good broth (No. 99) into the saucepan to loosen the glaze, remove the cinnamon, and throw the sauce over the turnips.

968. Onions, with Cream.—Peel twelve medium-sized, sound onions; pare the roots without cutting them, and place them in a saucepan; cover with salted water, add a bouquet (No. 254), and cook for forty-five minutes. Lift them from the saucepan, and lay them on a dish; cover them with half a pint of cream sauce (No. 181), mixed with two tablespoonfuls of the broth they were cooked in, and serve.

969. Fried Onions.—Peel, pare, and slice round-shaped, four medium-sized onions. Lay them first in milk, then in flour, and fry them in very hot fat for eight minutes. Lift them up and lay them on a cloth to dry. Serve on a dish with a folded napkin, with a little fried parsley.

970. Stuffed Onions.—Peel six medium-sized Spanish onions; empty out the centres with a vegetable-scoop; parboil them for three minutes, and turn them upside down on a cloth to drain. Fill the insides with sausage forcemeat (No. 220). Line the bottom of a sautoire with a piece of lard skin, and one carrot and one onion, both cut up; lay the onions on top, and moisten with half a pint of broth (No. 99). Cover with a buttered paper; then put it in the oven to glaze for forty minutes, taking care to baste frequently. Place them in a hot dish; strain the gravy over them, and serve.

971. Minced Onions.—Peel and pare three medium-sized onions; cut them in two, and mince them into fine slices. Place them in a sautoire, with half an ounce of butter, and let them get a good golden color on the stove for ten minutes, tossing them briskly. Place them in a bowl, and use when required.

972. Glazed Onions for Garnishing.—Select one quart of small onions; peel the sides only, and pare the roots neatly, being careful not to cut them. Place them in a sautoire with half an ounce of clarified butter, and sprinkle them with half a pinch of powdered sugar. Glaze them in a slow oven for fifteen minutes; place them in a stone jar, and use for garnishing when required.

973. Sorrel au Maigre.—Pick off the stems from half a peck of sorrel; wash it in several waters, drain, and chop up with a head of well-cleansed lettuce. Add half a bunch of chervil, and chop all together very fine. Place all in a saucepan, stir well together on the hot stove for three minutes, and then place it in the oven until the vegetables are well dissolved; then add an ounce and a half of butter, and stir again for about ten minutes, or until the sorrel is reduced to a pulp. Season with a pinch of salt and half a pinch of pepper, and pour into it a thickening of two egg yolks and half a cupful of cream; stir well, without boiling, and serve.

974. Sorrel au Gras.—Dissolve the same quantity of sorrel as in No. 973, adding enough butter to form it into a perfect pulp (one ounce and a half will answer); stir it until it begins to bubble; then moisten it with half a pint of gravy or good stock, roast-beef gravy, or reduced broth. Cook it for five minutes, and use this purée as a sauce for various meats.

975. Stuffed Peppers.—Fry for one minute only, six medium-sized green peppers in very hot fat; drain and skin them properly, and cut a round piece off the bottom to use for a cover. Remove the insides, and fill them with a good sausage forcemeat (No. 220); put on the round cover previously cut off, and lay them on an oiled baking-tin. Moisten the peppers lightly with sweet oil, and place them in a slow oven to cook for fifteen minutes; then arrange them on a hot dish, and serve with a gill of demi-glace sauce (No. 185).

976. Green Peas à l'Ancienne Mode.—Take three quarts of unshelled, young, tender green peas; shell them carefully, and keep them wrapped up in a wet napkin until needed. Clean, drain, and tie up a lettuce-head; put it in a saucepan with the peas; season with a pinch of salt; cover with a glassful of water, and add a quarter of a pound of very good butter. After cooking for a quarter of an hour, remove the lettuce, and when ready to serve, thicken the peas with three spoonfuls of cream, diluted with one egg yolk, adding half a pinch of white pepper, and a spoonful of powdered sugar. Let all thicken together for five minutes, and serve immediately in a tureen.

977. Green Peas à la Française.—Shell carefully three quarts of fine, young, tender, fresh green peas, and place them in a saucepan with one ounce of butter and half a cupful of water. Knead together with a wooden spoon; strain off the water, and add a bouquet (No. 254), one small onion, a well-cleansed lettuce-heart, half a pinch of salt, and a teaspoonful of powdered sugar. Cover the saucepan, and cook very slowly for half an hour; remove the bouquet and onion; lay the lettuce upon a dish, incorporate into the peas half an ounce of fresh butter, and cook until it thickens, which will require at least five minutes. Pour the peas dome-formed over the lettuce, and send to the table.

978. Green Peas à l'Anglaise.—Procure the same quantity of green peas as for No. 977; put them in a saucepan, and cover them with boiling water. Add a handful of salt, and boil quickly, without covering, for fifteen minutes. Skim the water as soon as the scum rises. When done, strain them through a colander, return them to the saucepan, and toss them well, adding an ounce and a half of fresh butter. Dish them in a vegetable-dish, place another half ounce of butter in the middle, and serve.

979. Green Peas à la Bourgeoise.—Shell three quarts of tender green peas; put them in a saucepan, and toss the peas quickly in a gill of light roux (No. 135); moisten with a pint of boiling water, adding half a pinch each of salt and pepper, a bouquet (No. 254), and a raw lettuce-heart. Reduce it for twenty minutes, or until all the juice has evaporated; then add two raw egg yolks well beaten, with three tablespoonfuls of sweet cream. Stir quickly for four minutes, without allowing it to boil, and then serve, removing the bouquet.

980. Green Peas, with Cream.—Put one ounce of butter in a saucepan with one tablespoonful of flour kneaded well together. Dissolve it; then add the shelled peas as for No. 977, a bouquet (No. 254), a quarter of a bunch of chives, a pinch of salt, and half a pinch of pepper. Cook in their own juice for twenty minutes, then take the saucepan from off the fire. Pour the gravy from the peas into another vessel, add to it half a cupful of cream and a teaspoonful of powdered sugar; pour this sauce over the peas, and heat up once again without boiling, for two minutes, before serving.

981. Green Peas, With Bacon.—Brown in a saucepan half an ounce of butter with two ounces of small, dice-shaped pieces of bacon, and when of a good golden color, take them out, and put a spoonful of flour into the fat to make a roux. Moisten with a pint of white broth (No. 99); replace the bacon, add the raw shelled peas, as for No. 977, one whole onion, a bouquet (No. 254), and half a pinch of pepper. Cover, and let cook on the corner of the stove for thirty minutes; place in a hot, deep dish, and serve.

982. Potatoes, Boiled Plain.—Take twelve medium-sized, fine, sound potatoes; wash them thoroughly, peel off a piece of the skin, about half an inch wide, around each potato, to ensure mealiness, and lay them in a saucepan, covering them with cold water, and adding half a handful of salt; place the lid on, and cook for forty-five minutes. Drain, lay a napkin on a hot dish, in which you envelop the potatoes, and serve.

983. Broiled Potatoes.—Peel six medium-sized, sound, cooked potatoes; cut them in halves; lay them on a dish, and season them with a pinch of salt. Pour two tablespoonfuls of melted butter over them, and roll them well in it. Arrange them on a double broiler, and broil them on a moderate fire for three minutes on each side. Place them in a hot dish, with a folded napkin, and serve.

984. Potatoes à la Génevroise.—Peel, wash, and drain four medium-sized, sound potatoes; cut them into julienne-shaped pieces, and wash and drain them again. Season with a pinch of salt and half a pinch of pepper. Butter lightly six tartlet-molds with clarified butter; cover the bottoms with grated Parmesan cheese; arrange a layer of potatoes on top, sprinkle more cheese over them, and continue until all are filled, finishing by sprinkling cheese over the surface and dropping a little clarified butter over all. Set them on a very hot stove for two minutes; then place in a hot oven, and bake them for twenty-five minutes. Unmold, and place them in a hot dish, with a folded napkin, and serve.

985. Potatoes, Maître d'Hôtel.—Take eight medium-sized potatoes, boiled as for No. 982; peel them, cut them into slices, and place them in a saucepan, with an ounce of butter and a pinch of chopped parsley, and season with half a pinch each of salt and pepper, the third of a pinch of nutmeg, and the juice of half a lemon. Warm all together, toss well, and add half a cupful of cream; heat slightly once more, and serve.

986. Potatoes, Parisienne.—Take six good-sized, well-cleansed potatoes; with a round vegetable-spoon cut out the Parisian potatoes; then put them in fresh water; wash well, and drain. Melt an ounce of butter in a sautoire, throw in the potatoes, and season with half a pinch of salt. Place the sautoire in the oven; cook for twenty minutes, and serve on a hot dish with a folded napkin.

987. Potatoes à l'Anglaise à Crû.—Wash well six medium-sized, sound potatoes; cut them into quarters, pare them neatly, clove-garlic-shaped; wash again, drain, and place them in a saucepan. Cover with water, throw in a heavy pinch of salt, put the lid on, and cook for twenty minutes. Drain, and put them in a saucepan, with an ounce of butter, a pinch of chopped parsley, heat slowly for five minutes, toss gently, and serve.

988. Potatoes à l'Anglaise.—Wash well six good-sized potatoes; boil them in salted water for forty-five minutes; peel, and cut them each into quarters. Melt an ounce of butter in a saucepan; add the sliced potatoes, half a pinch of salt, and the third of a pinch of pepper. Cook them on a very slow fire for five minutes, tossing them well, and serve on a very hot dish, sprinkling a little chopped parsley over them.

989. Potatoes, with Bacon.—Cut one ounce of bacon or pork into small pieces; put them in a saucepan, with half an ounce of butter; cook for five minutes; add a spoonful of flour; stir, and brown well for four minutes. Moisten with a pint of white broth (No. 99), and cook for five minutes longer. Put in eight well-peeled, washed, and sliced raw potatoes; season with half a pinch of pepper and the third of a pinch of nutmeg; lay the lid on, and cook for twenty-five minutes. Then skim off the fat, and serve in a hot, deep dish.

990. Potatoes à l'Italienne.—Boil eight medium-sized potatoes in boiling water, as for No. 982; peel, put them in a saucepan, and mash them. Add a piece of butter of one ounce, and a piece of fresh bread the size of a French roll, suppressing the crust, and soaking it in milk. Add two more tablespoonfuls of milk, in order to form a pliable paste, three fresh egg yolks, and the whites of the three beaten to a froth; season with half a pinch of salt, half a pinch of pepper, and the third of a pinch of nutmeg. Mix well together, and pile it high on a baking-dish; pour over it a little melted butter; sprinkle a little Parmesan cheese over; place it in the oven, and after ten minutes, when of a good golden color, serve.

991. Potatoes à la Lyonnaise.—Cut eight potatoes, boiled, as for No. 982, into round slices; lay them in a frying-pan with an ounce and a half of butter, and the round slices of a previously fried onion, and season with half a pinch each of salt and pepper. Cook well together for six minutes, until well browned; toss them well, and serve with a pinch of chopped parsley sprinkled over the whole.

992. Stuffed Potatoes.—Wash and peel about six large potatoes; cut them, lengthwise, in two, and scoop out the centres carefully with a knife or spoon. Fill the cavities with a sausage forcemeat (No. 220), letting it bulge out a little on the top; butter a baking-pan, arrange the potatoes on it, and cook in a slow oven for half an hour, or until nicely browned, then serve.

993. Fried Potatoes.—Peel and wash six large potatoes, cut them up into fine slices, a quarter of an inch in thickness; plunge them into very hot, clarified beef suet or fat, and cook slowly. When they are soft, lift them out with a skimmer (it generally takes ten minutes to cook them); heat the fat again to boiling-point, and put the potatoes back. Smooth them down with a skimmer, and after two minutes they will swell up considerably; lift them out with the skimmer, drain, sprinkle a pinch of salt over, and serve on a hot dish with a folded napkin. These potatoes answer for garnishing chops and other meats.

994. Potatoes Sautées au Beurre.—Peel and clean eighteen small, round, raw potatoes, new ones if possible; place two ounces of butter in a saucepan; place it on a hot fire, adding the potatoes; cook them until they are a golden color, which will take fifteen minutes, then drain. Sprinkle over them a pinch of table-salt, and arrange them on a dish without any further seasoning than a little chopped parsley; then serve.

995. Potatoes Sautées.

—Take eight good-sized boiled and peeled potatoes (No. 982); cut them in slices a quarter of an inch in thickness; place them in a frying-pan with an ounce and a half of good butter. Season with a pinch of salt and half a pinch of pepper; toss well for eight minutes, dress on a very hot dish, and serve with a little parsley sprinkled over.

996. Potato Balls.—Peel, clean neatly, and boil in salted water for thirty minutes, eight good-sized, sound, round, yellow potatoes; drain and return them to the same pan, and mash them well, adding two egg yolks, and the whites beaten to a froth, three tablespoonfuls of cream, a teaspoonful of chopped parsley, very little chives, half a pinch of salt, and the third of a pinch of nutmeg. Mix well together for two minutes, and dip about half a tablespoonful at a time into frying batter (No. 1185). Slide them into very hot fat, and leave them in for three minutes; this swells them, and forms them into a species of fritters. Place in a very hot dish with a folded napkin, and serve.

997. Potato Croquettes and Quenelles.—Peel, wash, and drain nicely eight medium-sized mealy potatoes; cut them in quarters, put them in a saucepan, cover them with water, add a pinch of salt, cook for thirty minutes, and drain. Lay them in a mortar with an ounce of fresh butter, pound them well, and add three raw egg yolks. Season with half a pinch each of salt and pepper and the third of a pinch of nutmeg; mix well, and then divide into twelve parts, shaping each one like a cork, or any other shape desired. Dip them separately into beaten egg, and roll them in fresh bread-crumbs; fry a golden color for three minutes, and serve on a dish with a folded napkin.

998. Mashed Potatoes.—Peel, wash, drain, and cut into quarters eight good-sized potatoes; put them in a sautoire, cover with water, add a good pinch of salt, and boil for thirty minutes. Drain, rub them through a purée strainer, and put them in a saucepan with an ounce of butter, and half a pinch each of salt and white pepper. Stir well, adding half a cupful of hot milk, until it becomes of a good consistency. Serve, garnished with six pieces of bread fried in butter.

999. Potatoes à l'Hollandaise.—After boiling eight good-sized potatoes as for No. 982, peel, and cut them into quarters; put them in a sautoire with an ounce of butter and half a pinch of chopped parsley; season with half a pinch each of salt and pepper, toss them gently, and warm them slightly for five minutes. Place in a hot dish, and serve.

Sweet potatoes à l'Hollandaise are prepared the same way.

1000. Potatoes à la Gastronome.—Peel, clean, and with a No. 3 tube cut twelve medium-sized potatoes into inch-and-a-half-long pieces. Place them in a saucepan; cover with water, add a pinch of salt, and cook for twenty-five minutes. Drain, and place them in a hot dish; pour a gill of hot Périgueux sauce (No. 191) over them, and serve.

1001. Potatoes à la Bignon.—Prepare twelve potatoes as for No. 982; empty them with a potato-scoop, leaving the bottoms uncut; blanch them in boiling water for two minutes; drain, and fill them with sausage forcemeat (No. 220). Lay them in a buttered sautoire; place it in the oven, and cook for twenty minutes. Use for any garnishing desired.

1002. Hashed Potatoes, Sautées.—Hash eight medium-sized, cold, boiled potatoes; place an ounce and a half of good butter in a frying-pan, add the potatoes, season with half a pinch each of salt and pepper, and toss them well in the pan for two minutes. Give them the shape of an omelet, and let them take a golden color, which will require five minutes. With a spoon take up all the butter which lies at the bottom of the pan; slide the potatoes carefully on a hot dish, and serve.

1003. Hashed Potatoes, with Cream.—Hash eight cold, boiled potatoes, and place them in a sautoire; add half a cupful of cream and half an ounce of butter; season with half a pinch each of salt and pepper, and the third of a pinch of nutmeg; stir well with a wooden spoon for five minutes, until well heated, and serve.

1004. Hashed Potatoes, with Cream au Gratin.—Prepare the potatoes as for No. 1003; place them in a dish (a silver dish preferred); sprinkle over them two tablespoonfuls of grated Parmesan cheese, and two tablespoonfuls of fresh bread-crumbs; spread well over them a piece of butter the size of a nut; then place the dish in the oven. After ten minutes, when a good golden color, serve.

1005. Potatoes en Surprise.—Prepare some potatoes as for croquettes (No. 997); form them into twelve balls the size of a good-sized egg; scoop out the centres, and fill in with a salpicon (No. 256). Close the opening with a little more potato; dip them in beaten egg, then in fresh bread-crumbs, and fry them in very hot fat for three minutes. Lift, drain, and serve them on a hot dish with a folded napkin.

1006. Potatoes à la Duchesse.—Place some croquette preparation (No. 997) in a bag, and squeeze it upon a buttered baking-sheet, forming it into any shape required, and with a light hair brush cover the surface with a beaten egg. Brown lightly in the oven for eight minutes, and serve for various garnishings.

Balls can also be formed about the size of an egg; spread a little flour on the table; place the balls on top, and flatten them, shaping them nicely; cover the surface with a beaten egg; brown lightly in the oven on a buttered baking-sheet for eight minutes, and serve.

1007. Potatoes à la Rice.—Peel, wash, and drain eight medium-sized potatoes. Cut them into half-an-inch-square pieces; place them in a frying-pan with an ounce and a half of butter; season with a pinch of salt, toss well, and let them get a golden color (fifteen minutes will suffice). Drain the butter from the bottom of the pan, and place the potatoes in a hot dish; sprinkle a pinch of chopped parsley over, and serve.

1008. Potatoes à la Windsor.—Peel, and clean nicely, twelve large potatoes; cut them into balls with a Parisian potato-scoop, then place them in a saucepan, covering them with water containing a pinch of salt. Cook for fifteen minutes; then strain them and place them in another saucepan with an ounce of fresh butter and a pinch of chopped parsley. Warm them well for five minutes, and add the juice of half a lemon before serving.

1009. Potatoes, Château.—Cut six medium-sized potatoes into quarters, and pare them like cloves of garlic; wash them well, and drain. Fry them slowly in moderately heated fat for ten minutes; lift, drain thoroughly, and put them in a sautoire with half an ounce of butter. Season with half a pinch of salt, heat well for two minutes, and serve.

1010. Potatoes, Soufflées.—Peel eight good, mealy potatoes, and cut them into even pieces a quarter of an inch in thickness, shaping them as oval as possible. Fry them in moderately heated fat for eight minutes; then lift them out, and lay them aside for a few moments; plunge them into boiling hot fat, and the potatoes will swell considerably. Drain, and serve them on a dish with a folded napkin.

Sweet potatoes soufflées are prepared the same way.

N. B.—When cutting the potatoes for a soufflée, a continuous, sharp, and rapid cut should be made, so as to have them to perfection.

1011. Potatoes, Saratoga.—Peel and clean six medium-sized potatoes; cut them with a sharp Saratoga potato-knife into thin slices; place them in cold water, wash thoroughly, drain, and plunge them into very hot fat for eight minutes. Take them out, drain thoroughly, and sprinkle over them half a pinch of salt. Serve them on a dish with a folded napkin.

1012. Potatoes à la Hanna.—Peel, wash, and drain six medium-sized potatoes; cut them into as thin slices as possible; then wash them well again. Take a flat mold large enough to contain the potatoes, butter it well; put in a layer of potatoes, then a very light layer of grated cheese; season with a very little salt, and the same of pepper. Cover with another layer of potatoes, season again the same as before (the whole not to exceed half a pinch of each); then spread half an ounce of butter over them. Place the mold in the oven, and cook for thirty minutes; remove, turn it upside down on a hot dish, unmold, and serve.

1013. Potatoes, Julienne.—Peel and clean six medium-sized potatoes; cut them into square pieces two inches long by the third of an inch wide; wash well, and drain; place them in very hot fat for six minutes, then lift them out, and lay them on a cloth to drain. Sprinkle half a pinch of salt over, and serve them on a dish with a folded napkin.

1014. Potatoes en Paille (Straw).—Prepare the same as in No. 1013, cutting a little thinner.

1015. Rice, Plain Boiled.—Clean and wash neatly a quarter of a pound of Italian rice; place it in a saucepan with a pint and a half of cold water and a pinch of salt; put the lid on, and boil for twenty-two minutes. Pour through a colander, being careful to let it drain thoroughly without crushing the rice, otherwise it will be spoiled. When well dried, return it to the saucepan, put the lid on, and leave it on the corner of the stove to dry gradually for five or six minutes. It will now be ready to use as required.

1016. Rice à la Ristori.—Wash well and drain a quarter of a pound of good Italian rice; shred two ounces of bacon into small pieces, and place them in a saucepan with a medium-sized, chopped-up, raw cabbage, letting them steam for thirty minutes. Add a pinch of salt, half a pinch of pepper, and a teaspoonful of chopped parsley; put in the rice, and moisten with half a pint of white broth (No. 99). Cook for fully a quarter of an hour longer, and serve with grated Parmesan cheese sprinkled over it.

1017. Risotto à la Milanaise.—Chop rather fine one good-sized, very sound, peeled onion. Melt two ounces of very good butter in a saucepan on a very brisk fire; add the onions, brown them for six or seven minutes, or until they have obtained a good golden color; then add ten ounces of well-picked Italian rice (a heaped cupful), with two good-sized chopped truffles;

stir well with the spatula without ceasing for one and a half minutes, then add one quart of boiling and strained white broth (No. 99), lightly stir once only, and cook for fourteen minutes. Add six fine chopped mushrooms, and little by little, at intervals, another quart of boiling white broth—stirring almost constantly with the wooden spatula while cooking, very rapidly, for ten minutes more. Season with a heavy half-teaspoonful of salt, a light saltspoonful of white pepper, adding one and a half ounces of grated Swiss cheese, and a heaped teaspoonful of Spanish branch saffron, diluted in two tablespoonfuls of hot white broth, and strained. Cook for three or four minutes longer, stirring continually meanwhile; then pour it into a hot soup-tureen, and send to the table with a little grated Swiss cheese, separate. A little beef-marrow can be added to advantage, by making a small cavity in the centre, while yet in the pan, one minute before the time to serve, and plunging into it one tablespoonful of marrow.

1018. Oyster-plant Sauté au Beurre.—Scrape nicely a large bunch of fine oyster-plant; plunge it into cold water containing two tablespoonfuls of vinegar, so as to prevent it from turning black. Take it from the water, drain, and cut it into two-inch-long pieces. Place them in a saucepan, with two tablespoonfuls of vinegar and two tablespoonfuls of flour; mix well; cover with plenty of cold water and a handful of salt; put the lid on, and let them boil slowly for forty minutes. Then drain, and return them to a sautoire, with an ounce and a half of the best butter procurable; season with half a pinch of pepper, the juice of half a lemon, and a teaspoonful of chopped parsley. Heat well for five minutes, tossing occasionally; then place them in a hot, deep dish, and serve.

1019. Oyster-plant à la Poulette.—Scrape nicely a good-sized bunch of fine, fresh oyster-plant; plunge it at once into acidulated water, and when well washed, drain, and cut it into two-inch pieces. Place them in a saucepan, and boil them in plenty of water, adding two pinches of salt, two tablespoonfuls of vinegar, and the same quantity of diluted flour. After forty minutes, or as soon as they bend to the finger, they are done. Lift them out, drain them well, and serve with a pint of hot poulette sauce (No. 598) poured over them.

Printed in the USA
CPSIA information can be obtained
at www.ICGtesting.com
CBHW080601091024
15572CB00022B/1776